THE HON. NATHANIEL FIENNES 1608-1669

A Colonel in the Parliamentary Army commanded by William Waller at the taking of Winchester in December 1642. He and his troop were accommodated in Winchester College for several days. He is said to have saved William of Wykeham's Chantry and Monument from spoliation by Waller's riotous troops.
(Courtesy Lord Saye and Sele)

SAWYER'S COLLECTION

CIVIL WAR
IN
WINCHESTER

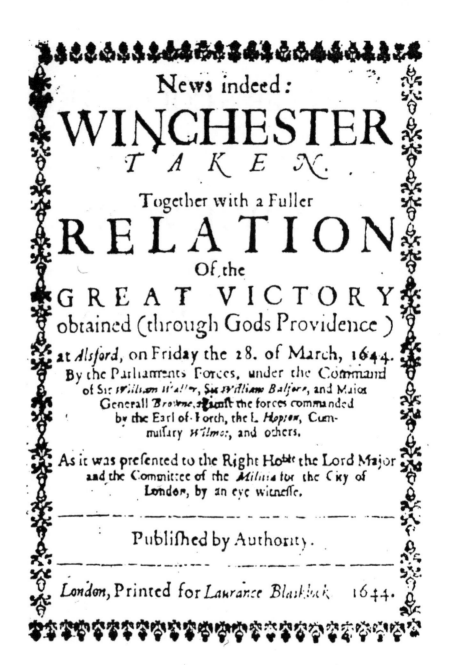

News indeed :

WINCHESTER
TAKEN.

Together with a Fuller

RELATION

Of the

GREAT VICTORY

obtained (through Gods Providence)

at *Alsford*, on Friday the 28. of March, 1644.
By the Parliaments Forces, under the Command
of Sir *William Waller*, Sir *William Balfore*, and Maior
Generall *Browne*, against the forces commanded
by the Earl of Forth, the L. *Hopton*, Cum-
missary *Wilmot*, and others.

As it was presented to the Right Hoble the Lord Maior
and the Committee of the *Militia* for the City of
London, by an eye witnesse.

Published by Authority.

London, Printed for *Laurance Blacklock* 1644.

"WINCHESTER TAKEN"

Cover of a tract published in London after the Battle of Cheriton fought on the 29th March 1644.
Winchester was not taken by Parliament until October 1645.

(B.M. Thomason Tract E.40.1 – Winchester City Library R9234)

SAWYER'S COLLECTION

CIVIL WAR
IN
WINCHESTER

An anthology
of contemporary 17th century
writings
collected by

RICHARD SAWYER

ROWANVALE BOOKS

Rowanvale
Books

Published by **Rowanvale Books**,
69, Beech Grange, Landford, Salisbury, Wiltshire, UK.

Copyright © 2002 by Richard Sawyer

ISBN 0 9530785 5 8

Printed and bound by The Cromwell Press.
Typesetting by Rowanvale Books.

Dedication to D.D. 1983

ACKNOWLEDGEMENTS

I have listed in the bibliography the many libraries who have helped over a long period of time. In particular, I would like to thank John Hardacre, editor of the Winchester Cathedral Record, also Philippa Stevens, the staff at the Winchester City Library and the staff of the National Portrait Gallery.

I acknowledge too, the help and encouragement of Tony MacLachlan, author of "The Civil War in Hampshire", and the team at Rowanvale Books.

Further, the delight of Andrew Sollars' photographs.

CONTENTS

ILLUSTRATIONS

CIVIL WAR IN WINCHESTER

THIS collection of contemporary writings of the Civil War period has been made over many years, acknowledgements to the very many authors and libraries who have been quoted or have contributed is expressed in the text and index of References.

The narrative and comments are mine, the quotations, some lengthy, tell their own tale, sometimes pleasantly exaggerated with spellings amusing to read and perhaps difficult to interpret but tiresome to copy, yet done here to give a feeling for the time in which they were written.

In spite of the many depredations, plunderings and spoilations the City survived; just as happens today the contemporary reporters saw only with the eye they wished to see with and embellished their reports to suit their readers.

The narrative covers the vicissitudes of truly loyal and Royal City from the proclamation of King James and the greeting given him on his visit to Winchester in 1603, until the Restoration of King Charles II in 1660.

There is a description of beautifying the Cathedral at the instigation of King Charles I and the state of the Town and Cathedral before the War, also account of the pillaging and spoilations wrought by Sir William Waller's Parliamentary troopers.

In 1643 the Castle was seized and fortified by Sir William Ogle for the King. Winchester then became a Royalist Garrison town until the King's armies, under Sir Ralph hopton, marched out to be defeated at the Battle of Cheriton, on the 29th March 1644, to change the course of the Civil War in the South.

The Castle, under its gallant commander Sir William Ogle, held out for the King for a further eighteen months until beseiged and taken by Lieutenant General Oliver Cromwell in October 1645.

Related too are subsequent troubles with plague, politics and proposals for the demolitions of the Cathedral and Castle.

Perusal of the subject index alone will set off many different trains of thought, wonderment and in many cases surprise.

Richard Sawyer, a Chartered Surveyor by profession, but now retired and who was responsible for the care of the fabric of many parish churches throughout the Diocese, is known for his interest in Civil War history particularly The Battle of Cheriton.

He has here opened up his collection of notes and contemporary writings, for others to enjoy, on the events that occured in Winchester during those troublesome times.

He served in the Royal Hampshire Regiment during the War was wounded at the Battle of "Hunts Gap" in North Africa, taken prisoner and survived to return home to read his own obituary notices.

As President of the Winchester Chamber of Commerce in 1958 and as Chairman of the Welcome to Winchester Guides for many years he has encouraged Tourism with the wish that people should understand the purpose of our historic buildings and enjoy stories about those who built them, lived or worked in them, together with the great historic personages connected with them.

Chapter 1

THE CITY FLOURISHES

Portal the Great
Hall of Win'
Castle p. 33

T HE proclamation of King James I from Winchester Castle by the High Sheriff Sir Benjamin Tichborne, in March 1603, without waiting for an Order in Council, marked a decided change in the City's fortunes as will be seen in many unexpected ways.

As a reward for his loyalty Sir Benjamin was granted the Castle for his life. In return he was to provide a lodging for the King when he visited the City.

King James made his first visit with Queen Anne of Denmark on the 20th September 1603. Their Majesties were received by the Mayor and Twenty four with great solemnity and were presented with two silver cups.

In the speech of welcome the Recorder said,

Nichols
Progresses of
James I p. 274

> *"If my tongue, the natural messenger.*
> *of the heart and mynde, could so lively*
> *expresse, most high and mighty Prince and*
> *our deere and dread Soveraign, the*
> *exceeding joy and gladness of this your*
> *Highness' ancient Citty of Winchester —*
> *whose now decayed walls and ruynous*
> *buildings presenting to your Majesties view*
> *a desolation, are again re-edified with the*
> *joy and comfort of yourMajesties presence*
> *and access to this place."*

The Royal Court remained in Winchester until the 4th October when King James received the Spanish and French Ambassadors.

Within a month, because of the Plague in London, this City was chosen as the venue for the great State Trial of Sir Walter Raleigh, for his alleged part in the "Main Plot", designed to put Arabella Stuart on the throne in place of King James.

Orders were given to make ready the College and Wolvesey Castle to provide accomodation for the judges, public officers, peers of the realm and numerous attendants who would be at the trials.

Sir Walter Raleigh and the other conspirators were conveyed by carriage from London to the Castle here in Winchester, guarded by warders from the Tower of London. They were met at on the 9th November at the County boundary at Bagshot, by the sheriff's son Sir Richard Tichborne "to be well and strongly guarded by fifty light horsemen through Hampshire."

Kirby, Annals of Win' College p. 300.

Sir Walter Raleigh was arraigned on the 17th November in the Great Common Hall, as it was termed, tried by his peers, found guilty and condemned to death. However his sentence was stayed at the last moment. He was then commited to the Tower, released and then fourteen years later by a legal barbarity executed. While in captivity he wrote his famous "History of the World", a copy being in the Cathedral Library.

Nichols p. 295

The prosperity of the City, brought about by the throng of people attending the trials, and hopes of a continuing Royal presence and favour, was short lived.

Portal. 83 n.1

In the words of a contemporary solicitor John Trussel written about 1645,

"But when King James of pious memorye
(the plague in London raging heavely)
was heere well pleased to appoint his Court
and howld the terme, then hither did resorte
more noble men and honable peers
than had before in many score of yeers
appeered; who on generall summons hither came
about the arraignment of some men of name
And spent their mony heer, my inhabitants
pickt, then their crums up and sodred upp
*   their wants*
Then I with some more confidence did presume
my former state in somesort to assume."

Trussel.
Benefactors to
Winchester. f. 95.

However, revival came in quite a different way, through the church rather than the state, due to the appointment as Dean, a Scotsman and Royal chaplain, John Young in 1616. In that same year his father, Sir Peter Young, although a layman, was made Master of St Cross.

Initially Dean, John Young was often absent in Scotland on Royal business and for a while John Trussel acted as his bailiff until the appointment of John Chase, a notary, as Chapter Clerk in December 1622. John Chase was responsible for reassembling the Cathedral library and muniments after they had been twice ransacked during the Civil War. Chase was to be remembered as a man with an orderly mind but scrawny hand writing, who brought a degree of management into the business of the Chapter.

The accession of King Charles II to the throne and appointed of William Laud as Archbishop in 1625 brought about a sense of urgency and reform into church affairs. Soon began the long process of restoring and rebeautifing the Cathedral after years of neglect following the Reformation. It started with the provision of a new bell frame and rehanging of the bells. That year too saw John Harris, a Prebend of the Cathedral, made Warden of College. Lancelot Andrews was Bishop at that time being succeeded by Richard Neale in 1628 and Walter Curle in 1632.

As part of the process of restoring discipline and dignity into church proceedings Bishop Curle expressed displeasure at the way the cathedral was being used as a public way, between the Close and College to the City. To abate the nuisance Dean Young cut a new passage through at the south west corner of the Cathedral, now called the 'Slype'. It caused some small disturbance, among the prebends who objected to part of their properties being pulled down, which the Dean had to resolve.

Young's Diary. Ed by F.R. Goodman p. 4

p. 76

p. 26. 103.

To mark the new slip way, on the south west buttress of the Cathedral, at the west end of the passage, is inscribed this injunction in latin.

Locke
In praise of
Winchester.
p. 117.

```
ILL                 PREC
   \                    \
    AC                   ATOR
   /                    /
H                   VI
```

AMBULA

That way worshipper this way traveller walk.

Over the arch at the east end, (this was repositioned when the new south buttresses were built in 1912), also in latin, was written,

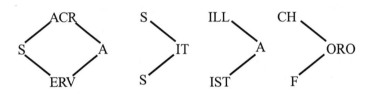

```
   ACR          S          ILL         CH
  /   \            \           \           \
 S     A            IT          A           ORO
  \   /            /           /           /
   ERV          S          IST         F
```

Let that way be consecrated to the choir.
This way serve for the market.

Also was written "private property has yielded to Public Utility. Proceed now by the way which is open to you."

As part of the reforms and beautification, so strongly urged by Laud and supported by King Charles, and with Dean Young in close contact with His Majesty, it is not suprising that a major scheme of restoration should be devised for the Cathedral supported by King.

Young's
Diary
p. 102.

The first scheme was to be the 'Arching of the Tower'. That is to say adding a vault to the tower so that the vaulting would be continuous from the west door to the presbytery. There was discussion at the time how it should be done. At this period, strangely, the Gothic style was chosen and it is constructed in timber and not stone. The contract for the "arching of the toure" was signed on the 16th June 1634. The work taking about a year. In April of the next year an agreement was reached with Jerome the painter for painting and gilding the new vault.

Royal Arch'
Institute.
1924.
p. 329.

On the 31st August 1636 King Charles brought his Queen, Henrietta, of France to see this magnificent ceiling fresh and colourful, with its painted and gilded bosses and conceits including portraits of Charles and Henrietta Maria, together with other heraldic devices.

Coffer
Accounts
Sept. 1636.

M. Toynbee.
in H.F.C.
xviii 1
p. 17.

In the centre of the roundel is the emblem of the Holy Trinity encircled with a chronogram in which the large letters are picked out in red to read,

sInt DoMus hVjVs pII reges

nVtrItII regIna nVtrICes pLae

May pious Kings be the nursing fathers and pious Queen the nursing mothers of this church

MDC VVVVV IIIIIIII
1634

Jervis.
Woodwork
in Win'
Cathedral.

This great roundel forms the hatchway through which the bells are hoisted up into the bell chamber from the floor of the choir. The vault now apparently supported by stilts of small clustered columns, above the great Norman capitals originally had corbels of figures painted like the figure heads of a ship. These are now preserved in the south triforium.

King Charles was delighted with the new vault but expressed dislike of the arrangement at the entrance to the choir. This was then through the space, under the pulpitum and between the Rood and the choir, used as the Chapter House. This space now forms the dais behind the nave altar.

Clarendon & Gale.

The King's Surveyor General, Inigo Jones, was employed to remove the pulpitum and to build a new screen at the entrance to the choir. In complete contrast to the new vault the screen was designed in the Renaissance style, and to please His Majesty he included two niches in which to place statues of King James and of Charles. There can be little doubt that the screen must have received royal approval and encouragement.

Blakiston. Inigo Jones's Screen. in W.C.R. No. 45.

These statues, in bronze, were to be placed on either side of the doorway to the choir. They now stand on each side of the great west door and are the work of Hubert le Sueur, a celebrated 17c sculptor. He was a pupil of John of Bologna and came to England in 1628.

Frequent mention will be made of these bronze statues during the course of the narrative for they suffered great indignities during the Rebellion.

Another major change made in the Cathedral was the re-ordering of the presbytery with new Holy Table and rails, (The Laudian altar rails are now in use in the lady Chapel.) A wooden reredos or screen with an ornamental canopy, said to have been given by King Charles, was set behind the Holy Table. It displayed the Tables of Commandments.

Jervis. Woodwork in Win' Cathedral.

It was this wooden screen, behind the altar, which protected the Great Screen from the fury of the Parliamentarian troopers a few years later.

Fragments of the canopy and of Inigo's choir screen are preserved in the south triforium with the figure heads from the tower vault.

Bussby. The Great Screen of Win' Cathedral in W.C.R. No. 47.

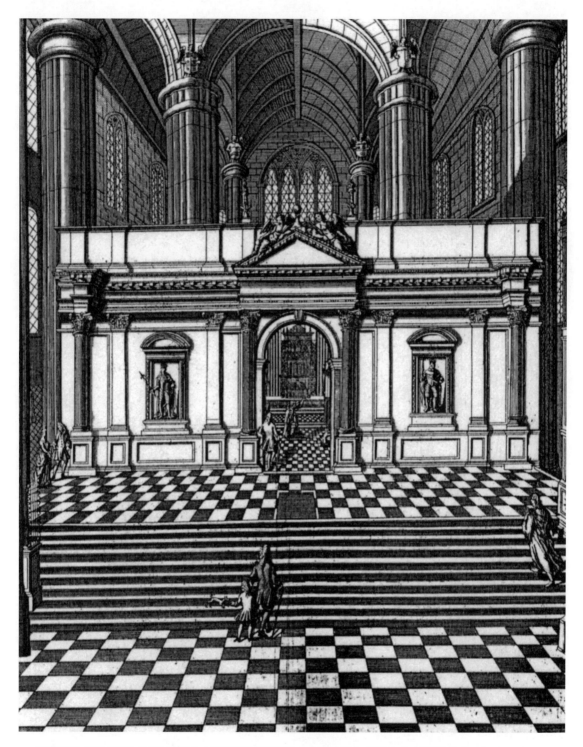

INIGO JONES' SCREEN AT THE ENTRANCE TO THE CATHEDRAL CHOIR

Shows Hubert Le Sueurs' bronze statues of King James I and King Charles I of 1638. Through the doorway may be seen the screen behind the High Altar which saved the Great Screen from further spoilation, after the Reformation

(Gale and Clarendon's History of the Cathedral of 1715)

At a time of developing political and religious differences and the taking of sides for King or Parliament, a moment to stop the calender of events and to take a contemporary view of the City itself as seen through the eyes of Lieutenant Nowell Hammond who visited the City in August 1635. That was shortly after the vault to the Cathedral had been completed and before the building of Inigo Jones' screen had commenced.

Hammond.

> *"I found her (the City of Winchester) situated, in a rich valley invironed round with great hills, a sweet and pleasant river gliding by and through her, encompassed with a wall near two miles about, and a ditch without with six gates for entrance.*
>
> *In the lowest part of her eastward, almost through every street, runs a pleasant river or small stream. Some part of the ground within her is unbuilt especially on the north and west sides which is converted with orchards and gardens and little pastures.*
>
> *There is also the ruins of two famous monasteries in her which are lamentable to behold.*
>
> *The goverment of this city is by a Mayor with his four maces and twelve Aldermen who sit to distribute justice at a hall which some times was an Hospital. (St Johns)*
>
> *She has but one Captain and his company but a small one."*

"The City and her suburbs doe equally
challenge their shares of her churches
seven being without the walls with the
College (and) that over King's Gate;
and seven within the walls with their
brave old Mother Cathedral which I found
faire and long being 200 of my paces,
the longest I dare say except old St Pauls
   Saint George on horseback on the top of
her flat bottom'd steeple to be sentinel
and give notice of her governours
prerogative prelacy of that high noble order
 in the Court.
   Her quire up to the high altar is equal
with that of (Canterbury) the roof whereof
is stately fair and rich to adorne, which
and to beautify the same, a great sum of
money hath been very lately bestowed with
the arms of the King and Queen and many of
the nobility richly gilded."

Hammond
p. 44.

One may wonder if the "St George" was a large weather vane. The Bishop of Winchester is Prelate of the Order of The Garter whose insignia is St George. For his part Jerome the painter was paid thirty pounds for painting and gilding the new vault.

Young's
diary
p. 44.

Hammond continues with a lengthy description of the choir and monuments, which will be referred to in detail later, as will also reference be made to the Mayor and his maces. The ruins of the two monasteries were those of Hyde Abbey and the Nunnaminster. The seven churches without would have been College Chapel and St. Swithuns over Kingsgate, both mentioned by Hammond; plus St. Michaels, now used by College; St Peters Chesil, a redundant church used as a theatre club; St Johns, still a parish church; St Martins Winnal, rebuilt in 1850 but finally demolished in 1969. The seventh church was St Bartholomews Hyde.

See p. 48
below.

a "Friend to
Winchester."
B. Arch'
Assoc' 1845.

The seven churches within the City were St. Maurice, then recently repaired (the Dean and Chapter had subscribed 40 shillings in 1630), St. Lawrence, to be ransacked and torn during the war; plus the old St. Thomas church, St. Clement, St. Mary Kalender, and St. Peter in Colebrook Street. These four have now completely disappeared. St. Peter Macellis, marked out on the pavement at the rear of God-be-Got House was then already in a ruinous state, while the Chapel of St. Johns Hospital was being used as a school, not being restored to its proper use until 1838.

Nowell Hammond continued with his tour to the west side of the City.

Y's D.
p. 86.

Leach.
Win' Coll'.
p. 331.

> "Upon a high mounted hill, a strong
> and spacious which is very
> ancient, yet not much recinated (sic);
> for of late yeers it hath been much
> repayered and beautify'd by the late
> Lord Treasurer of England. (Richard
> Weston Earl of Portland)
> This castle is built four square
> with four great towers at the corners
> two of them round and two square.
> The hall, kitchen, guard chamber,
> privvy chamber, the Kings bed chamber
> and many other faire chambers for the
> noble officers and court traine all
> made very compleat and handsome at the
> Earls great cost.
> So many stayers and ascents as are
> up to the hall, from the first entrance
> of the ascending bridge so many are
> there down again under (to) the castles
> deep vaults and cellars where the
> keepers may securely quater themselves
> if any occassion bee."

Hammond.

See J. Milner's sketches.

> *"From hence I march'd downe again*
> *to see what manner of hall and*
> *table that brave and warlike worthy*
> *Brittish Prince kept above 1000 years*
> *since, which are both fit for so royall*
> *a Prince where the one exceeded in*
> *longitude (King Arthur) and the other*
> *did in rotundity (King Henry VIII).*
> *I found the hall 50 paces long and*
> *very broad with two rowes of goodly*
> *marble pillars. For the other his*
> *Table as thy call it with his whole*
> *jury of couragious warlike Knights*
> *round about it shew'd no end of his*
> *bounty."*

Hammond.
p. 51

To illustrate the ceremonial and pomp displayed in the City in 1635, and this must have been the same at the trial of Raleigh, Hammond then describes "although it be a little digressing" the

> *"proceeedings of the Court of Eyre*
> *then meeting on circuit in Winchester*
> *under The Noble Earl of Holland, Chief*
> *Justice of Eyre in all his Majesties*
> *Forests Chases and Parks on this*
> *side Trent, with the assistance of two*
> *judges, the Lord Chief Justice of the*
> *Common Pleas (TheLord John Finch) and*
> *the chief justice of Chester (Sir John*
> *Bridgeman)*
> *On Monday morning His Lordship came*
> *from Sr William Udalls House Accompani'd*
> *with the Earl of Southampton, who was*
> *deeply interested in this business, with*
> *divers Knights, and Gentlemen of the*
> *Shire thereof, (White Breconsaw and*
> *brother of 'Dame' Alice Lisle), and*
> *his Attendants, making in all about*
> *200 horse and 10 coaches.*

D.N.B.

Hammond.
p. 52.

Hammond.
p. 52.

"The Mayor with his Brethren in
scarlet received his Lordship at
the East Gate on the same morning
it being St Bartholomew's day (24 Aug),
the Saint, though not their owne
St Swithun, entertaining him with
weeping tears, which soundly washed
the Scarlet weeds of their grave
Worships. Then after a small time of
repose at Capt Tuckers house, not far
from that gate where his Lordship lay,
by the said two judges in their scarlet,
Mr Mayor and his Aldermen in theirs;
Mr High Sheriff, with all his in theirs;
Colours, some twelve of the Kings Guard
with their Royall Badges; The Kings
trumpetters, and the High Sheriffs,
was he guarded in this majestick manner
to the Great Hall where they sat in
Royall state, most of the Knights,
Esquires and chiefe Gentlemen of the
County bearing offices in New Forest,
Wulmer Forest and Chale Forest attending
at this great and high Court.
Heere was exceeding great crowding to
see and heare such a splendid sight."

Schellink's
View.

Hammond's description of the castle does not tell of the great ditches or barbican on the west side, although he did mention the bridge. A pictorial representation was given by Speed in the margin of his map of 1611, which shows the Motte of the Castle at the south end, with a tower at each corner, and bridge on the west side. It does not show the great shell Keep depicted in Schellink's drawing made soon after the Civil War.

Of the towers described by Hammond, the two round ones, which were in reality oval, and had been built in Edward III's reign. The square and older west towers were built in Henry II's time. The position of the road leading to the bridge probably followed the line of Mews Hill which ran up westwards past St James chapel. Surprisingly the barbican, which guarded the entrance to the castle across the bridge, was not mentioned by Hammond.

The domestic buildings, built in the bailey would have been in the centre of the whole castle complex, and contained the privy chamber and the King's bedchamber provided by the Sheriff, Sir Benjamin Tichborne and his wife Amphillis Weston for King James and the Queen in 1603.

Monument in Tichborne Church.

Although Sir Benjamin had been granted the castle it seems he preferred his own home at Tichborne where for several years on August 29th he entertained the King and by so doing fulfilled his obligation to provide accomodation for His Majesty. His son Sir Richard Tichborne apparently took up occupation of the castle on his marriage to Susanna Waller. Susanna was the heiress of Sir William Waller of Old Stoke and Parneholt with West Bere Forest. Sir Richard Tichborne was a Knight of the Shire and in 1614 was appointed by King James as his Ambassador to Elizabeth of Bohemia. Three of Sir Richard and Susanna's children were christened in the Cathedral between 1615 and 1624, and there is a floor slab marking the grave of their infant son Richard in the retro-choir. When Sir Benjamin died in 1629 Sir Richard moved out to the family home at Tichborne, at the time the castle was granted to Sir Richard Weston, King James' advisor to the Queen of Bohemia and subsequently his Lord Chancelor. The relationship between Amphillis Weston, Sir Benjamin Tichborne's wife, to the Chancellor is not clear but Sir Richard Weston's succession to the castle may well have been a family arrangement endorsed by His Majesty in the formal grant.

V. C. H. IV. p. 440-1

Vaughan. Win' Cath'. p. 225. 272.

Vaughan.

Richard Weston died on the 13 March 1635 having, as Hammond related, expended a large sum on repairing and beautifying the apartments in the Castle. He was buried in the north chapel of the Cathedral retro-choir, the Guardian Angels Chapel, where the south wall was appropriated for his monument in which lies a superb bronze life size effigy of the Earl traditionally ascribed to Hubert Le Sueur. It is known that Richard Weston commissioned Le Sueur to make the equestrian statue of King Charles that now stands at Charing Cross. It seems likely that he was also responsible for commisioning the Cathedral's bronzes of King James and King Charles besides ordering an effigy for himself which was later placed on his monument.

Clarendon & Gale.

Blakiston in W. C. R. No. 50.

The Castle then passed to Jerome Weston, the Second Earl of Portland, until 1638 when it was granted to Sir William Waller later to become the Parliamentary General responsible for despoiling the cathedral. Waller too had been entrusted with the care of the Queen of Bohemia, being an Officer in the English forces at the Battle of Prague in 1620. This Sir William Waller, now of Winchester Castle, was a distant cousin of William Waller of Old Stoke (Stoke Charity) and was therefore related to Susan Waller Lady Tichborne.

Adair.
A Roundhead General.
p. 65.

D. N. B.
Finch.

Further, William Waller (the General to be) had just married Lady Anne Finch, who was related to Sir John Finch the Lord Chief Justice of the Common Pleas who had assisted at the Court of Eyre held in the Great Hall in 1635, and who as Lord Keeper was largely responsible for the "Ship Money" judgement of 1637 which had declared that tax to be legal and therefore payable.

It is remarkable how over such a period the Royal grant of Winchester Castle should have been so intermingled with personal service to King James, his daughter Elizabeth Queen of Bohemia and to his son King Charles by the Tichborne, Weston, Waller and Finch families.

Sir William Waller describes in his own recollections the trouble he had in putting the Castle house in order.

> *"At Winchester Castle, I ran a great*
> *hazzard of being buried under the*
> *ruines of an ould outwall, which I*
> *had been viewing, and considering how*
> *to have it taken down, and I no sooner*   Wallers
> *stept into the house (not above an*   Recollections.
> *easy stone's cast off) but itt fell,*
> *and covered all the place where I had*
> *been, and diverse yards beyond itt.*
>   *My dear wife (The Lady Anne Finch)*
> *had a deliverance of the very same*
> *kinde there likewise, having been to*
> *look att an ould staircase which was*
> *repairing, she was noe sooner gon, but*
> *the place where she stood fell, she*
> *could not but have perished in the*
> *ruines."*

To furnish his new home Waller moved into the Castle what he called "my vanity in furniture". Seven years later one learns a little about this furniture from an inventory of goods belonging to Sir William Waller listed a commissary's account book dated 6th October 1645 and therefore taken immediately after Cromwell's siege of that year,

> *"Seven stooles of Turkie worke.*
> *Two green chairs.*
> *Two stooles with hued and yellow work.*
> *Five old Irish worke stooles.*   Adair
> *One wood couch covered with b(r)aids.*   p. 34.
> *One old leather chaire.*
> *Four pieces of dornip hangings.*
> *Four picktoures Mary Magdalen,*
>   *lacred and an old woman"*

The restoration and reordering of the Cathedral together with the refurbishment of the Castle house and greater use of the Great Hall did indeed bring a transient sense of prosperity to a City which had regained its importance in Royal affairs.

John Trussel wrote as transcribed by Tom Atkinson,

Trussel.
f. 95.

"And then a many bounteous benefactors
of my encrease of strength Authors and Actors
did showe themselves, first Peter Symonds heer
founded Christs Hospital, Twenty pounds a year
ffor ever. William Symonds, Alderman
gave to my poor, And after he began
their followed many other Aldermen
as Burton, Ashton Edmonds, Thorpe and Marlyn
Yalden
which did bequeath mee legacies of plate
to howld my Maiors feast with greater state
But Pemerton their bounty did exceed
ffor he sufficient means hath given to feed
the belly of the poor and cloath their backe
and two pounds yeerlie to find cakes and sacke
ffor the Maior and his brethren, and a preachers
fee
ffor a sermon on St George his daye to bee
of Richard Budd in imitation
who to his never dying reputation
To the same purpose likewise and like end
his bounteous Charity freely did extend
Others gave stocks or worke to sett the poore
and bind apprentices; furthermore
The illustrious John Lord Marquis well incites
Southamptons Erle and many Lords and Knights
and other generous gentlemen to meet
and heer an horse race keep each Easter weeke
By theise and sutch like healpes my former
crosses
Were wipt away and many of my losses
recovered;"

To the great loss of the City and also the Cathedral the legacies of silver and gilt plate went into King Charles' coffers, in 1643, to pay for the War, but it still customary to display the City Plate at the Mayor's Feast, or Dinner. And the Mayor continues to offer hospitality if not as then in cakes and sack but in the form of sherry and snacks.

Richard Budd by his will of 1630 left £40 to the Dean and Chapter, if they would have the great bell of the Cathedral church tolled for condemned criminals before their execution, and also cause to be read a prayer on their behalf. A new bell frame for the Cathedral was referred to by Dean Young in his diary for that year, Budd's gift was an expression of public interest in the bells and this with the other gifts of an awareness of the needs of the poor.

The custom of tolling the great bell for condemned criminals only ceased with the abolition of the death penalty in the 1950s.

Sermons and lectures were an essential part of church services. In the Cathedral Statutes of 1638 precise rules were set out for sermons to be preached every Sunday and in addition on the "Accession Day of the King" (27 March) and on the "Fifth of November in memory of our deliverece from the destestable Gunpowder Treason" of 1605.

The mention of a sermon to be preached on St George's Day, 23 April, in St Lawrence's Church is a reminder of Hammond's reference to the Patron Saint of England and the St George on horseback atop the cathedral tower. St George was certainly a popular figure at that time.

The City was becoming a lively place and since the accession of James I and by the continuing interest shown in the cathedral by Charles I prosperous. Some how or other the Winchester Races continued to be run right through the troublesome days to bring a little and much needed trade, relaxation and pleasure. After the Restoration it was the Winchester Races which attracted king Charles II to the City.

Chapter 2

DIFFERENCES AND
DISSENSIONS

THE imposition of Ship Money in 1638 showed up great differences between the Church represented by the Dean and Chapter in their Close, and the State by the Mayor and Corporation in the City. A struggle developed to such an extent that both the Dean and the Mayor were summoned to appear before the King in person in the Star Chamber at Whitehall. After an initial victory for the Dean the conflict finally ended in a political victory for the Corporation and no little dissension in the Close.

City Charters
& Mss. 1951
Exhibit No 70.

The altercation began with a demand from the Sheriff of Hampshire for payment of the taxes due for Ship Money. The Close being rated at £20 and the City at £200.

The City then imposed a share of their £200 on the Close, but the Dean and Chapter who had promptly paid their £20 imposed direct by the Sheriff refused payment as naturally the Dean was unwilling to pay twice especially as his treasurer held a receipt. The Mayor for the City's part determined to impose his authority over the whole City, clapped into Westgate prison two singing men, servants of the Cathedral who lived in the Close, for non payment of their rate.

Win' Cath'
Documents
2 p. 2

Y's D.
p. 113
128.

It was not so much the amount of money involved but who was to have jurisdiction over the Close. The power of the Church against that of the King, embodied in the Mayor by right of their Royal Charter.

H. N. Q.
VI p. 140.

The outward sign of the Mayor's claim to jurisdiction was shown by Mayor Ralph Riggs, as was customary, by carrying the City's Maces into the choir of the Cathedral when attending services.

W. C. D.
p. 5.

The first round of the contest was won by the Dean who obtained an Order through the Star Chamber requiring the Mayor to release the prisoners and not carry the Maces into the Cathedral without the Dean's Consent. Furthermore to enforce this the granting of the City's new Charter was witheld on the King's direction.

Sir Simonds D'Ewes wrote in his, "A Journal of Parliament" 23 February 1640.

> *"A petition was pressed by the Maior*
> *and Commonality of Winchester against*
> *the Dean and Chapter for that in a*
> *controversie between them the matter*
> *was brought by the Churche men to*
> *the Councell Table where it was ordered,*
> *that the Maior should not carry the*
> *Ensigns of honour of Maioralty when he*
> *came within the Close or pale of the*
> *churche, though the honour of having a*
> *Mace borne was granted by Charter ect.*
> *It was referred to a Committee that did*
> *take consideration of the Councell Table,*
> *although there was some doubt how to*
> *meddle in it because it is meere matter*
> *of honour and noe freehold, which was*
> *entirely vested in the Kings Good will*
> *and pleasure."*

D'Ewes
Harlian Ms
162 f 251a.

By 1640 the political temper of the country had changed and King Charles found he could no longer dictate to the Star Chamber its decisions.

On a new petition from the Mayor the previous Order was cancelled and in 1641 a new Order was made giving the Mayor jurisdiction over the Close and the right to again take the Maces into the Cathedral.

The dispute was marked by much pettiness; the Dean depriving the Mayor of his customary seat, and by the Mayor arriving late for the services.

In Dean Young's own words there was "a great difference betwixt the Church and the Cittie."

Y's D.
143.

The custom of the Mayor attending a service in the Cathedral preceeded by the Maces continues today on Civic Sunday, the first Sunday after Mayor making, and again on Law Sunday.

THE WEST GATE TO THE CITY 12th C.

(18th C. drawing by A. Shepherd – Winchester City Library collection of Etchings)

Nationally the fierce struggle that arose over the religious dissensions between the Established Church and the Non-Conformists was brought to a head by Archbishop Laud's excessive zeal. It was the use of the High Commission Court used to impose his policy of "Uniformity" which eventually led to the formation of the Puriton Party.

Religious dissension first showed in the Cathedral in November 1629, the year King Charles dissolved Parliament, when Dr Moore was charged by his fellow prebends for not conforming with the Archbishop's instructions in doctrine and procedure. In reply Dr Moore

Y's D.
p. 84.

> *"Denayed that he ever spoke anie thing against boweing at the name of Jesus, but Dr Kercher stated that Moore had spoken in front of the Chapter in sermon in his hearing, against that, against standing at the Gloria Patri and (against) bowing, or crouching as he called it, towards the Communion Table."*

Dr Moore declining to accept the Dean's authority resigned, or was compelled to do so, his appointment as a prebend, and when he came to deliver his last sermon he did so without wearing a surplice. Dr Moore must have been a man of strong convictions and courage.

Leach.
p. 344.

The wearing or not of surplices became quite an issue, some time later, it was in 1643, Winchester College received instructions that the young scholars "ought not to be pressed or imposed upon" to wear surplices "it being against law and liberty of the subject."

On the 18th June 1635 Sir Nathaniel Brent, Archbishop Laud's Vicar General, came to Winchester to make his 'Visitation' to the Cathedral and College. He came into the City in the Dean's coach, Dean Young had gone out to meet him, alighting at the City Gate. Sir Nathaniel expected

Y's D.
p. 105.

Win' Cath'
Statutes.

> *"the Mayor and Aldermen s(h)ould have*
> *met him, as at other places, but they*
> *dide not. Then the gentleman ap(p)aritor*
> *carried a mace before him -."*
> as the procession proceeded to the Close.

The Mayor and Corporation were clearly opposed to Laud's injunctions and they and their maces were not going to be put into a position of subjection to the Archbishop's representative.

The political cum religious conflict engendered by the King's dismissal of Parliament, displayed here by the fractious behaviour of the Mayor continued for several years. As another example, on the 26th July 1640 the Dean recorded this incident. The Mayor and Aldermen, who had arrived late for the service turned round and went out finding the way obstructed by the Archdeacon, kneeling at the Commandments, and who would not give way to them.

The Dean endeavoured to keep the peace with the City and even after the Order of 1637 had been recinded in favour of the City, he was still able to persuade the Chapter to present the customary sugar loafe to the Mayor.

Truly a sweetener.

At the end of 1641 the whole town, both Church and City were much divided. Within the Church it was between Conformity or Presbyterianism. Amongst the Corporation and City it was for King or Parliament. Sides were beginning to be taken, shortly, very shortly, they had to be for there was anxious talk of war. Come Christmas 1642 there was indeed Civil War, and as it developed into bitter struggles one sees in Winchester that it was the religious differences in the Nation that displayed themselves as being paramount by the ransacking of the Clergy and the Cathedral here in the City by the Parliamentary armies.

Nevertheless the City of Winchester was and remained true to the Crown and King Charles throughout suffering many many hardships for its loyalty.

Chapter 3

PREPARATIONS FOR WAR

MILITARY preparedness prior to a war has little changed over the ages, usually too little, too late and no money to pay and equip an army. It was so in the 17th century.

Of the Trained Bands Winchester had "but one Captain and his company small". Its Captain in 1625 was Sir William Sandy(s) of Mottisfont

"Both my father before me and myself having been Captains of the City of Winchester these forty years."

The next year, 1626, the City did consider it necessary to employ Sergeant Prince, a soldier who came out of the Low Countries, to train them. At that time there were frequent musters held on Magdalen Hill, which lies on the east side of the City. Some of Sergeant Prince's recruits no doubt embarked at Southampton on the ill fated expedition to La Rochelle led by the Duke of Buckingham, who for his failure was murdered at Portsmouth by Lieutenant John Felton in 1627.

In 1632 there was a sudden sense of urgency for in that year there were four musters, held on June 1st and 28th; July 4th, and August 6th, to which Winchester College sent two men instead of the usual one, paying them two shillings for each muster and sending one shilling and six pence to the Muster Master, as a gratuity, at the end of the exercises.

If the College had to send men so did the Dean and Chapter have to make their contribution by sending four men to "Ye muster" at a cost of four shillings and in addition six shilling and eight pence was paid to

"Blisset for scouring ye armour"

Hammond.

C. S. P.
1625. p. 49.

H. N. & Q.
VII p. 54.

Kirby.
p. 319.

Y's D.
p. 175.

To illustrate the kind of arms and armour available for use in 1632, T.F. Kirby lists, in his "Annals, of Winchester College", the stock held in college from that time until the end of the Civil War apparently without ever being used.

Kirby.
p. 319.

> *Imprimis One blacke demi-launce with*
> *demi pauldrons.*
> *Another demi-launce lent to Bishop*
> *Bilson.* (The Bishop died in 1616).
> *Item One white demi-launce with custres*
> *and pauldrons.*
> *Four blacke corseletts with murreons.*
> *Item Four white almond rivetts with sculls.*
> *Item Three sheaves of arrowes, two paire of*
> *plate sleeves and eighteen other*
> *arrowes.*
> *Item Six calivers with eight flaskes and*
> *three touch boxes.*
> *Item seven flaske leathers and three hangers*
> *one hand weapon with pikes and a*
> *gunne at ye ende.*
> *Item One poleax, one sprinkle, one black*
> *bill, five pikes, two-demi launce*
> *stands and two light horse stands.*
> *Item One red horseman's coate and horseman's*
> *armour.*

p. 320.

A collection of medieval and Elizabethan armour hardly suitable for a trained body of troops but indicative of the type of arms immidiately available in the event of an invasion.

The black armour for a lancer had pauldrons or shoulder pieces for the lance; the white set of armour would presumably have been scoured and polished; and the four white almond (Allemand, German) rivetts were polished armour made up of small plates losely rivetted together. These and the scullcaps, or helmets, were more suitable for Gustavus Adolphus' troops. All very fine to look at, but by the 1640s obsolete and useless.

Nevertheless some of the items were formidable weapons such as the pole-axe and sprinkler. The calivers were small muskets suitable for horsemen and murreons were another form of helmet. The hand weapon with picks and a gun at one end might well have been more dangerous to the user then the enemy.

In that same year of 1632, that saw so many musters, a decision was made to put the city walls in order. Shortly afterwards the Mayor requested the Dean to put the South Gate in repair an ancient obligation imposed on the Prior in 1266 to maintain both South Gate and Kings Gate, for their part in supporting Simon de Montfort's rebellion during the Barons War.

Now, with a new civil war imminent, the walls and gates were to be put in order again.

> *19th Sept 1632.*
> *Item That everie yeare a 10th part*
> *of the Town Walls shall be bee repayre'ed*
> *by the Maior for the tyme beinge at the*
> *charge of the Chamber of the cittie;*
> *which if the say'd Maior, neglect to doe,*
> *there shall be deducted out of his*
> *allowance Ten pounds: And that there*
> *shall be uppon request deliver'd unto*
> *Mr Maior money out of the cofers for*
> *the same purpose.*

Archives of Win'. Ed by C. Bailey. p. 55.

From 1638 levies of troops were being made for King Charles' Scottish war and an army was to be assembled at York. Here in Winchester a great muster was to be held on Magdalen Hill. On the 6th of May 1640 Sir Richard Norton of Rotherfield, a royalist and then a Deputy Lieutenant of the County wrote these letters to his cousin Colonel Richard Norton of Soutwick, a friend of Oliver Cromwell and who came to be known as "Idle Dick Norton".

Norton's Letters.

*"May 6 1640, Sir R Tichborne and
Sir R Norton, deputy lieutenants of
Hants, to James, Duke of Lennox, and
Jerome, Earl of Portland, Lord
Lieutenants of the County; that May 4
we veiwed at Winchester the men to be
impressed for the King's Service, and
found many run away out of the country
and some present were unfit and had to
be refused. Those already impressed
were retained with difficulty owing to
the want of money. Impressed 1000 with
our own money until the money should
come in, and ordered coats for them on
our own credit. Uncertain whether
they will be ready to meet on May 10th
at Basingstoke; Drummers and drums
very scarce. The hardest work is
levying 50 horses for carriage.*

*May 12 the Hundreds of Odiham and
Alton for the most part refuse to pay
the coat and conduct money. The
soldiers for want of pay will mutiny.*

*July 1 Sir R Tichborne and Sir R Norton
met at Magdalen Hill Winchester. County
rated at £2500 and £500 paid by those nearest
us."*

Norton's
Letter Book.

The great cry was money for men, money for defences but
without Parliament to pay the subsidies King Charles and Laud
were unable to impose their will on Scotland. Presbyterianism
prevailed and the National Covenant bound the Scots

*"to defend the true religion and oppose
all innovations on the purity and liberty
of the Gospel"*

Puritans indeed.

King Charles' efforts to obtain money by the imposition of Ship Money, and devices of the Court of Eyre, revived so that the King could make claims and fines on encroachments of the Royal Forests, are but two examples of his method of taxation.

Another, which affected Winchester directly, was the expense involved by the City in trying to renew their Royal Charter. John Lisle the Recorder was never able to succeed in his efforts to obtain this from the King.

Yet other methods of taxation used to sustain the army were 'Free Billeting' of the soldiery, and a particular method noticed in Winchester, used by Captain Sands of the City's Trained Bands of whom it was said, he received money from the recruits impressed by the Deputy Lieutenants in order to secure their discharge. The money no doubt used to pay those who could not afford to buy their way out.

All through the Civil War both sides had their difficulties in recruiting and keeping their troops under arms due to lack of money for 'pay'.

By 1640 King Charles, in urgent need of money, called a Parliament but the House finding His Majesty unwilling to discuss their grievances refused to grant the Subsidies. This the 'Short Parliament' was dissolved after only three weeks.

By November the situation for the King had become desperate and a new Parliament was called, which by then was even more opposed to the King, and had become largely composed of Non Conformists. This the 'Long Parliament' impeached Strafford and Laud, introduced the Root and Branch Bill to abolish episcopacy, and by November 1641 was ready to present the King with the Grand Remonstrance passed by the House with the slender majority of only eleven.

The Remonstrance rejected by King Charles was followed at the beginning of 1642 by his attempt to personally arrest the 'five members' by entering the House himself but without succes for finding them absent he declared "my Birds are flown." Pym and the other members were carried back to the House by the jubilant Londoners in a great procession, while the King left London on the 10th of January, not to return for seven years and then for his trial and execution on the 30th January 1649.

The Winchester members of the Long Parliament were Sir William Ogle, who became an ardent Royalist and Governor of Winchester Castle. The other member was John Lisle the City Recorder and a follower of Cromwel. Lisle was one of King Charles judges and was assassinated in 1664, his wife Alice White Beconsawe, known as Dame Alice Lisle. Twenty one years later she was condemned in the Bloody Assise of 1685.

Jones.
M. PS. of
Andover

Living in the Castle at this time, 1642, was Sir William Waller. He had recently contested a by-election for Parliament at Andover and in a disputed result, decided upon in the House, his opponent Henry Vernon's election was declared void and Sir William Waller's good. This was on the 12th May. As a parliamentarian he certainly could be counted upon to vote with Pym.

It is significant that of the 28 members of Parliament in Hampshire only eight were in sympathy with the King. It is not therefore surprising that the House had voted by 107 to 102 in favour of Waller known to be sympathetic to the Parliamentary cause.

With such differences between king and Parliament, and within Parliament itself, armed conflict seemed to be inevitable as each side tried to impose its will on the other.

Furley.
Quarter
Sessions
Gov't.

In April 1642 Quarter Session government of the County, administered from the Great Hall of the Castle, was suspended. The King issued his Commissions of Array and Parliament passed an Ordnance of Militia.

The Commanders of the Militia, in sending their letters of support to parliaments Ordnance were careful and ambiguous in their statements loathing to take the fatal plunge into war.

1642 "*On the 21st of June the Deputy Lieutenants and the colonels, captains and officers, with the 'cheerful' assent of the soldiers of the trained bands of the county (above 5000 men, besides a great many volunteers) presented a declaration to Parliament.*

   They humbly acknowledge that the Ordinance of Parliament concerning. the Militia doth much conduce to the defence of the true Protestant religion, the defence of His Majesty's sacred person and the preservation of the publique peace and privelege of Parliament against the evills that threaten them by foreign invasion and declared that 'with great sense and grief of heart' they could not but apprehend the continuall practises and attempts of the malignant party to invalidate the said ordinance, wickedly endeavouring to crosse the settlement of the militia by colour of a proclamation set forth in His Majesty's name, forbidding the execution thereof which we humbly conceive to be illegal.

   They therefore tendered their lives and fortunes to Parliament in maintainance of the said Ordinance."

V. C. H. V. p. 337 Quoting from Thomason Tracts

The Lords answered that they were determined to uphold the true religion and the King's authority,

"*not withstanding any danger and hazards that for that cause may befall them.*"

SIR WILLIAM WALLER 1597-1668

Waller was a Parliamentarian General who allowed his troops to despoil the Cathedral and loot the City in
spite of being a Freeman of the City and owner of the Mansion in the Castle.
(Artist unknown – Courtesy National Portrait Gallery)

The County of Hampshire was clearly in favour of the Parliamentary party but in the event Winchester and Basing House became Royalist Strongholds. As an indication of Parliament's fears for the attitude of the City, and ordinance was issued for the seizing and removal of all warlike stores from the storehouse in Wolvesey.

C. S. P.
Add.
16256-49
p. 128.

> 22 July 1642
> *"And whereas in the Store House at*
> *the City of Winton there are Six Field*
> *Pieces,with double carriages, Nine*
> *sows of lead, five dry vats of match*
> *with spoons, ladles and brushes, and*
> *iron bullets for the pieces; which*
> *said pieces and ammunition aforesaid*
> *are belonging to the said County of*
> *Southampton. And whereas it is not*
> *convenient for the use and service of*
> *the said County that those Pieces and*
> *Ammunition aforesaid should remain and*
> *continue in the said Store House.*
> * It is ordered by the said Lords and*
> *Commons that the said Pieces and*
> *Ammunition aforesaid shall be carried*
> *and conveyed into some more convenient*
> *place of the said County, as the Deputy*
> *Lieutenants, or any two or more of them*
> *shall nominate or appoint."*

Journals
of the
H. C.
July 1642,
quoted in
H. N. & Q.
V. p. 85.

Parliament was just in time for on August the Second Lord George Goring declared for

"THE KING ALONE"

and seized Portsmouth Castle.

The reaction of the parliamentarians, led by Sir William Waller, was swift. By the end of August Portsmouth had been retaken for Parliament, the Isle of Wight seized and Southampton secured.

All this in Hampshire before the King had hardly raised his Standard at Edgehill on the 22 August 1642.

War had been declared, Winchester started to arm as the corporation, on the 18th of November, voted money for swords bullets and providing the Citie arms.

Meanwhile the King had set up his headquarters at Oxford and as was usual with him, short of money, sent out letters asking for financial aid.

"To the Dean and Chapter of Winchester.
Charles R.
Trusty and well beloved we
greet you well.

It is well know to what streights
wee are put for moneys by reason of
the distractions and rebellious
attempts against us, which have
constreyned us to make use of the
good affections of our good subjects
to enable us to raise and mainteyne
forces for the defence of our Person
wherein as wee doubt not but to find
you forward and ready to contribute,
soe we have thought good by these our
letters to authorise you by such good
and speedy wayes as you shall conceave
best forthwith to collect such
contributions towards our saide greate
and extraordinary charge and expenses
as the Clergy belonging to our
Cathedrall and diocese of Winton shall
out of their good affections
contribute to us, and to send the same
to us with all diligence for the supply
of our private occasions for which
this shall be your warrant.
Given at our Court at
Maidenhead, the 10th day of November 1642
To our trustie and well beloved
the Dean and Chapter of Winchester."

W. C. D.
p. 54.

The Dean's reply was immediate, some plate was sent and the messengers given 20/- for their trouble. This may have provided financial help to the King but the Dean had to look to his own defences in a practical way. In his diary he recorded

Y's D.
p. 20.
150.

> *"Dec 2 1642. To the Commander*
> *Carmichael to guarde us, 20 lib."*

His plan did not quiet work in the way he had expected for the entry was endorsed.

> *"Of that 20 lib which I tooke for the Commander I sent by Mr Chanter to the Queer (choir) 10 lib and to the toune 10 lib."*

The Dean had much to be anxious about, for it was the declared intention of the House to abolish episcopacy, and in the churches to forewith remove the Communion Table from the east end of the church or chancel into some other convenient place, to take away the rails and to level the chancels. Crucifixes, pictures, of any person of the Holy Trinity and images of the Virgin were to be destroyed, and all tapers candlesticks and basons were to be removed from the Communion Table. Further it was also ordered "that all corporal bowing at the name of Jesus or towards the east end of any church chapel or chancel be henceforth forborne."

It was this order which proved to be indeed very cause and excuse for Sir William Waller's parliamentary troops to destroy so much in the Cathedral and Churches in the City of Winchester.

Trussel in his "Benefactors to Winchester" sadly writes,

"But alas the tyde is turn' d
And warrs my hopes of comfort have adjourned
And all this plate and stocks are rookt awaye
And nothing left the poore to paye
Most miserable what shall become of mee   Trussel
I nothing but apparant daunger see   f. 95
of utter ruine; like the anvil I
with many hammers beat uppon doe lye
ffor now the Cavaleers anon the troopers
To daye the Catholicks to morrowe dopers
Abuse my cittyzens and their howses rifle
And doe my quiett smother and my peace stifle
And all the miseryes that attend on warr
too visible in me increased are,
And all the blessings that attend on peace
doe every day mutch more then more decrease
The hope of thoroughfare or healp of trade
the use of fayers and markets are decayed
the former cours of Assise and Sessions is lost
and expectations of sutch meetings crost,
Tavernes and Innes have neither wine nor haye
To entertayne guests, all is fetcht awaye
And one uppon an other (in a maze)
with most dejected countenance stand and gaze
Children for meate, servants for wages call   f. 96
landlords for rent, But all want wherewithal
contentment to procure: The poore
                    want sustenance
and what was given for their mantaynance
is snatcht out of their mouthes: they are like to
and nothing least their being preserve (starve)
Heer ends the first sceane of my tragedye."

TV DeV IaM propItIVs sIs regI regnoquVe
        hVIC VnIverso

O goD noVV sheVV faVoVr to the kIng   Cave.
        anD thIs VVhoLe LanD   Win' Cath'
                                  Roof Bosses.

VDVIMIIVIIVVICVIV 1642 DVVVVVVIDIVVLLD

Chapter 4

THE TAKING OF WINCHESTER
CHRISTMAS 1642

Trussel.

> *"But now appears my greater misery*
> *ffor where before those that must bent the brow*
> *were but of meane or middle fashion, now*
> *all alike suffer, and both sides alike*
> *uppon mee as a washing blocke doe strike*
> *Lord Grandison heer with some troops of horse*
> *opposed by all the parliaments whole force*
> *They being mutch to strong, hee did retreat*
> *And hardly did into my Castle gett.*
>   *Retired into my Castle, Grandison*
> *from mee demaunds present provision*
> *or otherwise hee threttens fire: the sword*
> *on the otherside unsheathed is: The Lord*
> *is pacified with what the Maior did send,"*

Each side sent out parties ranging the country for men, arms and money. According to the Royalists the rebels were out for booty, and according to the parliamentarians the malignants were out for plunder.

Mercurius Rusticus the royalist newspaper wrote,

Mercurius
Rusticus.

> *"About December 1642, the Collonels*
> *Waller, Brown, and others, marching*
> *from Ailesbury to Windsor, and thence*
> *by Newbury to Winchester, their*
> *soldiers in the march plundered every*
> *minister within six miles of the road*
> *without distinction whether of their*
> *own party or of the other, whether*
> *they subscribed for Episcopacy,*
> *Presbytery, or Indepenency, whether*
> *they wore a surpless or refused it,*
> *only if they did not afforded them*
> *the less booty."*

At the beginning of December a party of Royalists had been in the Marlborough area and were returning with their plunder towards Oxford when they learnt that Sir William Waller was approaching from the direction of Newbury. The Royalists commander, Lord Digby, had gone ahead to Oxford with some of the troops and most of the plunder, while William Villiers, Lord Grandison, with 300 horse and Colonel Grey's dragoons 200 strong found themselves opposed by a greatly superior force blocking their way from Marlborough back to Oxford. They turned south through Andover towards Winchester in unfamiliar territory for Grandison's had been recruited in Somerset, and Colonel Grey's came from Northumberland. In the words of John Vicars the Parliamentary writer who said of the Royalists,

> *"fearing to be caught napping by*
> *active Sir William Waller and his*
> *force and the better to protect*
> *himself and his Cavaliers from the*
> *pursuit of the Parliaments force*
> *(Grandison) retreated to Winchester,*
> *a place not like to give him kind*
> *enterainment being full of Malignant*
> *spirits, who indeed were not a little*
> *glad at his coming, thinking*
> *themselves now secure from danger*
> *being under the wings of a bird of*
> *theire own feathers."*

Vicars.
Parliamentary
Chronicle.

On Tuesday the 12th of December the opposing armies clashed in the area of Wherewell. In the skirmish that followed the Royalists cut off a company of parliamentary dragoons, taking their colours. Contact with the rebels had been made but the flight to Winchester became a stampede.

Christopher Luckner, in command of the Royalists advance guard to their withdrawal on Winchester, drew rein at the North gate just as Lord Ogle was dining at the Chequers Inn (NatWest Bank) . He brought an order to the Mayor, Mr Longland, to provide Quarters for twenty five horse and dragoons. This was followed by the arrival at the City, of what was described as, six regiments. As the total strength was only about five hundred of Grandison's and Grey's regiments it would seem the Royalists were organised into six companies.

In the City the general alarm had been given and the call to arms made. The Parliamentarians for their part, incensed by the loss of their company with its colours and eager for the fray pursued Grandison to the town walls overtaking some of his horse before they could reach the safety of the City.

Some of the citizens came out to help the fleeing Royalists who

A True
Relation
of the
overthrow
give to the
Cavaliers
Dec. 1642
County
Archives
2438 b.

"finding it altogether unsafe to
keep themselves within the town and
give Parliaments forces opportunity
to beseige them for that they could
not be able to hold out long for
want of provisions they resolved to
march out and give them battel, and
accordingly put their forces into
battalia and marched out before the
Towne to a pitched fight which the
Parliaments forces perceiving, also
drew up their forces into battalia
and came up bravely to the charge
with their horse, there then being
a very hot skirmish for the time on
both sides. The Parliaments soldiers
followed their business so bravely
with undaunted courage that after
about half an houres fight they
forced the Cavaliers from their ground
and drove them into Towne again"

Or as was said by Nathaniel Fiennes serving in the parliamentary horse

Fiennes'
Letter
to the Lord
General.

> " We beat them back and
> surrounded the place with
> horse and dragoons."

and by the Royalists,

> "The rebells under the conduct of
> Sir William Waller sate down before
> the City of Winchester on Tuesday
> the 12th of December about twelve
> of the clock."

The excitement and noise created by Grandison's horse, galloping through the North Gate covered by musketeers, the rush to man the walls mingled with fear as it was realised that war, civil war, and all its horrors was literally on their threshold. All this must have raised cries of alarm, panic and despair.

It was certainly a bad moment for the Royalists, heavily outnumbered and ill provisioned. Further in the Castle the Sheriff had summoned all the soldiers (Commanders) and many gentlemen to a meeting to assess the County for maintenance of the King's Army. All were trapped.

The situation was, as Lord Ogle said of Grandison's resolution to stay in Winchester,

Ogle's
Engagements.
Add Mss
27402

> "contrary to all advise and reason
> to draw into Winchester Castle"

for disaster and ruin followed.

Grandison's and Grey's entire Regiments were destroyed, their officers and all the Sheriff's deputies taken prisoner and for two days the riotous and undisciplined Parliamentary troopers sacked the City.

When Waller arrived on the scene he found the gates shut, but knowing the town well, with his own house in the Castle, he at once invested and blockaded the City to prevent his enemy escaping. Then after making a further reconnaissance of the walls, while awaiting the arrival of his dragoons, planned an immediate assault.

The north wall was protected by a water filled ditch, and the east wall by the river Itchen. As the direction, of the approaching main body of his parliamentary force was from Andover, the natural place to be considered for the first assault would have been the west wall and there as described at the time it took place on that side of the town where the old walls had partially broken down, yet the side which had the deepest ditches and steepest banks. A likely place would have been about mid way between the West Gate and the Hermits Tower. A position now occupied by the County Council's multi storey car park in Tower Street.

Waller would have been anxious to take and secure the town before nightfall, with time to find billets for his troopers, and time to find provender for the horse. They had been on the march several days so there was to be no delay.

The attack took place about half past two, and after half an hours fierce fighting the wall was successfully stormed. Colonel Brown's regiment being the first to breach the wall and break into the town. This was about 3 o'clock.

The Royalists having no where else to betake themselves, fled into the Castle.

Fiennes briefly described the situation at that moment saying we

Fienne's
Letter.

*"forced an entry into the towne
but evening coming on (we) were
unable to take the castle, where
the sheriff had summoned all the
soldiers and many gentlemen to meet,
to assess the County for maintenance
of the King's Army."*

The Castle ill provisioned, unfortified and without ordnance was not to be the safe refuge Grandison hoped.

The best and most detailed account of the 'Storming of Winchester' was written by Vicars who continued his narrative saying, the Parliamentarians

"most valiantly pursued them to the town   Vicars.
walls where the most part of their Regiment
fiercly assaulted the Citie at one side of
it, and not withstanding the exceeding
high and very steep passage up to the
walls, even so steep that they had no
other way to get up but of necessity to
creep up upon their knees and hands from
the bottom to the top which was as high
as most houses, the enemy playing all the
while on them with their muskets and yet
slew but three men in this getting up, so
at last (though with much danger and
difficulty) our soldiers got up and plied
their business so hotly and closely that
they had quickly made a great breach in
the wall.

And here Colonel Browne's Sergeant Major
deserved much honour in this service, he
himself being one of the first that forced
upon the breach into the town, though the
enemies bullets flew thick about them, upon
sight of whose ever invinciple valour all
the rest of his comrades followed close
and drove the Cavaliers before them into
the midst of the towne, who having no place
else of shelter fled apace into the castle,
which yet was not so considerable a
sanctuary to defend them long, especially
it being destitute of ordnance, so our men
beset the castle round with musqueteers and
horse and lay per dues (they lay in hiding)
under the wall, so that not a man of
them could stir."

That evening Nathaniel Fiennes, who commanded the 36th Troop of Parliaments horse, billeted his troop in Winchester College. Fiennes had been admitted to the College as a Commoner in 1623 as of 'Founder's Kin'. William of Wykeham founded Winchester College in 1382, "Founders Kin" were descendants of his sister Alice Champneys.

T. F. Kirby in his "Annals of Winchester College" gives the following references to this occasion taken from the Bursar's book

<table>
<tr><td></td><td></td><td>s</td><td>d</td></tr>
<tr><td>Militibus Mri Fines</td><td>20</td><td>0</td><td>0</td></tr>
<tr><td>Quibusd. militibus relictis</td><td>5</td><td>0</td><td>0</td></tr>
<tr><td>Sex aliis militibus</td><td>2</td><td>0</td><td>0</td></tr>
<tr><td>Pro modio frumenti expens in militibus</td><td></td><td>5</td><td>0</td></tr>
<tr><td>Militibus quibusdam per Mrum Hacket et Mrum informatorem</td><td></td><td>5</td><td>0</td></tr>
<tr><td>Ric'o Frampton pro xij modiis brasii pro equis famulorum Mri Fines tempore guerrae</td><td>1</td><td>5</td><td>6</td></tr>
<tr><td>Pro le watch in hospitio Dni Custodis</td><td></td><td></td><td>6</td></tr>
<tr><td></td><td>28</td><td>16</td><td>0</td></tr>
</table>

Kirby p. 331.

Paid for Mister Fienne's soldiers, those that remained behind, and for six other soldiers; for a bushel of corn expended, and paid 5/- as a tip, to the soldiers on the directions of Mr Hacket (who was a Fellow of the College and presumably in Winchester at that time) and the Head Master.

Richard Frampton was the College brewer and he provided twelve bushels of mash for Mr Fiennes followers. Famulorem would imply personal servants, perhaps Frampton used the term in a slightly cynical way. The last entry 'for the watch' or guard to the Wardens house was interpreted by Kirby as suggesting Nathaniel Fiennes slept in the Warden's Lodging with a sentinel at the door.

Fiennes had arrived with his troop on Tuesday. The next morning he watched the surrender of the Castle, as will be related in a moment, and remained in the City until Thursday. Some of his troop were sent away as escort to the prisoners, while six others joined those that remained of his troop, in what must have been in the circumstances a very comfortable billet.

The College accounts record sixty one-pound loaves being provided for the men's supper and breakfast.

There is no indication of the number of men billeted, but if the College had to pay £28 16s plus free bread and fodder for a single troop, one may wonder what had been the cost of billeting Wallers entire army, said to be 5000 horse and dragoons who somehow or other crowded into the town to find shelter from the cold December nights.

There is no evidence of any spoilation of the College at this time, or at all during the Civil War. The College was allowed to retain their revenues, Parliament taking care not to in any way to interfere with the schools, other than that they should conform in religious matters.

In the town, as the weary troopers and the much troubled citizens tried to settle down for the night in an uneasy sleep, the silence broken by the calls of the sentries, the clatter of hoofs and rumblings of carts as preparations were being made to lay siege to the castle.

To intimidate Grandison's small command the Parliamentarians

> " Seised upon four pieces of ordnance which was in the Towne and drew them up against the castle to batter the same, where upon the Cavaliers conceiving themselves to be all dead men, (like the City Malignants about their petition) cryed for quarter upon any tearms, which upon conditions was granted."

A True Relation.

Portal.
p. 34

Vicars relates that at about ten or eleven o'clock a great quantity of faggots and pitch barrels were prepared ready to fire the Castle Gate and as the position of Lord Grandison became no longer tenable he sounded a parley which was accepted.

After some debate, articles and conditions were agreed upon, namely

> *"That they should all yield themselves*
> *up prisoners to the Parliament, and*
> *resign the Castle unto Sir William*
> *Waller's custody and possession.*
>
> *Their arms, horses, money, and all, to be*
> *seized on by Parliaments' officers*
> *in arms."*

The Articles for the surrender of Winchester being,

> *"That the whole force in the castle*
> *be fortwith brought into a field at*
> *the town's end near the castle.*
>
> *That no violence or incivility be*
> *offered to the Commanders and other*
> *Gentlemen and that they be preserved*
> *as far as in us lies from all plundering*
> *and rioting.*
>
> *That we represent to the Lord General*
> *the Earl of Essex why they should be*
> *returned again to the King's army,*
> *having given up themselves and the*
> *Castle on these conditions.*
> > *Signed*
> > > *Grandison.*
> > > *Richard Willis.*
> > > *Ralph Hebberne."*

H. M. C.
Report 13
Vol I. p. 79.
13. Dec 1642.

Of the sad events of Wednesday morning Nathaniel Fiennes said

> *"The next morning Lord Grandison*
> *came out and surrendered the castle*
> *upon conditions, but we were unable*   Fiennes.
> *to enforce the observancs of the*
> *Commanders and Gentlemen from violence*
> *and pillaging."*

Thus the Castle fell to Parliament; those surrendering were abused and havoc was to be wrought on the City.

Chapter 5

THE TOWN AND CLOSE
PLUNDERED

WHILE Grandison and five or six others were negotiating with Waller the 'Conditions' for the surrender of the Castle, the Mayor was trying to settle the terms to avoid the town being set on fire and looted.

Trussel.

"They were glad to compound for £1000
to save the City from pillage."

Trussel said this was agreed in writing

"They underhand did give me assurance
I should be exempt from further greivance ."

Alas, the conditions and terms agreed with Grandison and the Mayor with Waller were soon, too soon, broken by the jubilant and riotous Parliamentary troopers, who when they fully appreciated their total victory and that the town was theirs, rebelled against their officers and pillaged the Royalist prisoners.

And then, on the pretext that the town's ransome had not been paid, they rioted and went on the rampage seeking loot and revenge on the townsmen who had sided with the Cavaliers.

Parliaments 'Eye Witness' reported

Sterley.

"The greatest opposition we had in
taking (Winchester) was from the
Townesmen who have sufficiently
paid for it."

However, as will be seen, some in the town were eager enough to see the Papists pillaged.

To repeat a small part of Fiennes' letter and then to continue in his words,

> *" The next morning Lord Grandison*
> *came out and surrendered the castle*
> *upon certain conditions, but we were*
> *unable to enforce the observance of*
> *the condition for the protection of*
> *the commanders and gentlemen from*
> *violence and pillaging, for the*
> *(Parliamentary) soldiers were in such*
> *a state of mutiny that the officers*
> *and gentlemen were not only some of*
> *them stripped and pillaged but put*
> *in fear of their lives, whilst some*
> *of the soldiers actually shot at*
> *their own officers who tried to*
> *prevent this violence"*

Fiennes.

Cornet Sterley who took part on the assault of the walls wrote,

> *"The prisoners were despoiled contrary*
> *to the articles of surrender even to*
> *their clothes, four or five pulling at*
> *one cloak like hounds at the leg of a*
> *dead horse."*

Sterley.

It was said of Sterley, disgusted by the behaviour of the soldiers and many other disorderly passages, that only his zeal for the right cause prevented him from leaving the army. The surrender utterly complete the mutinous troopers then finding themselves master of the place ran riot through the Town and fell upon the Close on a pretence of a search for hiding Cavaliers.

Godwin.
p. 45.

*"They seized upon the Prebends horses
and demanded their persons with
threatening words..."*

*"...our soldiers most notably plundered
and pillaged their houses taking
whatsoever they liked best out of
them but chiefly some Papists houses
there, and the sweet Cathedralists in
whose houses and studies they found
great store og Popish books and
Crucifixes which the soldiers carried
up and down the streets and market
place in triumph to make themselves
merry"*

Vicars.
quoted in
W. C. D.
p. xxiv.

Trussel retells the story of the destruction wrought by the
Parliamentarians this way,

*" But the other being entred, doe pretend
the conquest of mee, and as if conquerors
made all the inhabitants in mee sufferers
by plundering whome they pleased and
              slaughtering those
whome they malignants stild: and for a close
unto their stomaches they spoyld all the meate
That was for either horse or man to eate
They then demand to have a thousand pound
or else my howes should be fired round
This mony hardly gathered, At length payd
And nothing that they did demaund denayed
They under hand did give to me assurance
I showld exempted bee from further greivance
Then did departe. But yett before they went
like candlesnuffe behind they leaft a sent
so stinking that it did the nostrills stuff
of all, for all might take the same in snuff
ffor after I had Composition made
because the mony was not forthwith payd"*

Trussel
f. 96.

Chapter 6

SPOILATION OF THE CATHEDRAL

"They in the interim in a pert derision
Of order, Disaplyne and trew Religion
my great Church entred and so prophanely abused
That Turcks the same could not more baselye have
        used
With Dunge of horse and man (an act most vile)
The Church and Chauncell they att once defile
The Bible, organs and Communion table
They teare, pull downe and make unserviceable;
The cushions, hangings and quier ornament
They most prophanely tare and baselye rent;
The urnes of Brittishe, Saxon, Danish Norman Kings
And sacred monuments, as unworthy things
and those reserves of Kings, Queens and mitred
        Prelatts
Which Bishopp Fox had placed their, theise zelotts
did them demolishe and their ashes flung
Amongs their owne filth and their horses doung
And having leaft nothing undone that night
expresse their mallice or declare the spight
to King and Church, prowd in their villanye
(as being theirin not surpast by any)
In triumph they departed, leaving mee
To tast the leeze of their impiety."

Trussel.
f. 95.

From this description of the despoiling of the Cathedral by Waller's troopers, it is possible to imagine them entering by the west door and riding down the nave, a large and open space, to face the new Inigo Jones choir screen with the bronze statues of King James and King Charles, standing as on guard in their niches at each side of the entrance. There those troopers, compelled to dismount before entering the choir, hacked at and discharged their muskets at those hated Royal effigies. Then having gained an entrance to choir and presbytery they wrought the further havoc described by Trussel.

WINCHESTER CATHEDRAL NAVE

The open Nave as it would have appeared to Waller's marauding troops
(Britton' History of the Cathedral 1818)

There they pulled the beautiful Renaissance painted mortuary chests, scattering the bones of the Kings and Bishops. This particular act of desecration is recorded on one of the coffers replaced at the Restoration.

Clarendon
& Gale

In hac cista A. D. 1661 promisque
Recondita sunt ossa Principum et
Praelatorum Sacrilega Barbarie
dispersa A. D. 1642.

Brayley.
p. 66

In this chest in the year 1661 were promiscuously laid together the bones of the Princes and Prelates which had been scattered about by sacriligious barbarism in the year 1642.

From the 'chauncell' or presbytery the troopers then went into the retro-choir to cause further destruction to the Chantries, the Lady Chapel and the mediaeval glass.

Returning by the south presbytery aisle to the south transept, they rampaged through the library looking for apparently nothing more than silver, and ransacked the vestries searching for plate and any other treasures that could be easily converted into money.

Frustrated by lack of loot they bedecked themselves with vestments returning to the nave to remount and gallop out. Yet, perhaps caught by the lustre of the great west window, depicting the Saints and so recently repaired by Dean Young, they then

Y.'s D.
p. 25

may have halted to fire a salvo of musket shot into the glass in what was to them a final "feu-de-joie"

When Lieutenant Hammond visited the City his route around the Cathedral almost exactly preceded that followed by Waller's desecrating troopers, so it is of very cogent interest to follow Hammond's description in detail and compare this with the contemporary accounts of the destruction. Hammond's visit coincided with the completion and painting of the tower vault in 1635, and before the building of Inigo Jones choir screen.

HAMMOND'S DESCRIPTION OF THE CATHEDRAL IN 1635

CHOIR
Stalls

"Brave old Mother Cathedral which I found faire and long being 200 of my paces, the longest I dare say exept plaine old St Pauls
Her quire up to the high altar being 60 paces long, the roofe whereof is stately fayre, and rich to adorne which, and to beautifie the same, a great Summe of Money hath beene very lately bestow'd with the Armes of the Nobility richly gilded.
And as above on the Roofe, so over the Deanes, Prebends, and Quiristers Seats is rich Joyners worke; but more remarkable artificiall, and rare Postures, ravishing the eyes of the beholders, in a lively wooddy Representation, Portraits, and Images from the creation, to the Passion which though it tooke me some time to take (my notes), yet I thought it neverthelesse not idely, ill spent time, for me to decipher the same"

Hammond.
p. 48.

Hammond described in great detail the pictures which were in the panels above each stall, which are now painted blue and decorated with stars. They must have been loose panels to have been so easily pulled down and trampled upon, for all were destroyed.

Hammond's description of the pictures in the panels is given on page 250.

ORGAN

"The organs in this church are not exceeding faire nor rich, but sweet tunable, and sweetly played on, by one of the rarest organists that this land affords, who is now of his Majesties Chappel. The Quiristers were skillful and the voices good, where they sing sweet and heavenly Anthems."

Hammond.
p. 46.

Matthews
ORGANS
in Win'
Cath'.

The organist referred to by Hammond was Thomas Holmes, he was succeeded by Christopher Gibbons in 1638. The organ was destroyed in 1642 when Gibbons left Winchester to fight for the Royalist cause from Oxford.

MORTUARY
CHESTS

Hammond.
p. 46.

*"Her monuments are many, fayre and
ancient especially 10 in little wooden
gilt Coffers, are wrapt, and shrin'd in
lead, the bones of 4 Saxon Kings,
2 Danish Kings and 4 Bishops and a Queen
which were taken up, and preserved by
Bishop Fox, when he built up that part
of the Quire where they were interr'd:
They are equally plac'd and fix'd
between the Quire and the High Altar,
on the top of the wall. 5 on one side
and 5 on the other vizt.
King Canutus and his son Hardicanute
both in one, and 4 more Saxon Kings,
Egbert, Elfred, Adulphusand Gilsus,
with their Crownes on the top of those
boxes. On the north side is Queen Emma
and her sonne, and 4 Saxon Bishops with
the miters thereon."*

There are now six mortuary chests, four of Bishop Fox's time, and two made after the Restoration in which to place the relics which had been carefully swept up and somehow preserved after their desecration by the troopers.

According to the inscription on the four coffers of Bishop Fox's time, those on the north side contain the bones of Kings; Edmund, Edbert and Kenulph: while those on the south side hold the bones of Kings; Adulphus (Ethelwulf), Kinegils and Edred. The two Restoration period chests in which were promiscously laid the bones of the Princes and Prelates contain the relics of Kings; Cnut and Rufus; and Queen Emma. Bishops; Wina and Alwyn. However, it is not now accepted that the bones of William Rufus rest under the 'dos d'ane' marble tomb in the centre of the choir, described by Hammond as then being near the high Altar.

RUFUS'
TOMBE

*"The plaine Marble Tombe of William
Rufus, in the fashion of a coffin, south
against the High Altar, Saint
Swithuns Shrine. In a neat wrought
Chappel, with French Cane (Caen) stone,
artificially cut and carv'd, lyeth the
foremention'd Bishop Fox. Under that his
Anatomy in a grate; he was founder of
Corpus Christi Colledge in Oxford, his*

FOX'S
CHANTRY

*curious neat Closet by it, wherein is
artfully cut and richly gilt, the
Churches Armes, the Cross Keys with the
sword joined with his owne, the Pellican
picking her breast.*

PRESBYTERY
VAULT

*Also the Club, Sword, Darke Lanthorne
and Hand, The Post, Scourge, and Whip,
the Speare, Spunge and Buckett, the side
and hands streaming Blood, the 3 Nailes
Cords, Etc: the three Dice, with Angells
between every one of them. The seeling
is very rich, with the Armes of King
Henry 7th, his owne, and the Colledges,
and the Churches alone, very finely gilt.*

GARDINER'S
CHANTRY

*Over against this on the north side of
the High Altar and St Swithuns Shrine,
is another neat built Chappel, call'd
Bishop Gardiner's, answerable, and in
imitation of this, though not so rich,
nor so artificially wrought but of the
same modell and height, under which lyes
his Anatomy as in this.*

BEAUFORT'S
CHANTRY

*Between these 2 monuments of an equal
height, right against each other. Th'
one Cardinall Beaufort's marble Tombe,
the top and roof of Cane stone, and
artificially wrought, he lieth in brass,
his statue upon itt in wood; This
Cardinall Bishop was the Founder of that
Stately Hospitall thereby, called St Crose's.*

Hammond.
p. 47.

WAYNEFLETE
CHANTRY

The other is Bishop Wainfleete with 4 Columne
Pillers of Marble most artificially cut and wrought
of Cane stone as Bishop Fox's is."

The effigy on Beaufort's tomb was destroyed during the
Civil War and replaced soon after the Restoration. The effigy has
17th century shoes. Hammond then goes by Wayneflete's chantry,
passing the tomb he attributed to the legendary King Lucius. This
is now ascribed to Bishop Godfrey de Lucy the builder of the
Retro-choir. The tomb robbed of its brass embelishments rests in
front of the entrance to the Lady Chapel.

In the Lady Chapel itself a great deal of damage was done
to the furniture and the great Jesse Window installed in the late
15th century and vandalised by the Troopers.

Hammond then described the Tudor "X" purple velvet
chair, known as Queen Mary's chair.

Hammond.
p. 47.

LADY
CHAPEL

"Close by lyeth King Lucius, the first
Christian King of England under a plaine
Marble stone, like a coffin with 7 Pummels
of Brasse like a Cross. The faire
gravestone of Pryor Westgate thereby.
In the Lady Chapell is Pryor Silkstead
and Pryor Hunton under 2 faire Marble
Gravestones of 3 yards long. These 2
founded this Chappell as appeareth by the
badges they gave it, the gilded Tun and
Steed all over the roofe, pretty Conceits
that Pryors and Officers then used.
In the Chappell are 3 fayre Windows, one
at the East end thereoff, in which is
painted the Genealogie from the Root of
Jesse, 14 Generations; another on the North
side contayning the History of the
Revelation with the Saints praysing and
glorifying God. In the South window which is
the third, is the History of the Nativity of
our Saviour. In this chappell is placed the
Purple Velvet Chayre, wherein (if you
beleeve Mr Verger) Queen Mary did sit, when
she was marry'd to King Philip in his
standing posture.

GUARDIAN
ANGELS
CHAPEL

In a little Chappell on the North
side of the Lady Chappel in a vault
is interred Sir Richard Weston Earle
of Portland, and Lord Treasurer, so
lately, as no Monument as yet made
for him.

Neer unto this on the wall is Sir
Thomas Mason a Privy Counsellor."

Hammond.

The bronze effigy of Sir Richard Weston by Le Sueur had not by then been placed on his tomb in the Guardian Angels Chapel. The Mason monument is in the Retro-choir on the north wall opposite Wayneflete's Chantry.

Hammond then returned to the choir by the south aisle, noticing a monument he describes as that of the Duke of Richmond. This monument is likely to be that of Richard, son of William the Conqueror, Duke of Beorn (Bernay) Normandy.

Crossing over to the north transept he next notices a monument to a "Templar Knight", the Crusader Arnaud de Gaveston, in a vault immediately to the west of the Chapel of the Holy Sepulchre now filled with part of the organ.

NORTH
TRANSEPT

"South of the Quire, close to the
wall, under a faire Marble stone
lyeth Duke of Richmond.

In the north cross Ile against
the Quire lieth a Templar Knight
of the Rhodes in a cross legg'd
Posture, a Coat of Maile, Cap a Pee,
with his sword drawne, his coat
of arms 6 wheat sheaves Argent
3 Bulls Gules with Bells about
their neckes. And by the Warlike
Knight is Domesday vault, where the
evidence of this Kingdome was kept
of old."

The effigy of the Crusader, Arnaud de Gaveston now lies in the north aisle of the retro-choir, while the shield slab which formed the base is now used as the front to the altar in the Guardian Angels Chapel. The Gaveston arms are quarterly; 1 and 4 or two cows passant gules collared and belled azure, for the Comte de Bearn to whom he owed allegiance; 2 and 3 azure three garbes (wheatsheaves) or, for Edward I Duke of Chester with whom he served in the Welsh wars; and overall a Cross of St George to shew he had crusaded with King Edward.

Hammond then moved back into the nave, crossed over to Wykeham's Chantry before returning to examine the Clerk Monument, then newly erected on the north wall of the aisle opposite Edington's Chantry.

The Clerk monument is in the then new Jacobean style, and the paint would have been fresh, colourful and a new attraction. Adjacent was the monument to the "son and Heyre" of Sir George Paulet (of Crondal). Hammond continues,

Hammond.
p. 48.

WYKEHAMS
CHANTRY

" *In the Church lyeth that great Favourer and liberall Mayntainer of Schollers Bishop Wickham, his Statue cut in Alabaster, in his Pontificall robes, with 3 Schollers at his feet, and is a curious decent Tombe: he vaulted the Roofe of this spacious church, and inlarg'd the Pillers, which are very fayre and large; hee was Founder of that stately Colledge there; of New Colledge in Oxford, and of a free schoole in Paris.*

There goes a story of this bishop; that he beg'd of the King, which whatsoever obtaines, is Bishop of the Diocesse which was (as it seem'd) more than the King knew when he granted it. Whereupon the King was duspleased and the Bishop displac'd and with the helpe of some backe friends at Courte, he was banished, and went to Paris:

"After the angry frowne of his displeas'd Prince was stopt by Death, this good old Bishop came over again and did those famous deeds, and was ever a great lover and liberal rewarder of Learning and Schollers.

On the North Ile of the church, is the Monument of two brothers of the surname Clarke wherewith I was so taken as take them I must and as I found them, I pray accept them.

Thus a union of 2 Brothers from Avington the Clarks family, were Grandfather, Father, and Son successively Clerkes of the Privy Seale in Court.

The grandfather had but 2 sons both Thomas
Their wives both Amys
Their heyres both Henry   VAUGHAN
                                        Win' Cath.
And the heyres of Henries were Inheretrix's
And both had 2 sons and one Daughter
And both their Daughters Issulesse
Both of Oxford : Both of the Temple   Milner A B.
Both Officers to Queen Elizabeth, and our
*   noble King James*
And both Justices of the Peace   Monument
Together both agree in Armes, one a   in South
Knight, the other a Captaine.   Stoneham
                                        Church.

Si quaeras plura, Both And so I leave them.

Neere this Monument, which I have set forth at large, is a neat one for the son and Heyre of Sir George Paulet.
On the South of the crosse Ile, lies an old Bishop in   Dickenson.
Marble, Founder of the Organs; And by him, which was the   on Clerke
last I saw, was the Monument of the last Pryor, and First   Monument.
Deane heere, his Name, Basing."

Hammond was then escorted to the vestry in the south transept passing the monument to the last Prior and first Dean William Kingsmill of Basing. This monument has dissapeared but its position is marked by a memorial on the choir screen.

Hammond.
p. 49.

> *"After I had taken a full view of*
> *the Monuments I was conducted into*
> *the Vestry, where I saw many rich*
> *Hangings, and Cloths. One of velvet*
> *wrought with Gold for the High Altar,*
> *which was given by Bishop Fox. Others*
> *of Cloth of Tissue and faire Cushions*
> *which were given by Sir John Paulet.*
> *Another of Cloth of Gold fill'd with*
> *Pearle wire. A rich and faire Canopie*
> *of Cloth of Cloth of Gold to carry over the*
> *King, 12 faire Cushions of red and*
> *blew Velvet with Lions and flower*
> *de Luce's in them wrought in Gold."*

The quotations of Hammond have been extensively given for, apart from their intrinsic interest, they help to give a feeling of the times. Too they help one to fully appreciate the effects of Laud's reforms, King Charles personal influence and Dean Young's vigour in making the Cathedral, as they saw it, a fit place in which to worship God. Further they describe the Cathedral with a sense of awe and delight at the colourful ceilings and monuments the fine joinery and splendid furnishings, the rich carpets and cushions. Also the gorgeous vestments and sweet tunable organs. The skillful quirister singing sweet and heavenly anthems.

A superb and colourful setting for worship. Contemplate on Hammond's marvellous word picture of the Cathedral in it's full glory, for that is what the Puritans destroyed.

The physical damage to the structure was not so great as to be irreparable, but there were permanent losses of mediaeval glass, statuary, ornaments, furniture, and decorations.

Who would gainsay that the Cathedral on the early morning of December the 14th 1642 was a magnificent and beautiful church. Of the first despoilation during the Civil War the Royalist Mercurius Rusticus, Bruno Ryves, relates,

Leach.
p. 342.

MERCURIUS RUSTICUS

*"On thursday Morning between nine
and ten of the Clock, they violently
breake open the Cathedral Church, and
being entred, to let in the Tyde,
they presently open the Great West
doores where the Barbarous Soldiers
stood ready, nay greedy to rob God,
and pollute his Temple.*

M. R.

*The doores being open, as if
they meant to invade God Himselfe, as
well as his possesion. They enter
the church with Colours flying their
drums beating, that all might have
their part in so horrid an attempt,
some of their Troops of Horse also
accompanied them in their march, and
road up through the body of the Church
and Quire, until they came to the
Altar, then they begin their work,
they rudely pluck down the Table and
break the Rayle; and afterwards
carrying it to an Alehouse, they set
it on fire, and in that fire burnt
the Books of Common Prayer, and all
the singing books belongig to the
Quire.*

*They throw down the organ, and
breake the stories of the Old and
New Testament curiously cut out in
the carved work, beautified with
colours and set round about the top
of the stalls of the quire.*

M. R.

*From hence they turn to the
monuments of the dead, some they
utterly demolish, others they deface
They begin with Bishop Fox, his
chappell, which they utterly deface,
they break all the glass windows in
the chappell not because they had any
pictures in them either of Patriarch,
Prophet, Apostle, or Saint, but
because they were painted coloured
glass.*

*They demolished and overturned the
Monuments of Cardinal Beaufort son to
John of Gaunt, Duke of Lancaster, by
Katherine Swinford founder of the
hospital of S. Cross, near Winchester
who sate (as) bishop of this See
forty three years.*

*They deface the monument of William
Wainflet, Bishop likewise of
Winchester, Lord Chancellor of
England and the Magnificent founder
of Magdalen College in Oxford which
monument in a grateful piety, being
lately beautified by, some that have
or lately have had relation to that
foundation, made the rebels more
eager upon it to deface it, but while
that colledge, the unparalleled
example of his bounty stands in
despight of the malice of these
inhuman rebels, William of Wainflet
cannot want a more lasting monument
to transmit his memory to posterity."*

The rebellious Parliamentary troopers then went to the Lady Chapel called by Mercurius Rusticus "Queen Maries Chappell because in it she was married to King Philip of Spain".

The marriage ceremony did indeed take place in the Cathedral but in the nave. After the wedding, Queen Mary and Prince Philip processed to the presbytery for further ceremonies, and while High Mass as being sung, they retired severally each to a side chapel for a said mass. It is possible that for Queen Mary, an ardent Roman Catholic, her Mass may have been said in the Chapel dedicated to the Blessed Virgin Mary, the Lady Chapel, from after whom she was named. This might account for the legend now recounted of the Lady Chapel being called Queen Mary's Chapel.

> *"From hence they go into Queen Maries chappell, so called because in it she was married to king Philip of Spain; here they break the Communion table in pieces, and the velvet chair whereon she sat when she was married.*
>
> (the chair is still there.)
>
> *They attempted to deface the monument of the late Lord Treasurer, the Earl of Portland (who died 13th March 1634) , but being in brass, their violence made small impression on it, and turn to his father's monument. which being of stone, was more abnoxious to their fury; here mistaking a Judge for a Bishop, led into the error by the resemblance or counterfeit of it a square cap on the head of the statue, they strike off not only the cap but also the head too of the statue and so leave it.*

M. R.

M. R.

*Amongst other acts of piety and
bounty done by Richard Fox, the 57th
Bishop of this See, he covered the
Quire, the presbytery and the aisles
adjoining with a goodly vault,
and gave new glasses (to) all the
windows in that part of the church,
and caused the bones of such Kings,
Princes and prelates as had been
buried in this church and lay
dispersed and scattered in several
parts of the Cathedral to be
collected and put into several chests
of lead, with inscription on each
chest whose bones lodged in them.*

*These chests, to save them from
rude and profane hands, he caused to
be placed on the top of a wall of
exquisite workmanship, built by him
to inclose the presbytery. There
never to be removed (as man might
think) but by the last trumpet, did
rest the bones of many Kings and
Queens as of Alfredus, Edwardus
senior, Eadredus the brother of
Athelstan, Edwinus, Canutus,
Hardecanutus, Emma the mother (to),
and Edward the Confessor her son,
Kiniglissus the first founder of the
Cathedral of Winchester, Egbert, who
abolishing the Heptarchy of the
Saxons was the first English monarch,
William Rufus and diverse others.*

*With these in the chests where
deposited the bones of many godly
bishops and confessors, as of Birinus
Hedda, Swithinus, Frithestanus
S. Elphegus the Confessor, Stigandus,
Wina and others.*

*But these monsters of men, to whom
nothing is holy, nothing is sacred
did not stick to profane and violate
these cabinets of the dead, and to
scatter their bones all over the
pavements of the Church, for on the
north side of the Quire they threw
down the chests wherein were
deposited the bones of the Bishops
and the like they did to the bones of
William Rufus, of Queen Emma,
Hardecanutus and Edward the
Confessor, and were going on to
practice the like impiety on the
bones of all the rest of the West
Saxon Kings.*

*But the outcry of the people
detesting so great inhumanity caused
some of their commanders (more
compassionate to these ancient
monuments of the dead than the rest)
to come in among them to restrain
their madness.*

*Those windows which they cold not
reach with their swords, muskets, or
rests they broke by throwing at them
the bones of Kings, Queens, Bishops,
Confessors, or Saints doing more than
£1000 worth of damage to the windows.*

*Those broke off the swords from the
brazen Satues of James I and
Charles I which then stood at the
entrance to the choir, breaking also
the cross on the globe in the hand of
Charles I and hacked and hewed the
crown on the head of it, swearing
they would bring him back to his
Parliament.*

Mercurius
Rusticus.

M. R.

*After all this, as if that they had
already done were all too little,
they go in their horrible
wickedness, they seize upon all the
Communion plate, the Bibles and
Service-books, rich hangings, large
cushions of velvet, all the pulpit
cloths some whereof were of cloth of
silver, some of cloth of gold.*

*They break up the Muniment House
and take away the common seal of the
Church supposing it to be of silver,
and a faire piece of gilt plate,
given by Bishop Cotton; they tear the
evidences of their hands, and cancel
their Charter;*

*In a word whatever they found in
the Church of any value and portable
they take it with them. What was
neither they either deface or
destroy it.*

*And now having ransacked the church
and defied God in his own house and
the King in his own statue. Having
violated the urns of the dead, having
abused the bones and scattered the
ashes of deceased monarchs
bishops, saints and confessors, they
return in triumph, bearing their
spoils with them.*

*The troopers (because they were the
most conspicuous) , ride through the
streets in surplices with such hoods
and tippets as they found, and that
they might boast to the world how
glorious a victory they had achieved."*

> *"They hold out their trophies to all*
> *spectators for the troopers, thus clad*
> *in the priests' vestments rode carrying*
> *Common Prayer Books in one hand and some*
> *broken organ pipes together with the*
> *mangled pieces of carved work but now*
> *mentioned containing some histories of*
> *both Testaments in the other."*

M. R.

Henry Cotton, donor of the stolen "Faire piece of gilt plate" was a former Prebend of the Cathedral. He was appointed Bishop of Salisbury in 1598.

Although the names of the Saxons Kings and Bishops were not accurately remembered, by Bruno Ryves in Mercurius Rusticus, he gave a remarkably vivid account of what happened on that black December day, even if slightly exaggerated as would be natural when confronted by such wanton destruction and despair aroused by at the loss of so many treasures.

Vicars the Parliamentarian when reporting to the House in London added this frightening postscript.

> *"Yea and they for certain piped*
> *before them with the organ pipes,*
> *the faire organs in the Minster*
> *being broken down by the soldiers*
> *and then afterwards cast them all*
> *into the fire and burnt them."*

Vicars.

It should not be thought that every Parliamentarian approved of such wayward and feckless behaviour. Nathaniel Fiennes disturbed by the ill discipline wrote,

> *"by the plundering and outrages*
> *commited in about the town the*
> *glory of the action was much eclipsed"*

Fiennes.

There is a legend long held and oft repeated by local historians, since the early 18th century, that William of Wykeham's chantry chapel was saved from destruction by Nathaniel Fiennes, the Second son of William Fiennes 2nd Lord Saye and Sele and the First Viscount.

The story is elaborated and embellished with pleasant exaggerations. Nathaniel Fiennes, who was born 1608, billeted himself and his troop on College on Tuesday 12th December not departing until Thursday the 14th, when he left for Portsmouth. He had witnessed the surrender of the Castle on Wednesday and it would have been on the Thursday morning he stood guard, so the story goes, over the tomb of Wykeham with drawn sword defying the rebels to lay a sacriligeous hand on the tomb and shrine of the Founder of his College. Fiennes had entered College in 1623 as a Commoner by right of being "Founders Kin".

There is apparently no documentary evidence for the story, but such lack of written evidence does not preclude an event occuring any more than the lack of a direct report of damage to Wykeham's monument, as was reported to those of Beaufort, Waynflete, or Fox's chantries, would indicate there was no damage to Wykeham's. In support of the legend Wykeham's Chantry most certainly did survive and the effigy with its three little figures at the Bishop's feet were not damaged and may be admired today. Nevertheless there was some damage requiring repair after the Restoration. Further the lack of damage to the effigy and that the brass inscribed strip around the top of the tomb was not stolen as were all others seems unlikely to have been just providential.

To repeat Ryves' account in Mercurius Rusticus

M. R.

> *"Some of the Commanders more compassionate
> to these ancient monuments of the dead
> than the rest came in among them to
> restrain their madness."*

Also as has already been quoted, Fiennes himself said

> *"By the plundering and outrages*
> *committed in and about the town the*
> *glory of the action was much eclipsed."*

Fiennes surely must be considered to be a good and caring Officer. The saving of Wykeham's Chantry is a likely story. The legend should continue to prevail as indeed it has in the Fiennes Family for many generations.

Lord Saye and Sele writing in the Winchester Cathedral Record for 1955 says the legend is firmly established and to add confirmation wrote.

> *"The late Mr Whalley Tooker of Hambledon*
> *Hants, often told me that his ancestor*
> *Edward Walley was with Nathaniel Fiennes*
> *in this episode, but I have no mention*
> *of him. He is, however shown as Cornet*
> *Edward Whalley in the roll of John Fiennes'*
> *troop and may well have been there."*

Saye & Sele. in W. C. R. No. 24. 1955.

Peter Young, the Civil War historian, lists Edward Whalley as a Cornet in John Fiennes troop at the Battle of Edgehill. John and Nathaniel Fiennes were brothers. There is no record of John's troop being at Winchester at this time, and contemporary records hardly mention the names of any of the Parliamentary Officers at the taking of Winchester.

Young. P.

Edward Whalley was a cousin of Oliver Cromwell and became one of his generals later in the war.

To add a little confusion, the author of the 'Anonymous History of Winchester' published in 1772 (thought to be Porter) intrudes a different saviour of the Chantry who he names as one Cuff serving in Sir William Waller's army.

Anon.
I. p. 42.

"The elegant tomb of William of Wykeham
was happilly preserved by one Cuff a
rebel officer in Sir William's Army,
who having received his education at
the College of this City held himself
under an indispensable duty of
protecting with his life the monument
and remains of that munificent founder."

No trace of a Cuff has been found in the College records, nor does one appear as having served in Parliament's army, rather the Cuffs or Cuffauds were Royalists and took an active part in the affairs of Basing House during the sieges.

The story of the saving of Wykeham's Chantry, from the destructive troopers must have gone the rounds at the time as all good stories do. May the legend of Nathaniel Fiennes' deed continue to live.

At the Restoration a very great effort was made to restore the damaged monuments in the Cathedral. Some times when there was nothing left to copy a new effigy was made as that of Beaufort with his square toed figure crudely carved in stone which replaced the original wooden effigy described by Hammond.

Little imagination is required to visualise those Parliamentarians picking up the effigy of the Cardinal, the very representation of Papism so abnoxious to the Puritans, which being relatively light and portable was carried off in a mock procession, before being thrown with derision into the fire. There is no evidence for this suggestion, but it is made to demonstrate and illustrate the frenzy of the rioting and brutal soldiery.

Misconceptions on the amount of damage made by the Parliamentarians, to the fabric of the Cathedral stem from such remarks as this made by Brayley in 1804 when describing Wykeham's Chantry when he said.

*"The statues which adorn this chapel,
were destroyed in the time of the
Civil Wars, and many of the other
monuments were either mutilated or
erased. Since the Restoration it has
been twice or thrice repaired; and a
few years ago (1797) it was new painted
and partly gilded by Mr Cave of this
City. The charges of reparations are
defrayed by Wykeham's two foundations,
New College Oxford and Wichester College."*

Brayley.
p. 59.

In reality much of the destruction of the altars and figures to the niches here, and throughout the Cathedral were the work of the iconoclasts at the time of the Reformation. It would be extraordinary if this Chantry could last for ever without some repairs, attention and redecoration.

The cost of the repairs in 1664 was £24.5.2. shared between College and New.

This sum was made up of repairs to the fabric by a Mr Bird £11.7.0. For painting and regilding by a Mr Hawkins from Oxford £6.13.8. For making an iron hearse or frame for a pall 17s.6 and lengthening the cresting 17s.0. Also,

*"Pro xij ulnis canabi pro tegumento
ad statuam ad xxd per ulnam; et pro
conficiendo eodem."*

Kirby.
p. 353.

For twelve yards of cambric for the pall for the effigy at twenty pence per yard and for making it up. A fine white linen pall cloth.

John Lockett was paid £3.8.0. for making the 34 iron tridents which are still in position on top of the walls. The balance of 10s. 2d. being for drilling holes and preparing the monuments to take the iron frame for the pall.

It will be seen that most of the expense would have been for normal maintenance. The Iron frame and pall cover were additions. Hardly any of the expenditure could be claimed as War-Damage.

Chapter 7

LE SUEURS BRONZE STATUES OF
KING JAMES I AND KING CHARLES I

THERE is another story about the despoilation in the Cathedral often related but nevertheless repeated here as it is an essential part of the narrative of the destruction wrought by Waller's troopers.

It is about the much admired and much travelled bronze statues of King James I and King Charles I now standing each side of the great west door.

There existance is due to a dislike expressed by King Charles of the entrance to the choir. As a result Inigo Jones, the King's Surveyor General was commisioned to provide a new screen. An essential element of the design was that there should be a niche each side of the entrance filled with statuary in true Renaissance style.

However instead of the statuary the niches were filled with bronze figures, the contract for these being made on the 17th June 1638 which was witnessed by Inigo Jones,

W.C.D. II.
XXXIII.

"I Hubert Le Sueur Sculpter have bargained with the Kinge's Maagistie of Great Britain to cast in brass two statues of 5 foote and 8 inches high; one that representeth our late Soveraine Lord King James, and the other our Soveraine Lord King Charles for the sum of 340 lb of good and lawful money in England, to be paid in this manner Vizt 170 lb beforehand, and the other 170 lb after the work should be finished and delivered to the Surveyor of his Majesties works in March ensuing. And the said Hubert Le Sueur is to receive the aforesaid sums without paying any fees for the receipt thereof.
Hubert Le Sueur.

I was present and witness in this Bargain Inigo Jones."

In due course Le Sueur was paid the £340 by instalments plus £40 for conveying the statues to Winchester. This was not the end of the expense for in the Cathedral accounts for 1637-8 are these entries,

> *"Given to ye Kings workemen for*
> *setting up the Statues sent by*
> *his Majesty. £18-0-0*
> *Item to other workemen for*
> *helping about ye same £2-1-6."*

Y's D.
p. 175.

The statues would have been in position at the entrance to the choir by Christmas 1639. Three years later and just before Christmas 1642 the effegies were violently assaulted by Waller's troopers, as before quoted by Mercurius Rusticus,

> *"They broke off the swords from the*
> *brazen statues of James I and Charles I*
> *which then stood at the entrance to the*
> *choir, breaking also the cross on the*
> *globe in the hand of Charles I and*
> *hacked and hewed the crown on the head*
> *of it, swearing they would bring him*
> *back to his Parliament."*

M.R.

There is some mystery about what happened immediately after their battering. Apparently they were taken out of the Cathedral into the care of the Corporation for safe keeping, but some time later, when the City was under Parliament's control and soon after the King's Execution in 1649, they were taken out of store and sold by Edmund Biggs to Mr Newland of Portsmouth for £10.

a "Friend"
See p239 below.

In the temper of the times Mayor Biggs was probably glad to be rid of such, to him, embarrasing scrap and decided they should go to pot.

It was Ralph Biggs who when he was Mayor caused so much trouble over the maces and his seat in the choir. Edmund Biggs' vindictive act seems to have been followed by the misappropriation of the £10. The infamy was not, or could not, be disclosed until the Restoration and the Royalists were back in power, when an informer who styled himself "a friend of the City of Winchester," published a tract in which he wrote,

a "Friend"
See p239 below.

> *"two brass statues of King James*
> *and King Charles, standing in the*
> *cathedral Church, much burnt and*
> *damaged, and if continuing to stand*
> *likely to be wholly spoiled by*
> *souldiers, taken down by the then*
> *Mayor, in order to their preservation,*
> *but sold by Mr Edmund Biggs, and for*
> *ought that I could ever hear, by his*
> *single act; the money of them recovered*
> *is just joined to the rest for the*
> *same use."*

By the expression "is joined to the rest" the informer meant that the £10 paid for the Royal statues and recovered from Biggs, was added to the rest of the proceeds collected from the sale of bells taken from the dilapidated churches. The money was used towards the repair of St Thomas Church. Biggs was also no doubt compelled to disclose where the bronzes had gone to.

Certainly the Statues were found and the newly appointed Bishop of Winchester, Brian Duppa, in a gesture of thankfulness and in token of his loyalty to King Charles II, managed to recover the bronzes having paid ten times the sale price for their safe recovery. He was very well pleased with the purchase. Mr Benjamin Newland had of course taken the risk of being found in possession of such compromising material during the Commonwealth and felt compelled to bury the statues for his own and the "Kings" safety.

When sending the statues back to the Cathedral, the Bishop in his covering letter to the Dean and Chapter, effusively extols the virtues of Mr Newland. One hopes the repurchase price included the cost of cleaning, repairing and transport back to Winchester.

Bishop Brian Duppa wrote

"Mr Dean and ye rest of your Chapter.

This gent, Mr Benjamin Newland of the Isle of Wight gave me notice yt in the times of ye late distraction (wherein the churches themselves could not escape plunder) Two noble Statues in Brass of his now Majesties Royal Father and Grandfather were brought to Portsmouth to be sold by some persons, from whose sacrilegious hands he bought them with his own money to preserve them for such a hoped and happy Restoration. He kept them at first (as he saith) underground and afterwards very privately and brought them now unto me: for which I paid him £100 out of my own purse; which I think wel bestowed for ye Recovery of those Royal monuments, and shall send them unto you as a small Testimoy of the honor I owe unto the blessed memory of their sacred Majesties and the good affection I bear unto your Church of Winchester where they were first erected in the West End of the Quire.

W. C. D.
II. 103

I look upon the gents as one who
for his reall affection (generally
reported) unto the Church, justly
intitled unto a favor from the Church,
and therefore do recommend him (upon
any occassion which may be presented
to you) unto a kindness to be shewn
him, being he might have made (as I
am informed) a much greater advantage,
if he would have sold them heretofore
unto Aliens. So leaving him unto your
favorable consideration, I commend
you to the grace of the Almighty.
                    Your very affectionate friend

                    Br . WINTON

Wesminster this 18th of Decr 1660"

A close examination of the effigies show the scars of battle, and incidently that the bodies of both Kings are identical although the arms and regalia are differently arranged.

Blakiston
in W. C. R.
Nos 45-47.

After suffering such base indignities during "ye late distraction" the figures were restored to the niches in Inigo Jones screen remaining there until 1825, when the Renaissance screen was considered to be out of keeping with its surroundings. The "Kings" were taken down for repositioning on a new screen, while Inigo Jones masonry was dismantled. Some fragments are stored in the south triforium but the centre portion with the doorway is in the Museum of Archaelogy Cambridge.

A new screen in stone designed in the gothic style by William Garbett was then built, this too retained the central entrance flanked with pedestals for the Royal statues surmounted by pinnacled canopies.

In 1873 Garbett's screen was demolished and replaced by the wooden screen designed by Gilbert Scott, who made no provision for the statues.

The Sovereigns then took up a new stance at each side of the West Door where they remain undisturbed to this day. Not quite undisturbed for there has been yet another journey, in 1979, when Our Sovereign King James the Sixth of Scotland made a Royal progress to Edinburgh, for an exhibition. King Charles the Martyr remained on solitary guard until his Royal father's return. Both statues where at that time expertly cleaned and now stand on their alloted places for all to admire and ponder on an enduring loyalty to the Crown.

> *"This I must confesse was an unlucky blow but discourageth not, rather add vigilaunce to a just cause."*

H. M. C.
Report
No XIII
p. 441.

Chapter 8

CASUALTIES AND
CONTEMPORARY COMMENTS

SOON after the debacle a Royalist wrote on January 7th 1643 to Henry Mulliner, Taylor, at his house over against Magdalene College.

H. M. C.
Report XIII
Appx I. p. 84.

*"Though it was our mens misfortune
to to be so treacherously used at
Winchester, yet to give them their due,
no men could show more gallantry than
they did in that action, for when they
saw the enemy draw up so strong being
all engaged, Sir Richard Willis,
Sir John Smith - men of undaunted
resolution - with 18: more, stood
whilst my Lord Grandison with the
other forces made their retreat, and
being thrice charged by entire troops
still bravely repulsed the enemy and
broke them.*

*In Winchester; the spoiled the church
to the value of 7000 l. and, which hath
not been heard amongst heathen, they
broke the leaden tombs where-in the
bones of the Saxon Kings were kept for
a great monument of Antiquilty and with
these they broke and defaced all the
glass windows.*

*At Chichester they used the same
perfidious treachery they had formerly
shown at Winchester, and notwithstanding
Sir William Waller who commanded in Chief
their forces consisting of 2,500 horse
and foot, had subscribed these articles
that the gentlemen commanders should*

*"GO OUT OF THE TOWN ON HORSE BACK
WITH THEIR SWORDS, the common soldiers on
foot, leaving their own arms and colours
behind them undefaced for they had
burnt them at Winchester - yet when he
entered he observed none of these, but
presently seized upon all the commanders
as prisoners and pillaged them of
everything."*

The Parliamentary commanders Nathaniel Fiennes and Arthur Godwin in their report to their Commander in Chief The Lord General Essex deplored the excesses of the troopers, as related above and concluded their letter by saying the glory of the action was much eclipsed by the troopers riotous behaviour. From the minute book of The House of Lords one reads,

*"While if the arms and horse taken
had been more equally distributed,
the advantage to the State would have
been greater. We enclose a list of
the officers and gentlemen taken.*

*We recovered our Colours but the enemy
burnt their own during a desparate
resolution to make a sally in the night.*

Fiennes.

*We march this day to Portsmouth,
where we shall wait for orders, money
and reinforcements.*

*Our loss is only one Captain of
dragooners and four of five men, and
two or three hurt.*

*Lord Grandison has behaved very
fairly and hopes for better terms than
those granted in the field, because in
order to prevent more bloodshed he
delivered up the place which still had
some strength left."*

*"He (Grandison) and those taken with
him hope that if not allowed to return
to the King they may have the same
terms that were granted to those at
Portsmouth, but we only promised to
represent this to your excellency."*

The lists of casualities and the notes, have been compiled
from Cornet Sterly's report and other contemporary accounts
separated into Lord Grandison's Regiment, Lord Grey's Regiment
and the Gentlemen attending the Sheriff's meeting in the Castle, by
the help of the several Hampshire histories and in particular from
Peter Young's rolls of Royalist Officers given in his book "Edge
Hill 1642".

Lord Grandison's
Somerset Regiment of Horse

Col Lord Grandison. William Villiers.

                            he escaped captivity.

Major Sir Richard Willis. escaped.

Sterley   Sir John Smith. eager to make a sortie

                              but was over ruled.

Capt Garret. (Edward Gerard)
Capt Honeywood. (Philip)
Capt Barty. (Francis Bertie)
Lieut Williamson.

Young. P.   Lieut Booth. (George)
Cornet Bennet. (John)
Cornet Savage.

Colonel Grey's
Northumberland Dragoons
about 200 strong

Major Hayborne.		(Ralph Heborne)	Young P.
Capt Booth.			
Capt Brangling.		(Robert Brangling)	
Capt Wren.	P	(John)	
Capt Beconhear.		(- Birkenhead)	Sterley
Lieut Rodman.	P	(Edmond)	
Lieut Booth.	P	(Ralph of Wren's troop)	
Cornet Bradlines.		(Roger Brandling)	

Note, P = Taken prisoner to Windsor.

The following Officers Regiments have not been identified.

Lieuts Rogers.
　　　Elverton.
　　　Ruddry.
　　　Gwynn.
Christopher Luckner. This is probably
　　　Christopher Lewkenor of Chawton Hants
　　　the deposed Royalist Member of
　　　Parliament for Chichester.

Leigh &
Knight.
Chawton
Manor.
p. 98.

Gentlemen attending the
Sheriff's Meeting at Winchester
taken prisoner to Portsmouth

William Kingsmill had been appointed Sheriff in November 1642, Although his name does not appear in the list of those taken. The roll has been compiled from those listed by Portal in his history of "The Great Hall" and from Cornet Sterly's report. Sterly said that some of the prisoners were confined to the charge of Dr Layton the Keeper of the Lambeth House prison.

Alexander.		
Douce	Sir Francis Capt	of Winchester.
Foyle and		
his Son.		
Fuller	Douce.	
Griffin	Edward.	
Knowles	Sir Henry	
Mills	Sir John	of Southampton.
Norbury.		
Philips	Sir Thomas.	
his Brother James		of Stoke Charity.
Philpot	Sir George	of Swathlin
Powre	Sir Francis.	
Powlett	Sir John	of Hinton St George.
Powlet	John	
Ranford.		
Saunders.		
Sandys	Sir Henry	of the Vyne and
		Mottisfont.
Wells		of Brambridge.

Portal.
p. 34-5.

Lord Grandison, Sir Richard Willis and a few other officers managed to escape and were charged by the parliamentarians with breaking their parole; some said by the connivance of Colonel Urrey, whose house afterwards was plundered by the order of the Lord Mayor Isaac Pennington. Colonel Urrey demanded and was actually granted £400 (Compensation to be paid out of the monies collected the last fast day for the plundered ministers).

There seems little doubt that because of the rough treatment meted out to the Royalists in breach of the Articles, Grandison felt fully justified in arranging his own and other officers' escape, even if gold in handfuls was used to save themselves.

> *"Having as was supposed charmed their keepers with a good sum of money."*

Rushworth
II p. 92.

Of this incident Sir Edward Walker wrote to Montague Earl of Lindsay saying the Conditions were not kept,

> *"the rude multitude oversveaying theire officers so that our officers beinge detayned were enforced to make escapes as the Lord Grandison, Sir Richard Willis and some fewe others, but as yet your Lordships brother and Sir John Smyth are not come to us,"*

H. M. C.
Report 13
Appx I. p.79.

In London Parliament, desparate for some good news gladly paid Theodore Jennings £20 for being the first to bring the news of the 'Capture of Winchester', to the House. Immediately orders were given for bells to be rung and bonfires to be lighted.

Public thanksgivings were held on the following Sunday the 17th December in London, at Southwick and Westminster.

The House also ordered Sir Philip Stapylton, Colonel Hampden and Sir H Vane to thank Sir William Waller

Lloyd
Woodland.
p. 193

"for his care and vigilancy at Winchester."

Parliament had indeed won a great success. Winchester a potential Royalist stronghold had been captured and was securely in Parliament's hands. Two Royalist regiments had been destroyed and all their officers taken prisoner, and their troops dispersed many miles from home. Many of the principal Royalists in the County around Winchester had been taken prisoner. Further many horse had been captured from the Officers in Lord Grandison's and Lord Grey's regiments, from those gentlemen taken in the castle, from the Dean and Prebends in the Close and of course all the troopers and dragooners mounts. In addition there were all their arms and much other booty besides the £1000 paid by the City.

To end this unhappy chapter in the City's history, as if it had not suffered enough for its loyalty it received this Royal rebuke from His Majesty the King on December the 19th 1642.

The King's message to the
Inhabitants of Winchester.

"To our subjects of Winchester greeting.

Whereas we in our princely care
of you our subjects gave command
to our officers to draw to your said
City with a small number of forces,
for your defence, not destruction, to
the end that you might be preserved
from the violence of Our, and your
Enemies, not expecting but to have
received an answerable returne of
your loyalties towards us, But finding
that instead of friends you have
openly declared yourselves enemies,
and evil entreated those you had cause
to entertain with all love and respect,
flatly opposing our authority and
betraying those to ruin that were the
instruments of our presrvation.
Therefore Wee cannot but in justice
to Our owne Honour and those many
worthy Gentlemen which have lost their
lives and Liberties in the maintenance
of our just Cause but give way to a
vindication, for the satisfaction of
all those that have been so betrayed
and the recovery of Our owne Right and
interest which neither the law of God
or Man can deny us, nor the power of
you nor your Alies keepe from us, in
which (assurance) (as you have your
Allegience) So will Wee throw by all
respects or remembrance that you were
Our subjects."

County
Archives.
C. 2484.

BOOKS
& MSS
Exhibit
No 72.

Aghast at the severity of such Royal chastisement the Mayor replied justifying their conduct and confirming their loyalty.

"The Answer of the Inhabitants of the said Cittie to his Majesties message.

May it please your Majesty Wee your Loyal subjects have seriously considered the Summe of what is contained in your message, and having weighed our Actions in each particular we find no just cause of your Majesties high displeasure against Winchester, since what we have done, both the Lawes of God and Man authorise.
Had wee not sever all Presidents from Kingston, and many other place which might serve as a caution for us, happily we had beene wonne to give way to our owne betraying; But seeing so many examples, wee cannot be justly blamed for endeavouring to secure our Lives, and to keep our wives and daughters from rapine and inevitable destruction.
As touching Your Magesties sacred displeasure we are infinitely sorry that we should be so farre ingaged by our Consciences, to disobey your command, but being as it is we must be enforced to undergo the utmost event trusting onely in Gods protection by whose power we not dispaire but that at least your Majesty will plainely discerne the truth of all things, and we shall at length appear your most loyall and obedient subjects."

Chapter 9

GENERAL WALLER DEMANDS HORSES FOR PARLIAMENT'S USE

S IR William Waller after his success in December, satiated with loot, withdrew back to Portsmouth with his prisoners and then marched on to wreak similar uncontrolled havoc on Chichester.

Winchester shocked by events must have spent a very unhappy winter recovering from the barbarities perpetrated by the Roundheads. There was to be no respite.

In February Waller was given authority by the House to raise 3000 foot and 300 horse from the four counties of Hampshire, Surrey, Sussex and Kent for the service of Parliament.

After Waller had withdrawn, the City was re-occupied by the Royalists. Two of their Commanders, who are to play a large part in the actions to follow, Sir Ralph Hopton and Sir William Ogle, finding insufficient support in the County decided to withdraw their forces towards Wiltshire when they learn of the strength of Waller's army and his intention to march Westwards. The Royalist commanders debated whether or not to slight the defences of Winchester before leaving, although they do not appear to have done so.

On the third of March 1643 Sir William Waller again marched into Winchester. This for the second time but now on his way westwards, stopping to scour the City for money and supplies. This was for the second time the City was to be looted.

Trussel relates,

"They going afresh my miseries arise
ffor some of Waller and Hasleriggs Companies
gott entry and free quarter challendged

Trussel
f. 96.

Then them their Regiments straight seconded
When having all my late gott victualls spent
without allowance, therewith not content
littell reguarding what was done before
They doe demaund to borrow, not restore
ffive hundred pounds, which when I had procurd
much adoe, they then agayne assurd
That I from thence no more should be molested
which was by both the colonells protested."

And the same Parliamentary incursion as related by Godwin in his "Civil War in Hampshire" but with an unhappy and rather grim story at the end.

"On March 3, 1643, Sir William Waller marched
into Winchester, "and being an inhabitant and
a freeman of the City, he promised that no man
should suffer any loss or damage by him, and he

Godwin.
Civil War
in Hamps'
p. 73.

performed it for as much as it concerned himselfe,
but when he went away on Satarday (March 4) he
left behind Sergeant-Major Carie, with a troop
of horse, to levy £600 upon the same. A most
unreasonable sum to be imposed upon a town so
lately and so miserably plundered. But say what
they could in their own behalf, no less than £500
would be accepted, and that accordingly was
raised, viz., £350 out of the inhabitants of the
City, £150 on one Sir Henry Clerke, neighbouring
gentleman."

Master Say, a son of a prebendary of the
Cathedral, who probably fared none the better on
that account, had entrusted his horses for
purposes of concealment to his servant. Having
been betrayed by some of his neighbours, he was
brought before Sir William Waller, who questioned
him as to the whereabouts of the steeds. Master
Say pleaded ignorance, and was forthwith handed
over to the Provost Marshall, who received orders
to make him confess.

> *"This official conducted him to the George
> Inn, which dates back to the days of the
> Fourth Edward, and led him into what was
> long known as "the 18-stall stable". Placing
> a halter round his neck, the Marshal renewed
> his cross-examination. Obtaining no
> information, he hoisted him up to the rack,
> allowing him to hang until he was almost
> strangled, and then gave him a little
> breathing space. this process was repeated
> several times, until the spectators of this
> barbarous scene quitted the stable in
> digust. Finding torture ineffectual, the
> Marshal with many kicks and blows dismissed
> Master Say, who a few days afterwards was
> reported to be dangerously ill, a
> circumstamce scarcely to be wondered at."*

Godwin.
p. 83-4.

The reference to Master Say as son of a prebendary would seem to refer to the prebend's grandson. William Say was installed a prebend in 1583 when he was about forty, he died in 1615 at the age of 71 having served two Bishops as their chancellor. His monument is towards the west end of the north aisle of the Cathedral.

Sir Henry Clerke, the neighbouring gentleman who found the extraordinary large sum of £150 was of Hyde and Headbourne Worthy. He was the heir of the younger Thomas Clerke mentioned on the Clerke monument which so attracted Lieutenant Hammond when he visited the Cathedral in 1635.

See p. 54.
above.

The site of the stables of the George is now occupied by Barclays Bank in Jewry Street and was formerly part of the Manor of God-be-Got. It was leased by the Prior of St Swithun's in 1402 to Mark le Faire, who then built a new hostelry known as the "George". As the George Hotel it was demolished in 1956 as part of road widening scheme to St George's Street and Jewry Street.

Come April 1643 the Dean and Chapter had sufficiently recovered to hold a Chapter Meeting, not in the Cathedral but at Priors Barton, and John Chase felt able to return to the Cathedral to start putting things in order and writing an inventory of the muniments. While doing so he found his old list of church ornaments and apparently immediately put these in order annotating his inventory with the terse remark "stollen by the troopers" or just by this one word "sollen".

In Chase's memoranda on the muniments headed 10 April 1643 XIX Caroli Regis.

W. C. D.
II p. 57.

*"In domo Minumentorum Ecclesiae
Cathedralis Sanctae Trinitatis Winton."*

he says,

*"This should have been placed in
the beginning of this book, being the
first time that I began to order the
Minutment House (after the same was
the first time by the soldiers defaced
and spoyled time and divers writings taken
away....."*

This memo infers that he started putting the muniment house in order on the 10th April '43 but this particular entry was not made until probably 1650, and as Chase himself says "this should have been placed at the beginning of this book". Chase continues his memo by referring to a second spoilation in October 1646 thus implying that the entry was not made until after the second spoilation.

Chase, clearly confused by all the dreadful things that happend to his beloved books and muniments, misdates the second spoilation to 1646 when it is apparent it took place during Cromwell's siege of the Castle in October 1645, as will become clear later in the story.

See page
165 below.

WINCHESTER PLUNDERED
FOR THE THIRD TIME

12th JULY 1643

"Yet notwithstanding what they writt or spake
An other course to hinder me they take   Trussel.
ffor shortly after on markett daye   f. 96.
some of their troops in mee now reaks doe playe
ffor all the horses they could find they take,
On Maudlyn hill they their a horse markett make
And shortly after of them about seaven hundred
searcht all mens pockets and their houses
                                        plundered
leaving no meate, mony or armes behind
nor horse nor ought else good that they could
                                        find."

Sir William Waller was at this time ambitiously campaigning in the West against Sir Ralph Hopton, by coincidence it was on the following day, July 13th, that he was decidedly defeated at "Roundway Down".

Waller as always was in great need of supplies and money to pay and feed his troops. In response Parliament had urged its forces at Portsmouth to send urgently all possible aid. Thus it was that the City was plundered for the third time by Parliament's Forces. On this occasion they were led by Colonel Richard Norton of Southwick and Captain Francis St Barbe of Broadlands Romsey when hurrying through westwards on their way to assist Waller. Albeit too late.

Colonel Norton had left behind him in Winchester a small force with orders to search the whole town for arms and to make additional levies on the stricken City.

Captain St Barbe, only two month later, was killed at the First Battle of Newbury, fought on September the 20th 1643.

Trussel.
f. 97.

"Next Market day some others of their crews
all the Recusants howses search anewe
some of the men and all their horses they
To be redeemed agayne carried away
Then from the Committees comes a Commission
unto the Maior, with all expedition
of carts to make dew preparation
To Portsmouth all the ammunition
of goods and carriages which in store did lye
to be conveyed; which was perfomed accordingly
for all except the Guns. A precept then
from them is sent unto some Aldermen
nyne pounds per weeke to rate and collect
and send the Parliament; but for neglect
in levying yt come Nortons regiment
And to procure my further detriment
befaced my Market Crosse, an ornament
of great Antiquitie.
                    Into each house they went
and brought from thence what ever they could
                                        find
of armes or warlike furniture; behind
they did not leave a dagger, powder or match
But carried with them all that they could catch
Their skores they paid with Chalke, their
                                reckonings they
unto their hosts with filthy languadge pays
yf not with blows; All the recusants
And whom they pleased to nominate malignants
They re replundered and leaft them not
so mutch as pewter, bed, brasse spytt or pott
and they departed."

Trussel's simple doggerel verse has the ability to convey the sense of despair that had overcome "Mee" the City of Winchester during those troublesome days. This description of Norton's plundering troops is vivid enough but the ominous treat of yet more plundering if their demands are not met has a chilling feeling.

"But for neglect yt come Nortons regiment"

"Yt", an unusual word but one which seems to convey inevitability.

However in the event the Parliamentary army under Waller suffered a disastrous defeat at Roundway Down and again at Newbury forcing Waller to withdraw to Farnham enabling Winchester to again come under Royalist influence, but not without a great deal of further trouble. Much had been chalked up and old scores to be accounted for.

By August The City previously lost in the whirl of no-mans land, now found itself suddenly enlivened by a renewed confidence in the Royalist cause sent a party led by Colonel Henry Powlett, to Oxford to express their loyalty and to report on conditions in the City. Colonel Henry Powlett, the brother of John Paulet the Fifth and Loyal Marquis of Winchester. The name Paulet is variously spelt throughout the narrative according to the different spellings used by contemporary writers or as found on their monuments. Henry Powlett's monument is in the south aisle of the Cathedral retro-choir. He died in 1672.

Vaughan.

About the middle of August, Colonel Henry had received a Royal Commission to raise a Regiment of Horse in Hampshire. Towards the cost of this venture The Dean and Chapter received a demand from the king for a contribution, and in the Town, Colonel Powlett tried to impose a levy of £200 but as will be seen without success.

> *"Charles. R.*
> *Trusty and well beloved.*
> *Wee greete you well.*
>
> *Whereas wee are very well assured of*
> *ye fidelity and good affections of our*
> *right trusty and well beloved Henry Lord*
> *Pawlett to us and our service. And out*
> *of that asurance have granted him our*
> *Commission for our defence and for ye*
> *settling and securitie of this Kingdom*
> *And principally of our Contie of Southton*

W. C. D.
II. p. 55.

*against this unnaturell Rebellion, wh Regiment
by reason of ye present condition of his own
fortunes he is not so well able to rayse at
his own charge,wee doe therefore hereby
recommend him this Affayre unto you, desyring
you to assist him with yr voluntary and
free contributions towards the raysing thereof,
and to use you utmost industry yo persuade so
many of ye clergy as you shall know to be
able and well affected to us to contribute
likewise freelie to our said serice, and Wee
do assure you that yr faythfull endeavors
herein shall be very acceptable to us. And
we shall be ready to remember ye same upon
occasions for ye advantage. Soe not doubting of
your redie assistance in a worke that soe much
imports our service, we bid you heartilie
farewell.*

*Given at our Court at Matson ye 15 day of
August 1643.*

*To our trustie and well beloved the Deane
and Chapter of Winchester."*

W. C. D.
II. p. 55

Trussel tells of the imposition of a £200 levy and interestingly, or twice the value in broadcloth to provide the material for uniforms. When Powlett was denied payment, he rounded up forty or so parliamentarians, including the notorious Riggs of Mace and Royal Statues fame, and carried them off prisoners.

Godwin.
p. 53.

They had managed to send a message to Southampton, a parliamentary stronghold from whence rescue quickly came as Colonel Herbert Morley, a firm Puritan, and Governor of that town who arrived with a large body of dragoons and pursued the Royalists forcing them to release their prisoners.

In retribution Murford one of the parliamentarian Commanders placed guards over the city gates and rounded up a batch of Royalists intending to take them back to Southampton. Surprised and angered that the captured Royalists had no horses the troopers were set to plunder the City. This was to be for the fourth time. On an alarm of counter attack the troopers were called off and hastily withdrew to Southampton without their prisoners.

But a few days later Murford with renewed effrontry sent horse and carts to Winchester to fetch the four guns that had been used to intimidate Lord Grandison the previous December, and left behind by Colonel Norton's marauders in July for lack of transport.

Strangely the Mayor perhaps glad to be rid of the embarrassment allowed them to be carried off. Perhaps they were the guns referred to in a report of 1626 "as being cankered with rust and utterly unserviceable that lay in the store house at Wolvesey."

C. S. P.
1625-49
p. 49.

> *"They no sooner gone*
> *but to ad affliction to affliction*
> *A Partie came from Oxford and they crave*
> *Twoo hundred pounds in mony straight to have*
> *or twice the rate in broadcloth, which denyed,*
> *They Alderman Riggs with other more beside*
> *did hurry with them, and away they went;*
>
> *But shortly after Morlyes Regiment*
> *having placed att every gate a guard*
> *Hee for the Maior doth send, who come afterward*
> *sent for his brethren; they no sooner mett*
> *But presently on them a guard is sett,*
> *And all commaundered were to go horse back;*
> *But being answered that they all did horse lack;*
> *whilst they stood arguing, the Companyes*
> *some one way went and others otherwise*
> *To seeke for plunder every place was sought*
> *And what was fitting found away was caught;*

When on some soddayne newes away they went
leaving mee cause sufficeint to lament
So mutch the more by how mutch I could see
no likelyhood from sutch guests to be free.

Trussel.

From Momford at Southampton comes a kind
letter
with horse and carte within short time comes
hither
ffor the great peices, which as then were sent
(the maior sayd further daunger to prevent)"

Momford or Murford was the Parliamentary Governor of Southampton.

As an indication of the fluid state of the war, with Winchester in the eye of the maelstrom, the following month Colonel Sir Edward Ford, of Uppark and the Royalist Sheriff of Sussex, marched into the City with his regiment on Mayor making day. This would have been Monday the 18th September, the first Monday after the Holy Rood Day, Exalation of the Holy Cross, celebrated on September the 14th.

This marked the end of parliamentary dominance over the city for just over two years, that was until the City was beseiged and taken by Oliver Cromwell in October 1645.

Trussel.

"Then hither on my Maiors election day
Fourds regiment did come and went away
the thursday following, leaving all to paye
until the generall accompting daye
Thus sackt and ransackt, basely sat uppon
I unto heaven made my petition
that they would pleased bee some course to
invent
My now so thretned ruine to prevent
In thee meane time my enemies farr and near
in every skyrt and corner of the sheer
did play their parters wherof this was the end
to famishe mee and king Charles to offend."

Chapter 10

LORD OGLE TAKES AND FORTIFIES THE CASTLE FOR THE KING

BEFORE looking further into the City's troubles, a moment to review the general situation of the war in the South, after the Royalist victory at Newbury on the 20th September 1943.

In the early summer Sir William Waller had successfully marched into the South Western Counties where he was opposed by Sir Ralph Hopton. This autumn Parliament held the South Eastern Counties of Kent, Surrey, Sussex, and the Isle of Wight. They held too all the south coast ports, Portsmouth, Southampton. Poole and westwards. Also as an out post Parliament held Wardour Castle, thirty five miles west of Winchester.

The Royalist headquarters remained in Oxford and Basing house continued to be held by the Marquis of Winchester. Hoptons counter offensive and recent victories had forced Waller to withdraw to Farnham from whence he was able to recruit and re-equip and then lay siege to Basing House on the 12th November.

The Royalist strategy being to march into Sussex, obtain territory and therefore recruits and supples. Also to seize the iron works and gun foundries of the Weald. Further to gain control of a port through which arms could be brought in from the continent.

Parliament well knew, all through the war, the value of sea power and firmly held all the channel ports.

In Winchester with Parliament's forces roundabout in disarray, the City lay open to re-occupation by the Royalists and so the new Mayor (Richard Braxtone) wrote to Lord Ogle at Oxford inviting him to return.

The Anonymous historian's neat summary of the situation that autumn, although written in 1772, must have been based on local tradition and is given below. It is Ogle and Trussel who tell the contemporary story of the refortification of the castle.

Anon' tells how Lord Ogle at Oxford was prevailed upon

Anon.
II. p. 120

"to attempt the retaking of the castle, and of setting the prisoners at liberty. This enterprise was so effectually performed by his Lordship, that in three days he found himself not only in actual possession of the castle, but all the arms, ammunition, and effects of the enemy.

His first care was now to strengthn his newly-aquired garrison, and render it as inaccessible as art could invent, wisely considering that its situation rendering it the principle key of the whole western country, it might be made a convenient and serviceable rendezvous for his Royal Master.

He therefore lost no time in putting this business into execution; and happily meeting with the concurrence and mutual assistance of the Mayor and citizens, he not only re-fortified the castle, but put the city itself into a much better posture of defence than it had before; immediately after which, the western army marched into it, consisting of three thousand foot and fifteen hundred horse under the command of Lord Hopton; who with part of these forces took the route into Sussex and reduced Arundel Castle."

Godwin using Lord Ogles "Engagements" says

> *"On the way from Oxford. Andover was*
> *searched, and yielded four loads of*
> *match, two barrels of powder, and*
> *some fiften muskets. Towards evening*
> *the horse mustered upon the hill next*
> *to Wherewell. They refreshed themselves*
> *till 11 pm and marched at midnight.*
> * When they reached the North Gate it*
> *was immediately opened, and they marched*
> *into the High Street. The gates were*
> *shut, the guards were set, and 30 of my*
> *Lord General's convoy guarded the castle*
> *with muskets completely furnished"*

Godwin.
p. 105

The City Militia were called under arms, and Lord Gerard's brigade of horse came on the following Wednesday.

Trussel, more pithily, and writing very shortly after the event, recounts Ogle's first priority of putting the castle into a good state of defence, which required the clearing of the ditches of trees, shrubs and buildings to provide a field of fire. The work was not without its critics as is the way with any monies expended on defence.

> *"By Gods will to curbe theise insolents*
> *Sir William Ogle and the Regiments*
> *of Colonel Fourd and Bennet hither came*
> *and heer in solemn manner doe proclayme*
> *Sir William Ogle governor to bee*
> *both of the Countie, castle and mee*
> *When he endeavouring as by dewty tide*
> *against all inconveniencyes to provide*
> *and see all paces fitting fortified*
> *began his worcks the fitter to provide*
> *All interpossing obstacles to dispace*
> *and howses, barnes, and stables to deface*
> *trees to cut down and orchards up to grubb*
> *And whatsoever might seem to be a rubb*
> *In his Worcks way (however overprised)*
> *were clean removed,"*

Trussel.
f. 97.

Trussel.

"then some not well advised
who privatt profytt before publick good
ever preferr, before they understood
the end where forr, thinck by sutch meanes as
                                              theise
the cure wowld prove farr worse than the disease
Sutch as did gruth the chardg that the worck
                                              draws
did call them pytfalls to catch purblind dawes
And askt as yf theye were incompatible
whether the worcke or worckmen were more idle
But when they understand sutch worcks as theise
then lett them censure, till then howld their
                                              Peace."

Sir William Ogle, Governor of the Castle was a citizen of Winchester. He was one of the two members of Parliament for the City from 1640 until disabled by Parliament in 1643, his house being in Gold Street (now Southgate Street). Sir William was the brother-in-law of Sir Richard Tichborne whose father it will be recollected was granted the castle by King James the First. The relationship came about in this way. Sir William Ogle married Charity Waller of Stoke Charity; Charity's sister and co-heiress Susan Waller had married Sir Richard Tichborne. Further, Susan and Charity's father Sir William Waller of Old Stoke (Stoke Charity) was a fourth cousin of General Sir William Waller who had become the rightful owner in 1638.

APPX

Yet one further family connection; Charity Waller had firstly married Sir Thomas Philips and their two sons Thomas and James Philips served under their step father Sir William Ogle as part of the castle garrison.

Sawyer.
Battle of
Cheriton.

Thomas Philips was killed in 1645, and Charity Lady Ogle died during Cromwell's siege in October 1645 as will be related. (See appendix page 259).

Sir William Ogle for his service to the King was created Viscouny Catherlough in Ireland. His manuscript account of his actions during the Civil War is in the British Library.

After the death of Charity, Sir William married in 1648 another widow and heiress. She was Sarah Dauntsey the Widow of Sir Hugh Stewkely (d. 1642) of Hinton Ampner where her monument may be seen in the parish church.

Michaelmersh Church

Sir William Ogle died on the 24th July 1682. His monument is in the south aisle of Michaelmersh church.

Tradition holds that the ghost of Sir William may be seen riding the downs between The Wallops and Michaelmersh.

Chapter 11

HOPTON MAKES WINCHESTER HIS WINTER QUARTERS

THE City's past troubles become nothing compared to the grievous burden of a five month occupation by an ill disciplined untrained army of young men, seeking relaxation in excessive drinking and rowdism, common to all licentious soldiery in an over crowded garrison town.

Trussel's scathing condemnation, which shorly follows, needs reading twice, may be thrice to take in and fully comprehend what life in Winchester and the surrounding villages was like, and in what was to be a very severe winter.

To set the scene, Lord Ogle had arrived in Winchester about the end of September with his own small force plus the regiments of Colonels E. Ford and H. Bennet, perhaps a thousand or more foot and horse.

By October the military garrison had been increased by the addition of Colonel Gerard's Regiment of horse bringing the total strength up to some two thousand troops, compared to the population of the City of about 3,500. With the space available within the walls and castle and during the autumn tolerable.

The relationship between the City and the military remained good and in the City's Coffer Book there is an entry of 50 pounds being lent to Colonels Ogle and Gerard; perhaps paid under duress but never an indication of any repayment.

On Monday the 6th of November Hopton's army marched in from Andover after his recent achievements in the West. Having drawn on supplies from Oxford he marched out again to the relief of Basing House, being beseiged by Waller, which he accomplished by the 14th having driven the parliamentarians back to Farnham.

Colonel Gerard's Regiment was then Withdrawn to Oxford.

The deprivation and removal from Hopton's army of this well trained and equipped regiment of horse, when every available man was required to reinforce and exploit success after the Royalist's Western Army's recent victories was to prove in the long term a disastrous mistake. Although Hopton was soon afterwards reinforced with a considerable force of foot under Sir Jacob Astley from Reading, and Colonel Boles being sent from Wallingford to Alton, his need was for horse that by the time a contingent of Wilmot's horse, did arrive in Winchester time and tempo had been lost.

Hopton expressed his anxiety in a letter to His Majesty written from Alresford at the beginning of December.

> *"May it please your Highness,*
> *Your Highness' commands concerning Col*
> *Gerard's regiment, as all other your*
> *commands, I shall ever be most ready*
> *to obey. I shall only offer to your*
> *Highness my present difficulty, which*
> *is, that we being here, near the enemy,*
> *and our horse decreasing much, I am*
> *doubtful lest, in sparing a good old*
> *regiment, I may give the enemy too*
> *great an advantage upon me in this*
> *champaign country; unless your Highness*
> *will please to do me the favour to send*
> *me some other regiment that hath had a*
> *rest, till this be recreated. The truth*
> *is the duty of the service here is so*
> *great a necessity either of prevailing*
> *through all difficulties, or suffering*
> *them to prevail, which cannot be thought*
> *of in good English, therefore, if your*
> *Highness resume the horse regiment I*
> *should be glad to give these some ease*
> *as I could.*
> *I rest in all humility and faithfulness,*
> *your Highness'es most humbly devoted servant.*
>
> *Ralph Hopton"*

Godwin.
p. 136.
quoting
Hopton's
letter.

Notwithstanding the arrival in Winchester of two regiments of foot under the command of Sir John Berkeley recently raised in Dorset, they were of course untrained and slow moving, Hopton's need was for regiments of horse in the mobile and fluid conditions of a war of movement. He had already commited Sir Edward Ford's regiment to an eastwards thrust into Sussex and Sir Edward was back in his home territory at Uppark by the 1st of December guarding Hopton's lines of communication towards Arundel which was seized on December the 9th.

Thus in Winchester, apart from Ogle's garrison of the castle, there was a continuous movement in and out of the City of men and horse.

As the Royalists were better organised at paying their troops than the Parliamentarians, even if in arrears, it is possible that for a short time the City went through a brief period of prosperity due to the security provided by a strong military presence, so that morale rose and trading conditions returned.

The capture of Arundel marked the zenith of the Royalist penetration into Sussex, it also marked a too great dispersion of the Royalist forces over which Waller counter attacked with great advantage.

Firstly at Romsey, which had been garrisoned by Colonel Bennet, with about 200 horse supported by some foot commanded by Colonel Courtney, who was routed by a fierce and well planned raid by Colonel Richard Norton from Southampton.

Among the prisoners taken was Capt-Lieut John Norton, (brother of Colonel Richard), who was fighting for the King. The refugees fled to Winchester.

Secondly and almost at the same time, on December 12th Colonel John Boles at Alton was attacked and overwhelmed by a greatly superior Parliamentary force who had secretly made a night march from Farnham and were able to surround the town, encircle the Poyalists, and force them into the church before relief could be brought.

Colonel Boles with many other valiant defenders, not deigning to accept quarter, were killed in the church which can still show the bullet holes made by the assailants during that famous "Alton Fight".

Once again the survivors, these mainly from Lord Crawford's horse, fell back on Winchester for safety.

Colonel Boles funeral was held in Winchester Cathedral. The effect on morale in the City was considerable. Dean Young came out of hiding at Wallop and felt compelled to make a rare entry in his diary at that time.

"5s for torches at Co: Bools funeral."

The Colonel's memorial brass is in the Cathedral nave affixed to a column of the north arcade facing the nave altar. There is a replica of the brass in Alton church.

The memorial erected many years later, in 1689, date John Boles action as having taken place in 1641, whereas the correct date of his death was the 13th December 1643. Further it was John Boles who was killed and not his brother Richard as stated on the brass. John was the second son of John Boles a scholar of Winchester College in 1562, who died in 1610.

A MEMORIAL

Vaughan.
Winchester
Cathedral.
p. 186.

*"For this renowed Martialist Richard
Boles of the Right Worshipful Family of the
Boles in Linckhorne Sheire, Collonell
of a Ridgment of Foot of 1300, who for
his gracious King Charles the First did
Wounders at the Battle of Edge-hill.
His last action, to omit all others,
was at Alton, in this County of Southampton
was surprised by five or six thousand of
the Rebels; which caused him, there
quartered, to fly to the church with
near four-score of his Men, who there
fought them six or seaven hours;
And then the Rebells breaking in upon
him, He slew with his Sword six
or seaven of them. And then was
slain himself, with sixty of his
men about him.
1641*

*His gracious Sovereign hearing of
his Death gave him his high Commendation,
in that passionate Expression,*

*"Bring me a Mourning Scarf, I have lost
One of the best Commanders in the Kingdome"*

*Alton will tell you of that famous Fight
Which this man made, and bade this World good Night
His virtuous Life fear'd not Mortalyty;
His body must, his Vertues cannot die
Because his Blood was there so nobly spent:
This is his Tombe, that Church his Monument.*

*Richardus Boles Wiltoniensis in Art. Mag
Composuit posuitq: Doleus
An Dni 1689.*

Of this tragedy Hopton, with extraordinary trouble of mind, felt compelled to write from Winchester to his old friend Waller and now his adversary, this letter which brings to life the anguish of Civil War.

> *"To Sir W Waller.*
> *Sir - This is the first*
> *evident ill successe I have had. I*
> *must acknowledge that I have lost*
> *many brave and gallant man. I desire*
> *you, if Collonel Bolles be alive, to*
> *propound a fit exchange; if dead,*
> *that you will send me his corps. I*
> *pray you sende me a list of such*
> *prisoners as you have, that such*
> *choice men as they are may not*
> *continue long unredeemed.*
> *God give a sudden stop to this*
> *issue of English blood, which is*
> *the desire Sir of your faithful*
> *friend to serve you,*
>
> *Winton 16th Dec.   Ralph Hopton."*

Godwin.
p. 148.

To add to the troubles of an already overcrowded city, shortly to arrive were two further regiments of foot. Lord Inchiquin's Irish regiments under the command of Sir John Paulet, Sir Charles Vavasour and Hugh O'Brien, (Inchiquin's brother), who finding little room in Winchester some were sent to Alresford to find Quarters. These Irish were

> *"bold hardy men, and excellently*
> *well officered, but the common-men*
> *verie mutenous and shrewdly infected*
> *with the rebellious humour of England."*

Edgar.
Hopton
p. 146.

In December 1643 Winchester was indeed overcrowded with 5000 foot and 1500 horse in the neighbourhood, it should not be surprising that difficulties arose over discipline with responsibility divided amongst so many commanders. Even Ogle, as Governor of the City, found he was unable to exert overall command for the enforcement of law and order.

Hardly had Hopton recovered from the reverses at Romsey and Alton, than a third disaster befell him for he now found his forward outpost at Arundel beseiged and retaken by Waller for Parliament. This was on January 6th in spite if a determined attempt at its relief by a Royalist forced march from Winchester on the 26th December with 2000 horse and 1500 foot, which failed in its endeavour, due to the combined action of Waller from Farnham and Colonel Norton from Portsmouth who compeled Hopton to fall back on Winchester.

By the fall of Arundel the Royalist hopes for the taking of Sussex in the spring were shattered and Hopton found that even his position here in Winchester was vulnerable and he might be deprived of his winter quarters.

Immediately he set about strengthening the defences of the City by employing one thousand men to dig entrenchments and to build fortifications. These were no doubt influenced in their design by a Dutch Engineer employed by Ogle at the Castle at a cost of £80.

Godwin
quoting
on p. 165
Ogle.

Arms, men and horses were not the only things required for the war, and if the citizens had to provide free billet the Mayor and Aldermen had to give up their silver plate just as the Dean had on a previous occasion, all to go to the Royal Mint established in Oxford.

CITY PLATE

30th December 1643

Taken out thene of the Coffer these several
parcells of Plate, and delivered unto Mr Jasper
Cornelius, appoynted to receive the same for His
Majesty's use, by virtue of a letter sent from
His Majesty to the Mayor and Aldermen of this
Cytie for the loan of Money on Plate, for the
maintenance of the Army, by the consent of the
Maior and all the Aldermen of this Cytie.

BAILEY
Archives
of Winchester
p. 88

One Silver Ewer	*weighing*	32¼	*oz*
Three Silver Beer Bowles	*weighing*	34¼	*oz*
Two Silver Wine Bowles	*weighing*	15¾	*oz*
One Gilte Bowle with the cover	*weighing*	31½	*oz*
One great Silver Salt	*weighing*	28	*oz*
One Silver Tankard	*weighing*	19½	*oz*
One Silver Bason	*weighing*	74	*oz*
	Total	235¼	*oz*

Which according to the directions of the said
letter at 5s/-an ounce amount unto £58-16-3."

Silver then was a very much more precious metal than it is today. The present bullion value of silver is about £8 an ounce and this does not seem to bear any relationship to the value of the plate "loaned" to His Majesty.

"Now to read and re-read with a lively
imagination Trussel's account of all these
doings and troubles.

Trussel.
f. 98.

But when free billet went throughout the towne
And no man could be master of his owne,
When Common Souldiers must have bedding
                        found
When owner, wife and children on the ground
Chalke out their lodging:
                When the honest woman
must be as observant to her that is as common
as any barbar's chayre;
                When ragged groomes
in every howse must have the private roomes
to make them stables for their horses;
                  when boyes
shall uncontrowle make an obstreperous noyes
all the week long with horrid blasphemyes,
and execrable cursing rent the skyes
and all licentious courses are permitted
without controle
              And when yt had befitted
the officers the sowldiers to restrayne
from doing what they please and do not care

Then always sutch as live in Peace, whose eare
was never used to Drum and never were
acquainted with the incidents of warr
Doe presently traduce my Governor
for sutch disorders suffering, and not thincke
That att these tymes he may a littell wincke
Att faulters, until the garrison be setled
And every thing therein well ordered,

But when will that bee cryes the malcontent
whose beam'd eyes spie moates in this
                    Government
When to the castle all thats ours is sent
And we are made naked an indigent.

When our provision of wine bread and beer
ffuel and what els fytting shall appear
All in the castle stored, and we must lacke
meat for mave and clothing for the backe.

When all our ablest men must their reside
And heer the weake and lame and sick must hide
What can we looke for; But to live like slaves
or els bee quickly quarted in our graves?

Yet lett them thincke that thus their verduict
                               spend
Yts easier to fid fault then to amend
Particular losses for a publicke gayne
must be endured; then sutch playnts are vayne

I doubt not but if they will attend
That things now wrong will come to a right end   Trussel.
A pound of knowledg easily is outgone   f. 98.
with but an ounze of good discretion
and most non pleasing is the remedye
the which Despayre brings Necessity.

Hope well and have well thereon rest I still
And doe not doubt but that my Governour will
Ymploy his best endevors to amend
what is amys, the better to defend
himself from scandall and mee from disgrace
And prove himself well worthy of his place
ffor otherwise if hee in ether fayle
his Cross will be my losse, his blame my bale.

Yet geve me leave, without offence, to say
That by a mixt authoritie their may
mutch mischeife growe unseen, unpunished
ffor when the rod from th one to the other posted
Transgressions every where will multiplye
by being cherisht by impunitie.

Right noble Governour and worthy Mayre
Lett yt be therefore your conioyned care
To purge your government from these fowle
                              vices
To which the Devill by his wiles entices
Let not the synnes of Sodom unreprovd
nor Babilons faults in mee raigne unremoved.

Trussel.
f. 98.

But lett a martial sword or civil lawe
Cittizens and souldyers detayne in awe
ffrom wilfully offending god and man
with actions altogether unchristian

f. 99.

But when some officers doe night and daye
Drincke, dice and drabb, the souldiers thinck
they may
ffolow examples, But wanting wherewithall
this course of ryott to supporte, they fall
To private pillaging and publicke taking
what they can snapp, or else unto
skonce making.

Whilst my inhabitants to peace a frend
Doe silentlie what speech cannot amend
What souldyers plunder some shopkeepers dare
buye
Those doe encourage theise to the every

The souldiers love good liquor, night and daye
The alehouse keepers labour what they may
To brew strong heady drinck to beat the brayne
And by that course their Drunkeness mantayne

Nay which is worse they sell yt at that rate
Which vintners heertofore good wine sould att
Now every second howse almost is made
A member of the strong aledrapers trade

And yt ys greatly to be feard, unlesse
Some course bee tooke sutch members to
supresse
And good wholesome usuall beere be brewed
And the excesse of guzling bee eschewed
That more straung and strong fevers and
Dropsyes more
Will be this fall then were long tyme before."

———

CLARENDON.

"Due to the "terrible coldness
of the season Hopton chose to
repose himself in that garrison
till the weather should mend.""

Chapter 12

RECRUITMENT AND TRAINING
DURING THE WINTER OF 1644

DURING the exceptionally cold winter of early 1644, with deep snow making movement difficult, both armies withdrew into Winter Quarters.

For the Royalists centred on Winchester, after the debacle of Romsey, Alton and Arundel, it was time for Hopton to recruit re-equip and train his army in readiness for a spring offensive.

It was also necessary for him to secure his base of operations so that much time was spent in building defensive ditches or fortifications on the hills, on both the east and west sides. That on the east side, St. Giles Hill is more likely to have been the one known as Hopton's Sconce, the other was on the West Hill.

These two sconces are marked on Taylors map of 1759 as, 'old foundations', according to his key of characters. (Conventional Signs).

Milner in his 'History of Winchester' of 1798, wrote; "the field works on the east side were in the modern style of fortification, and were very perfect a few years ago on St. Giles Hill." Of those on the west side he said, "These are still discernable in what is called Oram's Arbour and the adjoining fields". The redoubts may have been similar to those later built during the Civil War at Newark.

At the Castle Sir William Ogle was busy rebuilding the defences with the guidance of his Dutch Engineer, victualling and stocking the castle itself with provisions, clothing, ammunition and other warlike stores. Ogle was also able to find some recruits to strengthen his own garrison.

Taylor's map.

Milner. J.

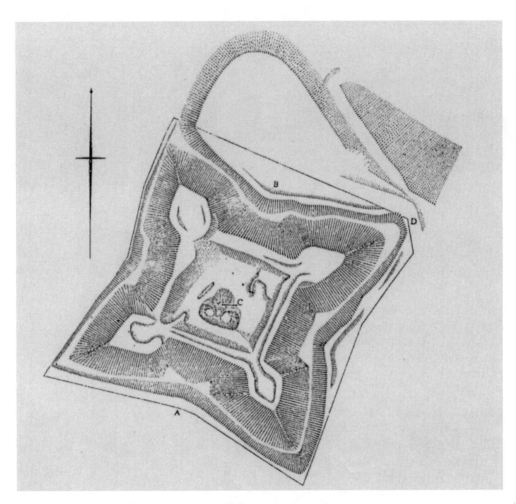

A "SCONCE", OR DEFENSIVE EARTHWORK

This plan is of "The Queen's Sconce" at Newark-upon-Trent built by the Royalists for the defence of Newark being besieged in 1645.

Hopton, too, was busy out in the County seeking recruits, not only to increase his strength but to replace the numerous desertions and casualties from sickness. It was said that he had collected such a bunch of raw recruits that when Lord Wilmot was ordered to withdraw his well trained horse back to Oxford he made a point of advising Hopton "not to engage his horse for they were new raised men and would never be able to do him any service for the present."

On the 1st of February Hopton was said to have 3.500 foot and 2,000 horse in Winchester. The strain on supplies and the continuing imposition of free billet so vividly described by Trussel must have been very onerous on the City itself.

By mid February, Hopton felt strong enough to send a reconnaissance party to Southampton. Possibly to gain information and keep his troops alert, but certainly as a good training execise. About this time there seems to have been talk of the army being ordered to withdraw to Marlborough, and whether the castle defences should be slighted.

Ogle was made of firmer stuff and certainly would not have yielded up his newly fortified strong point of Winchester Castle easily, any more that "The Loyal Marquis", John Paulet, was prepared to surrender Basing House. Further Ogle appears to have induced Hopton, ever ready to comply with orders, to see the advantage he had gained in the autumn and which he had consolidated during the winter, to express in a letter to the Royalist Headquarters at Oxford, that in the present circumstances a withdrawal from Winchester was not warranted.

Hopton in writing his own account of the 'War in the West', written in the third person, and some time after the event, reported,

Hopton's report,

> *"for the present the weather had*
> *releived him, so as he lay in noe*
> *danger, for the Enemy could not*
> *attempt him, that it might be hoped,*
> *that the wether might last till his*
> *recrewts, for which he had already*
> *dispatcht his orders, might be ready*
> *to come to him, that if there were*
> *any counsaillable meanes to preserve*
> *that County (Hants), so useful and*
> *so well affected to His Majestie it*
> *would very much import to his*
> *Majestie's service, that, if, by his*
> *quitting of these quarters, the Enemy*
> *should drawe downe to Winchester and*
> *possesse himselfe of that place, all*
> *the plaine of Wiltshire would lay*
> *open to him; He therefore humbly*
> *ofer'd it to his Majestie's consideration,*
> *whither His Majestie would be*
> *pleased to trust him with the time*
> *of his retreate; Which His Majestie*
> *most graciously did."*

EDGAR
p. 156
quoting
Hopton's
Bellum
Civile.

With the aid of levies made throughout the County and with other subsidies Hopton was not only able to maintain his army in supply and strength, but he had by March increased his force to about 6,000. No doubt with the assistance of a little forcible recruiting. This was in the circumstances a very considerable achievement.

In continuation of his training programme and the wish to show strength, strong patrols were sent eastwards deep into enemy held territory as far as Petersfield. Elsewhere, and to counter his previous rebuff at Romsey that town was raided, recaptured and many of Norton's Troops were taken.

As an example of the effects of free billet and the general shortage of food and fuel that winter, the Master of St. Mary Magdalen Hospital, which lay some two miles to the east of the City, felt compelled to write to Hopton complaining of the thefts and destruction of the Hospital buildings, and the use of the Chapel by the Royalists troops as a stable.

It has been too often claimed that the use of churches as stables was the prerogative of the Parliamentarians, as at Upham where in the church record will be found this entry made in 1642,

> *"Item*
> *For cleansing ye church against*
> *Christmas after ye troops had abused*
> *it for a stable for their horses 2s 6d."*

Anon.
II. p. 254.

The original entry made in 1642 was "used" for a stable, this was later changed to "abused". The abuse of St. Mary Magdalen Hospital was very considerable as detailed in the Masters Petition,

> *"To the Right Honourable Lord Hopton,*
> *Barron of Stratton, and Field Marshall*
> *General of his Majesty's Western Forces.*
>
> *The humble petition of the Master and*
> *the Almesfolk of the Poore Hospitall of*
> *St Mary Magdalen neare Winchester,*
> *sheweth.*
> *That the endowment of the sayd*
> *Hospitall is very meane and not sufficient*
> *to maintaine your Petitioners the poore*
> *aged people there, with necessary*
> *sustenance, and uphold the buildings without*
> *the pious and charitable benevolence of*
> *others.*
> *That sixteen acres of barren*
> *arable land and dry common for 120*
> *sheepe is all the land belongeinge to*
> *the sayde Hospital, which hath ben*
> *constantly manur'd and husbanded for*
> *the reliefe of your Petitioners.*

That about Christmas last,
thirty-six of their sheepe were taken
and killed by the souldiers of this
army, the residue of their sayde flocke
of sheepe they were for preservation of
them forced to convey them out of the
way, sixteen miles off, where they have
bin ever since kept at your Petitioners
charge, which your Petioners were
contented to suffer, without complaint
or trouble to your Lorship.

But your Petitioners doe
farther shewe that within four nights
last past, the souldiers keeping their
rendesvouse their, have not only
devoured nine quarters of their feede
barley for this season (being the full
provision for the same) and have broken
down and burnt up the great gates, all
doores, table boords, cupboords, gyses,
timber partitions, barnes and stables
there, but have also used violence to
the house of God; burninge up all the
seats and pues in the church, as also
the communion table, and all other
wainscott and timbers there, that they
could lay hands on: and have converted
the sayd house of God, the church, into
a stable for horses and other prophane
uses, to the great dishonour of God,
and griefe of soule of your petitioners,
beinge very aged and impotent persons,
and therby made destitute of the means
of having either temperall or
spirituall foode.

Anon.
II. p. 255.

Anon.
II. p. 256

*May your honor be pleased
therefore out of a charitable
commisseration of your petitioners, and
a religious considiration of the
premises, to give order for reparation
of the ruines of the sayde hospitall,
and to provide means that your
petitioners may, through your
lordship's goodness be settled in such
a condition as formerly they were,
havinge noe mean's but through your
boweinty to be otherwise relieved from
perishinge. So shall your petitioners
ever pray for your lordships encrease
of honour, and happy successe in thes
your most just and Religious
undertakings."*

Lord Hopton's answer was written on the back of the Petition reads,

*"I Desire Henry Foyle, Esq; and
Commisary Fry, to take consideration
of this petition, and to take such
order for the poore peoples reliefe
therein as to them shall seeme
expedient.*

RALPH HOPTON.

*Winchester
19 Martii, 1644."*

Hopton's aggressiveness that spring was further displayed in his determination to clear his rear of Parliament's strong point of Wardour Castle, which was beseiged and taken on the 18th March. Its commander, Edmund Ludlow, was taken prisoner and on being escorted captive to Oxford he passed through Winchester. In his memoirs Ludlow discloses that Hopton's Headquarters were in Eastgate House, and he tells of the civilities, courtesies, short tempers and heart pricking that was part of life during the Civil War.

"In our way to Winchester one
Mr Fisher, an acquaintance of mine,
then an oficer of the King's saluted
me and enquiring how I did, I
answered him ' As well as one could
be in my condition'; he thereupon
replying 'Why I hope they use you
civilly, do they not?' 'Yes' said I
'very civilly'
Sir Francis Doddington over-hearing
him, took it so ill, that he caused
him to be immediately disarmed,
telling him, that he was bold, to call
in question the usage of his prisoner.
Being arrived in Winchester, I was
staid at an inn till a private lodging
was provided for Sir Francis at whose
quarters, according to his promise, I
lodged, whilst in his custody.
Most of the officers about the town
came to me at the inn, several pressing
me to discourse, and particularly
concerning the justice of our cause.
I excused myself, by reason of my
present circumstances; by they still
persisting, I thought myself obliged to
maintain the necessity of our taking up
arms in defence of our religion and
liberties;

Ludlow's
Memoirs.
p. 83.

Ludlow.

*but some of them being wholly biased
to their interest, as they went from
me, met a relation of mine, one Col
Richard Manning, who tho a Papist,
commanded a regiment of horse in the
King's service, and told him, that
they came from one of the boldest
rebels that they had ever seen.*

*The colonel coming to visit me, what-
soever I thought, not to be so free with
them, lest they should do me some mischief.*

*The next morning, befor our departure
for Oxford Sir Francis Doddington brought
me to Sir Ralph Hopton's lodgings, which
being the headquarters we found there most
of the principal officers of that army;
where the general, after, he had saluted
me, demanded how I, being a gentleman,
could satisfy myself to bear arms against
my King: I told him, that, as I conceived
the laws both of God and man did justify
me in what I had done. 'Well' said he 'I
understand you are so fixed in your
principles, that I am like to do little
good upon you by my persuasions; but shall
desire the archbishop of Armagh to take the
pains to speak with you, when you come to
Oxford; and if he cannot work on you, I now
not who can."*

Archb'p of
Armagh.

While Hopton was preparing for the spring compaign and
to march eastwards, so was Parliament preparing to march
westwards. General Waller had been busy rebuilding the army of
the Southern Association, comprising the London Regiments
under Major General Browne, and the Regiments of horse, foot
and dragoons from Kent, Sussex and Surrey. These soon to be
reinforced by a considerable strength of horse commanded by Sir
William Balfour.

The whole Parliamentary army had orders to rendezvous at West Meon on the 25th March prior to marching into the West.

Waller's army totalled some 10,000 horse and foot and when ready to move he received the ambiguous orders from the Committee of Both Kingdoms that he was "Not to engage except upon advantage." Hardly an order designed to inspire confidence in a commander.

Meanwhile a decision had been taken to reinforce Hopton's army in Winchester. As part of the King's 'Old Army' marched from Oxford towards Winchester, Hopton rode north with Lord John Stuart to meet the King's Commander in Chief, Patrick Ruthven, Lord Forth, at Newbury.

The three Lords, Forth, Hopton and Stuart returned to Winchester on the 23 March with the Queen's Regiment. Additional regiments of horse foot and artillery under Sir George Lisle had been sent from Reading. All these contingents redezvoused on Hunton Down (two miles east of Sutton Scotney) before marching onto Winchester.

They were described as consisting of "mostly young boys torn from weeping mothers and masters who also want arms and military exercises".

On their arrival in Winchester the ever resourceful Governor Lord Ogle "caused them all to be accommodated in the City and suburbs."

By these very considerable reinforcements the total strength of the Royalist Army amounted to about 5,000 horse, 5,000 foot and eleven guns, perhaps a little superior in strength to Waller's army articularly in horse.

On the 24th March orders came from Oxford to march into Sussex. With both opposing commanders seeking a contest and both ready to move a battle became imminent and inevitable. Further to keep such large numbers of troops bottled up within the city walls would have created impossible conditions for discipline, supply and freedom from sickness and disease.

On Tuesday morning the 26th March 1644 a Council of War was held at Hopton's headquarters at which it was resolved to march immediately against Waller. To this council rather surprisingly the Governor of the Castle and City was called to give his opinion. Lord Ogle relates his part in the council's proceedings in the then customary third person.

Ogle's
Engagements.
Add Mss
27402.
f. 83.

"*Lord Ogle was desired by a messenger*
to come to my Lord Hopton's lodgings
nigh at Eastgate House: when he came
there he found the three Lord with all
the field officers sett in Councell.
My Lord Hopton said to my Lord Ogle
'Governor, tho you are not of the
Army; yet we have sent for you
to assist at this councell'
My Lord told him it was very improper
for him to give any opinion; where he
had not command; He desired to know what
was the debate, he was answered: that the debate
was to remove Waller's army out of
these parts, for it was a shame to let him
(approach so) neare; my Lord Hopton
desired my Lord Ogle to give his opinion;
he (Ogle) desired to know if it was their
joint opinion to march and remove him.
He was answered it was the resolution of
that councell; then he told them;
it would be to noe purpose for him to give
his opinion.
'My Lords' said Ogle; 'seeing it is yr
pleasure to have opinion I must
freely profess it fall not within
my understanding that you should
seek a formed Army well commanded
with raw men, new raised horse and
foot.'

*If Waller should come within a
mile of Winchester you might if
you thought fit drawe out and
fight them having this garrison
to back and supply you upon any
Disaster a safe retreat; but if
you march six or seven miles to
fight, you must carry your
provisions, and in this extreme
hot weather weary the soldiers
and (why) fight an Enemy who as
I am informed is marching away
to London'*
My Lord Hopton said, all this was but
one man's opinion; and soe continued
the Resolution to march immediately.
My Lord Hopton said, he wanting
provision to carry along with the army
must desire my Lord Ogle to furnish him
with what he could; he answered him,
that if he should doe so it would
disfurnish the Castle.
His Lordship replied, that he hoped
to come back with victory; but if it
otherwise he would most certainly
retreat to him at Winchester; and there
they should be able to supply what he
tooke from him with advantage;
Whereupon my Lord Ogle furnished him
six carts laden with biskett, cheese,
and divers other provision the
Wedneday following: he with the two
other Lords and all their forces
marched towards Waller who was as it
seemed, retiring towards London but my
Lord Hopton was minded to hinder their
retreat and to get before him and so
marched in great hast and did face him
at a place called Cheriton Downe."

Ogle.
f. 84.

-118-

The Royal army did not march directly to Cheriton but that evening moved out to a general rendezvous on Gander Down, three miles due east of Winchester, where they formed up and stood ready in "Battalia" to await the arrival of Waller's Roundheads whose advance guards had reached West Meon, and where opposing patrols clashed.

The voice of the City at these rapid changes of events was expressed by Trussel in these words,

Sawyer.
Ms
Battle of
Cheriton.

> *"But woe is mee whilst I am speaking this*
> *Affliction to afliction added is*
> *My foes reunite, my friends refuse to staye*
> *And my auxiliaries are drawne awaye*
> *Those regiments that heer were quartered and*
> *Were under the Marshall Generall's Command*
> *Honord Lord Hopton, are drawne forth to face*
> *Wallers Great body which comes on apace."*

Trussel.
f. 99.

400 troops were left to guard the Castle and Sir William Ogle tells the next part of the story, the Battle of Cheriton, one of the major battles of the Civil War, in but a single paragraph.

Godwin.
p. 198.

> *"Hopton marched in great haste to*
> *face Waller at a place called*
> *Cheriton Down where in all*
> *appearance Waller was worsted, but*
> *some of my Lord's horse charging*
> *unfortunately were routed and my*
> *Lord with the foot retreated in Great*
> *disorder towards garrison at Basing*
> *House and so left my Lord Ogle,*
> *contrary to his promise and having*
> *disfurnished his garrison of full two*
> *parts of his provision."*

Ogle.

Chapter 13

THE BATTLE OF CHERITON
29 MARCH 1644

ON Wednesday morning the 27th March the Royalist Generals rode out of Winchester, before dawn, to join the army already formed up on Gander Down, and where they were busy digging defences ditches. Immediately a strong patrol was sent to find and entice Waller's army on to the Royalists chosen battlefield, it being thought the open downland would favour their better trained horse.

Sawyer. Battle of Cheriton.

This was not to be, for Waller while apparently continuing his advance towards Winchester, suddenly turned off through Cheriton towards Alresford. A great chase began to be first into the town to man the barricades, the race was won by Hopton's dragoons.

The Royalists then moved their whole army to the downs south of Alresford denying Waller the quarters and supplies in Alresford, but more importantly it placed the King's army commanding Waller's supply routes to Farnham and London.

Waller was thus forced to halt and take up a position between Bramdean and Cheriton in "Lamborough Field", centered about Hinton Ampner House. (Lady Stewkely's house, formerly Mr Ralph Dutton's, now National Trust's).

All day Thursday the armies stood back from each other, except for some violent clashes between patrols as each side skirmished and manoevered for position.

The battle which ensued was fought in three distinct phases and opened at dawn on Friday the 29th when the Parliamentarians advanced on their right wing in an attempt to seize the high ground of Bramdean Heath to the east of Cheriton Wood.

BARON RALPH HOPTON 1598-1652

Lieutenant General of the West and Southern Counties. He defeated Waller at Roundway Down in 1643 but was bested by Waller at the Battle of Cheriton on 28th March 1644.
(Artist unknown – Courtesy National Portrait Gallery)

A counter attack led by Hopton was highly successful, Parliament's London Brigade were forced to a disorderly retreat. A victory for the Royalists. This engagement being called the "Battle of Bramdean Heath" as Lord Ogle had so succinctly said, "Waller was worsted". However Lord Forth, who as Commander-in-Chief of the King's armies, grievously failed to exploit this success.

After a lengthy pause while the opposing armies formed up in battalia facing each other, with Cheriton Down and East Down held by Sir William Balfour and Sir William Waller for Parliament, and Tichborne Down and Sutton Down held by the King's Old Army and Sir Ralph Hopton's army. The modern monument marks the centre of the Royalist position.

Between the two opposing armies lies the traditional site of the battle arena "Cheriton Field". This site is marked on I Taylors map of 1759, and on the first edition of the Ordnance Survey and on all subsequent editions. The map reference is SU 597295. Studies of the ground in relation to the numerous contemporary reports, pamphlets published in London and Oxford, and subsequent recollections of old adversaries, confirm this. Here was fought the Battle of Cheriton.

For some time the combatans stood watching each other, at a distance apart of extreme artillery range. The action was brought about by the impetuousness of a Royalist officer Colonel Beard who advanced too far forward without orders drawing the Royalist horse off their ground into the skirmish, until both armies became embroiled in a general engagement. The battle lasted well into the afternoon until the Royalists were forced to withdraw.

Lloyd.
p. 326.

The "commodius hollow that lay between them where many a gallant man met his grave" by tradition became "the lane which ran with blood".

This would have been one of the lanes in the middle of the battle arena.

The third and final phase of the day long action, called in the contemporary accounts "Alresford Fight" was a fiercely fought rearguard action carried out by Hopton, who very skillfully enabled almost the entire Royalist army to withdraw from the battle arena with a minimum of casualties together with all its cannon.

Contrary to Hopton's promise to Ogle that he would fall back on Winchester, in the event of disaster, the entire Royalist army withdrew to Basing House leaving Winchester isolated and unprotected to await the wrath and fury of a victorious enemy.

Of the many pamphlets, letters and reports written at the time this short article in "Bakers Chronicle" published in London the day after the Battle is a representative.

> *"Sir William Waller having taken*
> *Arundell Castle and gotten a commision*
> *to his mind, marched forward against*
> *the Lord Hopton whom he finds drawn*
> *out on Brandon Heath near Alsford with*
> *intention to fight, which Waller*
> *refused not, and so gaine an advantageous*
> *hill, from whence being forced he gets*
> *up to another whither the Cavaliers*
> *follow him, but at length the Parliament*
> *by the help of the ground and the coverts*
> *of trees and hedges did such execution*
> *upon the enemie, that after the loss of*
> *many persons of Quality beside a great*
> *number of the Vulgar Sort, they retreated*
> *in great Disorder; and drawing off their*
> *cannon towards Winchester wheeled off*
> *unseen to Basing House.*
>
> *Whence Hopton hastens to Oxford, and*
> *Winchester after this victory yields to*
> *Waller upon summons".*

Bakers
Chronicle.
p. 456.

Eye Witness.
Elias Archer.

Books & Mss
1951.
Exhibit No. 73.

Ogle.

To the Parliamentarians Winchester, or so it was thought, would be easily taken, so much so that

"WINCHESTER TAKEN"

was proclaimed in banner headlines in London.

This was not to be entirely true for the Castle held out for the King for another eighteen months.

Sir William Ogle tells the story of what happened in Winchester the night after the battle and the events in the City on Saturday the 30th

"That night a multitude of the scattered horse and foot came into Winchester; and it was daylight next morning before he could free the towne of them; which he did by assuming them that Waller with his whole Armie would come to Winchester and that the City was not to be defended.

This made them make haste to be gone Westward.

And about Eight of the clock on Sunday (this was Saturday the 30th) morning my Lord perceived Waller with the army marching down from Wallers Ash (Sir William Waller of Old Stoke's) towards Worthy, two myles from Winchester where upon he went into the City and called on the Mayor and Aldermen into the market place telling them that the City was not tenable against such forces and that they should enter it by force it must be plundered and ruined.

He gave them the keys of the gate and to offer him to come in without any oposition and that they might suffer noe prejudice by his soldiers which they did, and Waller with his Army came into the lower part of the city, and about the great church."

From this brief account, and those of the Parliamentary writers, it seems that as Waller approached the North Gate of the City a message was sent out to the General to say he was expected. This was confirmed by the "Kingdoms Weekly Intelligencer" and other reports by Vicars and "A Perfect Diurnal" who said "Upon the first summons the Mayor came out and opened the gate and presented the Keys to Sir William Waller. The Mayor and Aldermen declaring themselves for King and Parliament desiring to be preserved from violence which they were accordingly notwithstanding a small and inconsiderable number of the King's forces that were in the castle (said to be about 100 or 150 which if they do not run away will no doubt at a more convenient season bee forced to yeeld that, and themselves to Parliaments forces.)"

Perfect Diurnal. No. 36.

Vicars. No. 14.

Sir Arthur Hazelrigge, the commander of Parliament's cuirrassiers familiarly know as the "Lobsters", because of their heavy armour for man and horse, appears to have arrived in Winchester later that morning and then hastened back to London to report to Parliament the next day saying he "went to Wynchester, the town was open but the Castle shutt att their trumpeteer". The Intelligencer who also had been in Winchester in a lively bit of reporting said "the Keeper of the prison there, was so posset with fear, that he set eighty prisoners loose, taken at Romsey." These must have been the prisoners taken in Hopton's raid of the 13th March.

Haselrigg.

The Kingdoms Weekly Intelligency 2nd. April

Waller then summoned the Castle. Ogle Himself relates,

> *"He (Waller) sent three officers of*
> *Qualitye to my Lord Ogle to require*
> *that he should deliver the Castle to*
> *the Parliament; My Lord answered, he*
> *kept it by commision from the King*
> *and when he should receive his Majesties*
> *Order he would deliver it but not before."*

Ogle's Engagements.

Waller summons Ogle to deliver the Castle.

Ogle's
Engagements.

*"Then sent him word that if he would
not deliver it, he would burne his house
at Stoake Charitie; and fire the City:
He returned answer that he had
plundered all his house at Stoak; and,
for the house it was a very old one,
and none of his inheritance, and if he
pleased to burne the City it would make
a very spacious and faire garden for
the Castle.
Apon which answer he plundered five or
six of the houses of the best affected
Citizens for the King, and marched out
of the City at Kingsgate and drew up his
armie in the meadow about a half mile
from the City from whence he marched to
a little garrison at Christs Church and
took it at discretion making the Gentlemen
and soldiers all prisoners of warr;"*

Waller in haste to march Westwards to engage and capture as many as possible of the Royalist army assembled his horse in College Meads just south of Warden Harris's newly built Sick House of 1640, and galloped off to Romsey and on to Christchurch.

His inability to take the castle was due to a lack of foot soldiers to undertake the task, and the absence of any siege weapons or artillery. Many of Parliament's foot, particularly from the London Regiments declared that they had served their time without pay and they were going home as indeed they did. Under those circumstances the decision to by-pass the strong point of the castle and to pursue and destroy the fleeing remnants of the King's army was militarily correct even if in the event it was ineffectual.

The Parliamentarians feelings of anger and frustration in their failure to take the castle while searching for an excuse was expressed by Vicar's correspondent in this manner

> *"After our men had refreshed themselves,*
> *it was not thought fit that so brave an*
> *Army should spend an houres time about*   Vicars.
> *so petulent a designe as the reducing*
> *of that castle at such a time but rather*
> *with all vigilency to persue the victory*
> *and fall upon some other service of farre*
> *greater importance."*

Waller may have left the city in hurry giving his troopers little time to plunder, nevertheless the expression "they refreshed themselves" at the expense of the City was ominous. Waller however did leave a small detachment of an Hundred to watch the castle but the garrison together with the loyal citizens quickly disarmed them and took them prisoner.

Lord Ogle ever ready to seize the opportunity of restocking the castle with supplies, sent a night foraging party out to the deserted battlefield to pick up any things of value he could find.

> *"Sunday morning, my Lord Ogle drew his*
> *Regiments of horse and foot into the*
> *castle; having on Saturday night sent*
> *a party of horse towards Cheriton from*   Ogle.
> *whence Waller was gone; this party on*
> *Sunday morning brought in above three*
> *score barrels of powder, which they*
> *found in Carts upon the Downs with*
> *divers Arms and other provisions which*
> *were left behind (by) the Army."*

Within a week Waller was to return reinforced with detachments of the London Brigade who had remained with the Colours, and by then had come up to rejoin with the horse, when the City was again submitted to the dreadful vengeance of Waller's troops for their failure to take the castle from an unsubmissive Ogle.

Chapter 14

AFTERMATH OF BATTLE

THE Battle of Cheriton in which 10,000 troops on each side were engaged proved to be more a war of manoevre rather than a battle destructive of man power. Waller was certainly the victor on the battlefield, but was deprived of the immediate fruits of that victory through his inability to exploit his success.

Nevertheless the long term effect on the Royalist cause was profound. Never again was King Charles ever seriously able to get into a position to threaten London from the south.

Ever optimistic King Charles after the battle wrote to Prince Rupert.

Warburton.
Memoirs of
Prince
Rupert
II. p. 403.

"Nephew,

Indeed I have this advantage of you That I have not yet mistaken you in anything, as you have of me; as for your coming back towards Shrewsbury I do approve of it, and it is nowise contradiction to that opinion sent to you by Parsons for it was not only left solely to your judgement but it had a reference likewise to your strength, of which we had certain knowledge. And now it falls out of the better, because of the retreat that my Lord Hopton has made before Waller, where, though the loss was very inconsiderable, except the loss of some few brave officers, 400 being the most in all, both of horse and foot, the rebels loss being certainly more, some think twice as many; yet because they have something to brag on it may give them so much credit as to be able to recruit Essex's army, in which case it is requisite that yours be not far from me."

I hope in a few days to be able to
venture on another blow, for my foot
came off in good enough order; and
now I hear that the appearance of the
horse is better than we expected.
Warburton.
II. p. 403.
So referring the particulars of my
resolutions to my Secretary and the
clearing of mistaking to my Lord Jermyn
-in despite of all which, and what
else the devil can do, you shall still
find me

Your loving uncle and
most faithful friend

Oxford   Charles R.
1 April 1644."

King Charles may have been optimistic, but his secretary
Sir Edward Walker quickly appreciated the changed situation
and wrote these lines acknowledging this, which are given below.
Also quoted are the more familiar words of Clarendon taken
from his "History of the Rebellion". In his version of this turning
point in history but written many years after the event, Clarendon
had the advantage of hindsight and Walker's papers to study.

Sir Edward Walker, written in 1644.

"Parliaments success that day was
rather accomplished with marks of
victory, than any real proofs thereof,
Walkers
Discourses.
p. 7.
yet it was so great advantage to them
that thereby they necessitated His
Majesty to alter the scheme of his
affairs and in place of an offensive
to make a defensive war."

KING CHARLES I WITH HIS SECRETARY SIR EDWARD WALKER

This could depict King Charles dictating a letter to his nephew Prince Rupert relating the failure of the
Royal Army at the Battle of Cheriton in 1644.
(Artist unknown – Courtesy National Portrait Gallery)

Lord Edward Clarendon's version published in 1704

The Battle of Cheriton

*"broke all the measures and altered
the whole sceme of the King's councels
for whereas before he hoped to have
entered the field early and to act an
offensive part, he now discerned he was
wholly to be upon the defensive part;
and that was likely to be a hard part too"*

Clarendon.
1843 Edit'
p.480.

Parliament for its part learnt the lesson of the uselessness of an untrained ill armed army without a proper chain of command and supply. The failure to reap the reward of victory on the battlefield at Cheriton was the catalysis for the formation of the New Model Army, later to be so successfully wielded by Cromwell and seen in action here in Winchester in October year.

After "Cheriton" Parliament knew that the Royalist horse could be defeated. In addition the debacle of seeing their troops deserting for lack of pay at a crucial moment, gave them that incentive and sense of urgency they needed to create the well paid, armed and disciplined army that was to be the very means they achived their final victory.

Lord Essex, Parliament's Commander-in-Chief's anguish at the disarray in his armies, due to lack of pay, made him complain to Parliament a few days after the Battle in these terms,

"My Lords,

Upon the Victory God hath been pleased to give us against Sir Ralph Hopton, and the sense I have of any condition, (being General by your favour) that I am not able to prosecute this Victory, and that now the speech is general of His Majesty's taking the field; and by reason of the condition which the long delay of recruiting my Army and ill payment have brought me to, I am grown the pity of my friends and contempt of my Enemies, having as yet no Forces to take the field with, I am enforced to make this following Declaration.

Parliamentary History

'That it grieves me exceedingly to see so fair an opportunity lost of prosecuting the advantage which, by God's goodness we have gotten upon the enemy at this time, because the army is not recruited; so as I am altogether disenabled to move but must sit still and see this opportunity pass from me, I verily believe, of ending the bleeding miseries of this destructive war; whereas now the enemy will have time to recover and repair themselves before I can get into a condition to advance towards them."

Ponderous affairs of State but how fared abandoned Winchester. Two long passages from Trussel and Ogle tell what happened when the enemy without became the enemy within. It is the story too of a city that could lose nothing more, yet in spite of all the travail maintained its Loyalty to the Crown and which continued to say and pray,

"Protect thy Servant Charles my Soveraigne King."

Trussel.
See p. 139 below

Trussel.
f. 99

"To my no litle feare and fright, the nomber infinite
Of wounded and sick souldiers, day and night
brought hither into hospitall doe chaunge
my mansion howses, my inhabitants estraunge
themselves from their owne dwellings, being unable
to endure to bee encumbered with a rable
of miserable wretches, whose necessitie
enforce loud cryes to show their miserye
But meanes of help find none; the poore unto the needy
Complayne of want, but see no remedye.

The wounded dressings want, surgeos wherewithall
playsters to make; the sick and weake doe call
for comfort, but nor food nor phisicks found
to fill the stomacks or cleance the wownd
so that in everye street, most miserablie
they starving, pine, and famisht fall and dye
And both their deathes and buríalls commonly
want Christian rights and decent Ceremony.

Through out the streets are cryes and exclamations
For want of trade, and general lamentations
for private losses. But to this affliction
An other is added, that theirs no restriction
from hindring Markett people quietly
to bring mee provision, but that violently
their horse and carts are took away, And they
are forced for their redemption mony to pay
for feare whereof they doe forbeare to bring
provision to my Marketts so that everye thing
is sould att that dear rate that fewe are able
things needful to provide for hall or stable

These and suspitions of worse daungers make
the most of my best able to forsake
their shoops, trades, dwellings, And leave all
                              things heere
att six and seaven, And no way doe appear
ready or willing to geve contribution
or to the poore to render fytt solution.

But now to add more fuell to my woe
uppon the hill appears the insulting foe,
Who having from thence stormed mee doe provide
Themselves to quarter uppon every side;
And lately but too soone, break of daye   Trussel.
without alarum taken they find a way
within my walls to gett as well they might
when their was none opposed with them to fight
And had so many Stony frends within
To geve them notice which way to steal in."

Lord Ogle in continuing his recollections tells how Sir William Waller, who after his dash to Christchurch returned to Romsey, planned to retake Winchester.

Ogle refers to a Mr Callaway, a Parliamentarian living in Winchester who did "practice" with Waller. By the word practice he meant Callaway and Waller plotted how by deviousness the Castle could be taken by stealth.

"Then he came back to Rumsey where
he stay'd three daies which gave my
Lord Ogle suspect that he had some
design and soe it fell out, for he
having one Mr Callaway in Winchester
who did practice with him; their
designs proved to be that where as my   Ogle's
Lord Ogle did Quarter all his soldiers   Engagements.
both horse and foot in the City and
there being a good space of ground
betwixt the City and Castle in which
my Lord kept onely three score soldiers,
and the Southgate opening betwixt the
City and Castle, that if he could by
pretence open that gate; then all my
Lords soldiers in the City would be cut off and
he having so few with him in the Castle
it must of necessity be taken.
This afterwards was found to be the
design which my Lord could not foresee."

A MORTUARY CHEST IN THE CHOIR OF THE CATHEDRAL

(Photo by A. Sollars)

BISHOP WILLIAM OF WYKEHAM'S EFFIGY

(Photo by A. Sollars)

COLONEL JOHN BOLES MEMORIAL BRASS

Cathedral Nave Dias north side
(Photo by A. Sollars)

SIR JOHN CLOBURY'S MONUMENT 1624 – 1687

The monument in the Retro Choir of the Cathedral depicts a Martial Figure. He was a professional soldier who paid earnest attention to literature, a rare example among soldiers. He claimed to have assisted General John Monk restore the Monarchy in 1660.

(Photo by A. Sollars)

Referring to the events on the evening of the 6th April Ogle uses another word in an unfamiliar way. It is 'jealousy' in the sense of being supiciously vigilant of disloyalty.
"This doing wrong creates such doubts as these Renders us jealous and destroys our peace."

Ogle

Ogle wrote,
"But the night before late in the
evening, Mrs Calloway came to him (Ogle)
and pretended to give him good news
which she said had come from London,
but her discourse was so full of
idle words that he dismissed her and
began to have some jealousie that
there was some ill pretended by Waller,
who she did often name as an enemy to
her husband, who then lived in the
City and had a good repute.
    Upon my Lords jealousie of words
that past from her and after wondering
that Waller should be soe long at
Rumsey he drew all his soldiers horse
and foot into the castle; and told
them that they must all be in armes
that night in the works and to please
them distributed a great number of
coats and shirts amongst them which
my Lord Hopton had left in the town
with a hogshead of stronge beare and
having placed all the guards and
secured the sally ports about twelve
a clock my Lord Ogle laid downe in his
clothes to rest, all this he did
judging it not fitt to be secure an
enemy being so neare.

Towards day break he was waked
with a petard that had broken up
the Southgate and that Waller had
entered; My Lords soldiers who were
all upon the guards saluted him with
a great volley of musket which forced
him to detour (and) halt downe as
far as the great church having missed
his design of surprising the soldiers
in the City, he (Waller) plundered
three or four of the richest houses
in the City which were well affected
to the King and so with his companion
Callaway and his whole family marched
away towards London.
This Callaway had instructed him
in the whole design; after this there
were no more attempts upon my Lord
till after Naysby unfortunate battle."

Ogle's
Engagements.

The Battle of Naseby was fought 14th June 1645, when "The war was ended at a blow."

The story told by Ogle of the petard set against the Southgate was confirmed by Luke a Parliamentary scout in this terse report,

"On Monday last Sir William Waller
drew a party of horse and foot
together against Winchester and
because the gates where shut against
them he blew up the gates with a
petard, took 28 prisoners 1,000 arms
and plundered the Town and retreatd
To Romsey again next day."

Luke.
Scout Report.
No 87.

Another account of the forcible entry into the City was written by John Birch's secretary. Birch a Parliamentary officer serving in the London Brigade had been in action at Cheriton and after the Battle had been sent to Bishops Waltham to take the Bishop of Winchester's castle there which had held a small garrison for the King.

Local tradition holds that Bishop Curle was in his castle at that time, but succeeded in escaping in a cart, layer of manure being placed over him. Later the Bishop was in trouble again at the Siege of Winchester Castle from which there was to be no escape. Here at Bishops Waltham after a short investment, the castle surrendered to Parliament's forces on these terms,

Rushworth

> *"That the Commanders and Officers*
> *might march out with their horses*
> *and swords, and the common soldiers*
> *only with staves in their hands."*

From this diversion John Birch then marched to Winchester to join Waller's assault on the city. His secretary Roe was so involved in describing the heroic deeds of his master that he seemed to be oblivious of what was going on elsewhere at the time. Roe having described Birch's part at Cheriton, goes on to say how Winchester was surprised, but in this particular exploit his hero was at first misled by a guide. The guide was no doubt one of Trussel's stony friends who gave notice which way to steal in.

Birch. J.
Memoirs
written
by his
secretary
Roe.
p.11.

> *"At Winchester cittie your guide might*
> *well have caused you to miscarry; whoe*
> *being to guide you to a lowe place in*
> *the wall, your selfe being a stranger,*
> *when hee came about one hundred paces*
> *short, and the enemy fireing a few*
> *muskets (as he said) hee was so hastily*
> *taken hee must needs untruss, leaving*
> *you to find the lowest place in the wall*
> *yourself; which God soe directed you*
> *unto, that with the helpe of your*
> *ladders you were in before the enimy*
> *could make any head."*

Of the unhappy vicissitudes that followed Waller's forced entry, the 18c Anonymous historian summarised the situation and events that took place on Sunday the 17th April, and in writing his book it seems likely that he had read Mercurius Aulicus of the 13th April, written shortly after the event and in which he said

> *"Waller 'taught the Towne'*
> *a lesson for its intransigence."*

Anon' writes

> *"Waller himself, with all the forces*
> *he could collect, marched next day to*
> *this city, which he expected would*
> *voluntarity surrender upon the news*
> *of his last success, and the loss of*
> *their garrison under Lord Hopton; but*
> *after an obstinant dispute, wherein*
> *Waller got the advantage the Mayor*
> *and a number of citizens retired into*
> *the castle, which Waller likewise*
> *reconnoitred and attempted to reduce.*
> *Finding all his force ineffectual*
> *and the garrison under Lord Ogle*
> *determined to hold out to the last*
> *extremity, he turned his revenge upon*
> *the unhappy city which he plundered*
> *in the most brutal and insolent manner.*
> *When their brutal appetites were thus*
> *glutted with revenge, and Sir William*
> *Waller finding no hopes of reducing the*
> *castle and retired towards the*
> *metropolis."*

Anon.
p.124.

In the words of Mercurius Aulicus of April 13th 1644.

M. A.
p. 938.

> *"Sir William Waller is now at Rumsey,*
> *but it is uncertaine whether or no he*
> *will come to take possesion of his*
> *castle at Winchester, (uncertaine when*
> *he will. But tis certain he would have*
> *done, and was sent packing by the*
> *Governor). That because of the malignity*
> *of the Castle of Winchester which*
> *refuseth Sir William, therefore he*
> *taught the Towne, and rewarded his*
> *souldiers with the superfluilty of their*
> *Mammon, (Is all besides bare walls*
> *superfluous mammon?)*
> *He left not two Beds in all the towne."*

To Trussel must be given the distinction of concluding this chapter in the City's unhappy affairs. He claimed his story was too lengthy. Sad to say after this he laid down his vivid pen.

Trussel
f. 100.

> *"Entred, no scithian, Tarter Jew or Turck*
> *more insolence or Tirany could worcke*
> *against a Christian than theise dear*
> > *brethren did*
> *In doing that which charity doth forbidd*
> *Nay I say bowdly say it on good grownde*
> *In all the world no people can be founde*
> *of worse condition or of baser minde for they*
> *Leaft nothing unassayd that any waye*
> *might mischief mee (slaughter and fire except)*
> *ffirst in the shoppes the ware away they swept*
> *Then in each house cleane riddance they*
> > *did make*
> *And what is portable away they take*
> *What readily they cannot beare awaye*
> *They breake and spoyle,*
> > *And doe in what they may*
> *all things, that nothing may bee leaft behind*
> *wherein the owner any healp may find.*

Cubbards and chests and trincks they open teare
And purchase make of what they could find their;
Books of accompt, bills, bonds and evidences
Indentures, deeds and all conveyances
They tear and burne or otherwise deface
leaving my best friends in the worst bad case
Only a Rehab and some few favorites
escapt the daunger of theise Jebusites

Trussel.
f. 100.

Now what they said they would doe they have done
In making pore and rytch mens estate all one
The Rytch no rent, the pore their howses gett
The Rytch no money have, the poore no meat
The poor wowld rayment have, so wowld the other
ffor scarcly ether thereof have wherewith to cover
their bare; Lynnen and woolen so divided are
That pore and Rytch thereof have equal share
ffeathers the poor, bed tiks the rytch doe lacke
(with them the troopers cloath their Chivalls backe)

Orchards and gardens uninclosed stand
whereof both pore and rytch have like Commaund
their is no wyne, the pore and rytch I thincke
Content must bee with our owne country drincke

The pore and rytch may now for Company
Travayle on foot for horse theire is not any
The plate is gone, glasses are broke in peices
And rytch and poore are forced to drincke in dishes

Woe worth the while what shall become of mee
When poore and ritch are thus in one degree
When my inhabitants have nothing leaft
But are of stock and store and all bereaft.
And though they leaft mee in this wofull plight
Yet cease they not to worcke my more despight
ffor round about mee they in parties lye
to hinder all approaches of supplye
of food or fewell:

Rehab= a Syrian   Jebus= Jerusalem   Chivalls= Chevals, horses.

And yet everye way
doo Ambushes to slaye my people laye
And yt that Power that doth mans lief mantayne
prevent yt not wee shall bee starved or slayne

Oh thou, which art the Lion and the flower
Of Juda and Jesse, by the power
Protect thy servant Charles, my soveraigne King
And mee and myne under thy sacred wing

Trussel.

And lett those Rebells that do plott his harme
bee beaten down by thy all powerfull arme;
All thy good Blessings in abundance power
Uppon the endevors of my Governoure
Crown all his action with succesfull end
And from disasters him and his defend.
for next to thee on them I must relye
for being kept from death or slavery

Oh thou, the Prince of Peace and God of Warr
Whose providence seeth all things neer and far,
Preserve King Charles and prosper all his wayes,
And crowne with Peace and Plenty all his dayes
Safe keep his Nobles, Courage his cheiftayne
                                          give
And teach their souldyers in thy feare to live
Graunt all his subjects Love and Loyalty
And to mee pristine prosperitie.

Amen cryeth John Trussell.

Sit verbum vox viva licet
vox mortua scriptum
Scripta diu vivunt non

Trussel.

ita verba diu."

Chapter 15

A CITY BESET

GENERAL Waller had certainly won the field of battle at Cheriton, but because of desertions from his army, due to lack of pay and Parliament having no strategical concept, his forces were quickly dispersed chasing illusive Royalists, so that he was unable to pick the fruits of his victory. Winchester being a particularly valuable one, another being Basing House.

By mid June The Earl of Essex had to tell the Committee of Both Kingdoms that Waller would "do well to perform what he had already undertaken before he undertake a new business."

In the meantime the Royalists in Winchester had recovered their composure, and were reasserting their influence in the neighbourhood, enabling the Royalists' newspaper Mercurius Aulicus of the 2nd July to say,

> *"Since Alresford Fight the rebels*
> *have often faced Winchester Castle*
> *but have still been repulsed."*

Sir William Ogle undaunted by the disaster of April, and already with morale high, soon earned himself the title of "The Great Plunderer". He organised a marvelously successful raid on one of Parliament's supply convoys at Andover. This raiding party had bravely set out at the end of June towards Andover, perhaps with a little trepidation. Imagine the excitement as they marched back into the City laden with sixteen cart loads of booty, and, flushed with victory, Ogle was quickly able to make peace with the College from whom he had recently stolen fifteen head of cattle and some barrels of beer, by immediately repaying the oxen even if they had drunk the beer in celebration.

Godwin.
p. 226

"Sir William Ogle 'a great Plunderer' had sent out a force consisting of 50 horse, 60 musketeers and pikemen. The cavalry entered the town of Andover, the infantry having halted at a distance of some three miles. A convoy was intercepted and sixteen waggons laden with cloth cheese oil etc & 60 (or 94) oxen and 36 horses coming from the Western Counties were captured. With this plunder, which was valued at more than 6,000 pounds the cavaliers retired to Winchester. (Note- of the oxen, 60 plus the 32 hauling the 16 carts & 2 more)

Sir William Ogle had taken from the Master of Winchester College fifteen oxen and three hogshead of beer upon suspicion that he was a Roundhead. The College authorities sent a complaint to Oxford whereupon Sir William Ogle compensated them with fifteen oxen he had taken in a foray."

The effrontery of this raid caused quite a stir in London. Within a short time the value of the stolen goods had risen to £10,000.

Waller was at once instructed to order Colonel Norton (and he had the title of "The Great Incendary") back into Hampshire.

Committee of Both Kingdoms to Sir Wm Waller.

C.S. P. Dom
1644.
p. 300.

"Since the coming away of Col Norton's regiment from Basing Hants, there has been a great loss of cloth in that country; there was taken from Andover by the garrison of Winchester to the value of 10,000 L. The country press for the return of this (Col Norton's) horse and urge the promise of this committee that they should return when the Associated counties were come in."

> *"There are of them five troops, of
> which we desire that the Col. and
> three troops may return, and the
> other two troops Capt Potts and Capt
> Drapers may still continue there
> with you.*
>
> *We conceive it very necessary for
> the safety of that country and the
> trade from the West to London. And
> therefore desire you will, having
> consideration to the necessity of
> their service elsewhere speadily
> send them back."*

C. S. P.
1644.

Signed Wharton & Maitland.

It was some time before this letter from Colonel Edward
Massy, then serving in the West, reached the Committee in
London.

> *"I have received yours of the 2nd inst
> touching the Cloth taken into the
> garrison at Winchester, and will use
> my endeavours therein, but the Lord
> Hopton's forces have long lain most
> upon that passage, and his Majesty's
> army ever since upon our frontiers
> and neighbourhood, so that all our
> power has been hither to employed for
> securing of our garrisons and country
> from the power of the enemy."*

C. S. P.
1644.

At the beginning of August it was the turn of Ogle's
Winchester to be raided by a Parliamentary force, in an attempt
to kidnap the Mayor Mr Richard....on. The assault party led by
Thomas Bettesworth was foiled. Bettesworth, fifteen months
later, was to see his father appointed Governor of the Castle in
very changed circumstances.

Godwin writes

Godwin.
p. 232

> *"On August 4th it was reported from*
> *Southampton that 100 foot from that*
> *town, together with 4 troops of horse*
> *under Captain Braxtone, brother to the*
> *Mayor of Winchester, and Captains Fielder,*
> *Santbrook and Thomas Betterworth jun,*
> *(Bettersworth's home was in the Cathedral*
> *Close), were facing Winchester as the*
> *gates of both the city and castle had*
> *been, by the instigation of the clergy,*
> *shut against the forces of Parliament.*
>
> *Captain Tho Beesworth with some 14*
> *horse had ridden forth from the head-*
> *quarters which had been established*
> *within two miles of Winchester, in order*
> *to transact business with some other*
> *officers. He returned about midnight,*
> *and found his watch of horse not set*
> *which made him suspect the presence of*
> *a hostile force. None such appeared.*
>
> *Captain Bettesworth approached the*
> *city wall unseen, and entered an*
> *unguarded breach over a heap of rubbish.*
> *Two men were left in charge of the horse,*
> *and the rest hurried through the silent*
> *streets, hoping to secure the sleeping*
> *Mayor and certain Royalist clergymen.*
>
> *They were soon discovered. There was*
> *a hasty call to arms and they retreated*
> *in haste carrying off four prisoners,*
> *who were at once sent under escort to*
> *Southampton."*

This story of young Bettesworth's midnight foray made with an intimate knowledge of the streets and byeways, and his furtive dash and daring, provides in those few words the basis of an adventurous film script as would Ogles raid on the convoy of cloth at Andover.

In September, with the ebb and flow of warlike fortunes, the Royalist Army began to push eastwards again, but the regained strength of Parliament's forces, now back in Hampshire, were able to contain Winchester and lay siege to Basing House.

In an attempt to relieve the House, Colonel Gage, Governor of Oxford, led a force towards Basing calling on Ogle to provide 100 horse and 300 foot to help. Winchester must have had quite a sizeable garrison to be asked to send out such a strong contingent, however on this occasion Ogle was unable to help, as at that moment the City was beset by Colonel Ludlow. Colonel Ludlow was the Parliamentary Commander of Wardour Castle who had passed through Winchester as a prisoner in March and who had later been exchanged. His presence on this occasion led to another little episode of dare-and-do. This time one of breaking through the enemy lines on a swift horse to take a message to Colonel Gage.

> *"Lieut Swainly met me, sent by Sir*
> *William Ogle from Winchester to tell*
> *me that he durst not send his troops*
> *to assist me in regard some of the*
> *enemy horse lay betwixt Winchester*
> *and Basing."*

Godwin.
p. 253.
quotes from
Life of
Col Gage.

During the Autumn the King's army was again in strength in Hampshire. On October 18th King Charles stayed the night at Andover and there were suggestions he would go to Winchester, although it seems he travelled eastwards to Whitchurch.

Luke the Parliamentary Scout reporting on the strength of the King's army said on the 28th of October:

Symonds
Diary.
p. 142.

Luke.
Report
No. 63.

*"His majesty's Army consisting of
16,000 horse and foot with his train
of 36 pieces of Ordnance is come out
of the West, having victualled and
stored all his garrison to Winchester.
He intends to have releived Basing
House but was prevented by our armies
under the Earl of Essex, Earl of
Manchester and Sir William Waller who lay
thereabouts puposely to fight with him."*

The autumn Royalist thrust towards London petered out with the indecisive Second Battle of Newbury fought on the 27th October, and halted after Basing House had been relieved and a failure to reach Farnham, to which Waller's main force had withdrawn.

Ogle ever one to take advantage of the situation again sent out his raiding parties. This time to cut the London Portsmouth road. Highly worrying to the Parliamentarians even if only partially succesful to Ogle, who this time found the horse he had captured were more valuable than the goods.

Friday 1st November 1644.

Godwin.
p. 283.

*"A foraging party from Winchester
had appeared at Petersfield, and under
cover of fog plundered a Portsmouth
road wagon carrying off the eight
horses which drew it."*

In November one of Luke's scouts reported how Winchester was to provide Winter Quarters for a part of the Royalist foot. This report was followed by Mercurius Brittanicus giving this piece of Parliamentary sardonicism which was published on the 25th November.

M. B.

*"By this time Basing House is relieved
and the Winchester Gosse proud in his
conceit that his feathers shall not be
plucked this winter."*

A more domestic than military affair took place on the 14th November at St. Cross - a portent of the pervasiveness of the Parliamentary reforms being imposed and the lay intrusion into the Church - When Dr William Lewis, the Master of St. Cross, was displaced by an Ordinance of Parliament because it was said,

Godwin. p. 283.

> *"He hath neglected the government of the*
> *said House and adhered to those that have*
> *levied war against the Parliament and are*
> *are enemies to the King and Kingdom."*

Dr Lewis was replaced by the Parliamentary Member of Parliament for Winchester John Lisle, who later acquired one of the Close houses and became a Regicide. At the Restoration he escaped to the continent only to be assassinated in Lausanne. Cromwell had called him to the Upper House in 1657, his wife Alice thereby acquired the title "Dame". Retribution cruelly caught up with her many years later, here in Winchester, where she was condemned by Judge Jeffreys at the Bloody Assizes and executed in the Square in 1685.

Another tragedy of those times, equally poignant, now immediate to just before this Christmas of 1644, was recorded in the register of St. Maurice by the Rector.

> *"Chas Eburne was shot Decr ye 9th 1644*
> *and dyed ye same night at Christopher*
> *Hussey's, Alderman of Winton.*
> *Also Mr James Minjam and Richard Shoveler*
> *all three wounded in ye Soak near the East*
> *Gate and were Buryed ye next daye out of St.*
> *Maurice parish by me*
>
> *William Clun 1644 Ye Rector."*
>
> *"Vae Malum Belli Civilis"*

H. N & Q. IV p. 29.

Alas the evil of Civil War.

Chapter 16

PARLIAMENT TO ATTEMPT THE CASTLE

IN January 1645 Colonel George Goring, who had hoisted the Royal Standard at Portsmouth, three weeks before Edgehill, set up his Headquarters in Winchester as the Commander of some six thousand horse, some of whom were quartered in the surrounding villages and as far away as Andover.

With such a strong mobile force he raided as far afield as Gosport taking cattle, horses, sheep and pigs, and it was said at Romsey, not leaving a sheep or hog.

By the beginning of February Southampton was threatened, making it necessary for Parliament to move Sir William Waller back into Hampshire from Windsor where he had been training with the New Model Army under Fairfax.

Waller set out on the 12th of February with an army of 3,400 horse, 700 dragoons and some foot fully intending to take Winchester Castle, but the desertion of a trumpeteer, on the night previous to the intended assault, warned the garrison, and the intended scheme was abandoned, for unless the Castle could be taken by surprise siege weapons would be necessary. The presence of Goring's Horse, lying between Winchester and Salisbury, was a sufficient deterrent to the movement of such heavy siege weapons.

On March 2nd a personal tragedy befell the Castle's Governor by the death in a skirmish of his stepson Sir Thomas Philips. A party from the garrison, said by the Parliamentarians to have had "a great drinking day at Winchester and being elevated in their minds" rode out of Winchester two hundred strong, to engage a troop of sixty of Waller's force at Marwell Hall, the residence of Sir Henry Mildmay (another Hampshire Regicide).

In the ensuing skirmish Sir Thomas Philips, then a young man of twenty five, was killed. He was the elder son of Sir Thomas Philips of Barrington Somerset and Charity Waller of Stoke Charity. Shortly after Sir Thomas senior died in 1636, his widow Charity married Sir William Ogle and the young heir became Sir William's stepson and ward. Sir William Ogle had therefore seen Thomas and his young brother James grow up, the whole family were then living in the Castle. Young Sir Thomas Philips was buried at Stoke Charity on the 5th March 1644/5.

Three days later to further intimidate the garrison of the castle Sir William Waller reviewed 3,000 horse and dragoons near the City, but he was still not able to attempt the taking of the Castle. Nevertheless this dates the end of Royalist dominance in the neighbourhood.

In mid April a Parliamentarian body of horse, under Major Stuart from Southampton, approached the City daring Ogle to attack while enticing the Royalists towards a position strongly held on the road to Romsey. In the engagement that followed one of Ogle's troops was worsted loosing Lieut Coward killed, and two other officers and thirty troopers taken prisoner.

There can be little doubt that in these armed raids each side fought with determination and courage. There was no pretence. At that time Ogle could ill afford to loose a single man, but it did not stop his aggresive forays.

Parliament, increasingly exasperated by these, determined to "stop the insolencies of the garrison of Winchester" and that of Basing who "range and rage about the Country."

During the summer the Parliamentarians were again able to advance Westwards and Winchester was for a while left unmolested but in what was by then very hostile territory.

LORD GEORGE GORING 1583-1663

He declared for the King at Portsmouth to open the Civil War three weeks before Edgehill in October 1642.
In January 1645 with 6,000 Horse he made Winchester his headquarters.
(J. Thomson after Van Dyke – Courtesy National Portrait Gallery)

Parliament, who had intended that Fairfax should relieve Taunton, changed their mind and withdrew the army planning to attempt Oxford in a large sweeping movement. The army comprising seven regiments of foot with horse were about 11,000 strong, a formidable force which marched back eastwards through Romsey to pass Winchester and move on to Alresford, on about the 11th May. With such large numbers of the enemy passing literally within sight of the drawbridge, Ogle and his garrison could only quietly withdraw back into the castle and await events. They were of course unaware of Parliament's intention and the reason for their presence. There surely would have been many a sigh of relief as they watched their enemy march right by.

Godwin.
p. 309.

*"a fourteen mile march then brought
the army past Winchester to Alresford.
I need not acquaint you with our hard
march, hot weather and hard quarter,
but in all our march we have not seen
an enemy. We faced Winchester Castle
as we came by, but no enemy appeared,
nor any gun shot off against us"*

June 1645 seemed tranquil, Parliament's army had moved off northwards and at the beginning of the month the Royalists felt secure enough for the King to ask for, and Ogle to agree to part of the garrison being drawn off for convoy duties around Oxford. Although some sixty or so of the Royalist scattered horse arrived in Winchester after the Battle of Naseby, fought on the 14th June, the effect of the disaster was clearly not appreciated, it was business as usual with Dean Young riding into Winchester on the 23rd for a Chapter meeting, little knowing that this was to be his last meeting. He wrote in his diary

"I went from Wallop to Winton. Their at
the Chapter we swore the Receavour and
Threserur.
Mr Baying Lord Ogles secretarie leases us 3
houses gratis, which we turned to one lease."

W. C. D. II.
p. xxi.

Y's D.
p. 152.

To say business as usual of course could not really be so, in such circumstances, for apart from the presence of so many troops and recurring alarums the Town was subject to Martial Law. Quarter sessions had been suspended also the local City and Pie Powder (the Bishop's) courts as one is reminded by this brief and rather cryptic note taken from the archives of Winchester College,

"Sol Mro Bye promoventi causum
Collegii in petitione tradita
gubernatori per Ric Frampton X s.
Sol famulo Dni Gul Ogle Vicecomities
Barrington gubernatoris castri et
civitas tempore guerra j s."

Kirby.
p. 333.

It would have been to the ancient court 'de pie poudre' that Frampton, the College brewer living in the Bishop's Soke would take his case. There is no record showing how the case was dealt with. William Ogle's title as Viscount Barrington must have been one of courtesy derived through his wife Charity. Barrington was the former seat of the first Sir Thomas Philips. Ogle's title was Viscount Cathelough.

It was about this time, June '45 that the "Clubmen" were formed who set themselves up to defend their homes and granaries, from the marauding and foraging parties sent out by both armies. They were unarmed but quickly developed into a very considerable power which it was feared might develop into a new political force. Within three months of their foundation Cromwell was compelled to detach a regiment of horse from his army in the West to assist Colonel Norton supress the Clubmen in East Hampshire.

It is ironic that it was the Clubmen who complained of the ill disciplined soldiery taking their goods without payment and here Colonel Norton admits his troops were rebellious for lack of pay. On 26th September Colonel Norton The Governor of Portsmouth while waiting on the general to reduce Winchester Castle was ordered to immediately put down the Clubmen and with the assistance of the regiment of horse surrounded an assembly of Clubmen forcing them to yield to his greatly superior strength. Norton, with the usual exaggerations of the times, reported,

Godwin.
p. 322.

"There were only two towns that resisted us (Bishop Waltham and Petersfield) which were very ill affected and it pleased God to separate them from the rest before they gave us occasion to fall on them. I believe we took from them above 500 arms, their colours and drums. Truly it was high time, for it is evident by the heads of them that they intended mishief and I am persuaded it is the last and most devilish plot that the enemies of God and good men have left them. I have three of the most notorious rascals prisoners, though they are not the chief men and I hope to get the rest. I wish I might have power to hang some of them if they rise again.

In the meantime while I am serving the country abroad I am suffering at home. I wrote to the Lord General concerning my garrison. Truly I have not a penny to pay them on Monday seven night and if I am not supplied by the Excise men I am sure they will all Mutiny here for I am confident there is not a more disorderly soldiery in England.

H. M. C.
10th Report.
p. 163.

After Parliament's decisive victory at Naseby the "Business" of Winchester Castle was now to be seriously undertaken. Contrary to all previous procedures, the siege and reduction of the Castle and other obstacles to the reopening of trade routes and roads to the west, was now planned with deliberate determination. Plans were made to ensure proper and adequate supplies of pay, siege artillery, engineers and all the troops needed. There was to be strong leadership and a firm resolution.

PAY   24 July 1645
The House "Resolved that
Five thousand Pounds shall be charged
upon the Reseipt of the Excise to be
employed for the reducing of Winchester   Journal
Donnington and Basinge: of the
And Mr Lisle is to bring in an   House of
ordinance to this purpose.   Commons.

25 July
Order assented to and sent to the Lords,"
and agreed by them on the 26th July.

ARTILLERY   9 August
Proceeding of the Committee of Both
Kingdoms.

" The Governors of Portsmouth,   C. S. P.
Farnham and Southampton to send such   1645. p. 55.
Ordnance as the Committee of Hants
(shall require) for reducing Basing and
Winchester, not exceeding 12 guns with
their carriages, but having regard to
the security of their garrisons.
Warrant for gunpowder and other
necessaries required by the Committee
for Hants for reducing of Basing and Winton. "

ENGINEERS   25 July
From the letters of Sir Samuel Luke.
*"There being some service to be under-
taken against the garrison of Basing
House and Winchester requiring the
service of an engineer. The gentlemen
of Sussex, Surrey and Hants have desired
the help of your engineer who is at
Newport (Pagnell) and whom they will pay
his employment with them.*
*We desire you to accomodate- the service
with him and to send him to undertake
the work."*

15 August
*Captain Vanderboone to return to
Newport on completion of service at
Winchester and Basing.*
*(Note- capt Cornelius Vanderboone
was described as being an "Outlandish
and stout man".)*

Luke.
p. 365.

TROOPS and LEADERSHIP
30 September
A letter from Sir H Vane.
*"The rest of Fairfax's forces being
4 Regiments of horse and 3 of foot, he
has left for the present under the
Command of Cromwell, to take Winchester
and open up the passages between London
and the West."*

C. S. P. Dom
1645-6
p. 167.

RESOLUTION   26 September
*"Fairfax call'd a Council of War 'twas
resolved, that the main body of the Army
shou'd march to the West. and Cromwel
with a Brigade was sent before to attempt
Winchester and Basing-House which wou'd
otherwise interrupt the Intercourse between
London and Fairfax's Army."*

Rushworth.
p. 543.

Chapter 17

CROMWELL LAYS SIEGE

THE title "The Lieutenant-General" was used by all the contemporary writers to precede the name Cromwell. It was repeated so often that the words must have been on everyones lips after his successes at Naseby, the taking of Bristol in August, and more recently the taking of Devizes on the 25th September.

The Victorious general was perhaps in return unaware of the value of such publicity, but its effects on the morale of his troops, who were now well trained well disciplined and well equipped and supported with artillery, was decisive.

Two great Royalist strongholds Winchester Castle and Basing House each with determined and loyal commanders were to be broken and taken within a few days.

The Lieutenant-General arrived outside Winchester on Sunday night the 28th September 1645. Exactly one week later on Sunday night the 5th of October Viscount Ogle the Governor of the Castle and Town capitulated.

"Lieutenant-General Cromwell came before Winchester on the Lords Day at night and with him a party of horse and foot, viz of

HORSE   his own regiment,
Colonel Sheffield's regiment,
Colonel Fleetwood' and
Colonel Norton's regiment with some horse taken out of several other regiments to make them complete 2,000 horse; and of
FOOT   Colonel Montague's regiment
Colonel Waller's (Hardress) Some of Colonel Okey's dragoons were among the horse taken from other regiments. They had done good the Parliament good service by lining Lantford hedges at Naseby Fight."

Perfect Passages. OCT 1st 1645.

In addition to the regiments of horse and foot bringing up the rear with their escort of dragoons there was the trayne of artilery under the command of Captain Richard Deane, Cromwell's comptroller of artillery, comprising,

> A Whole or Royal cannon which could fire a 63 lb
>   shot
> Two demi cannons
>
> A great mortar piece which could fire a 13" shell
>   or granado weighing 60 lbs

Further there were the cannon sent from Portsmouth Farnham and Southampton also from Poole all served by gunners matrosses and pioneers with wagons for shot and powder.

As part of the Staff there was Captain Vanderboone the engineer, surgeons and ministers led by Hugh Peters. Also Cromwell's own minister and his secretary plus innumerable camp followers with the supply train including the "Press". The total strength of Cromwell's army may have been about 7,000 strong.

He was opposed by Lord Ogle whose garrison was about one tenth that of Cromwell's. A mere 700 who were secure in the castle, said to have been as strong a place as any in England, and which had been held for the King for two whole years. No one should doubt that Winchester was verily a Loyal City.

Immediately on Cromwell's arrival at Winchester the civilities and courtesies, a feature of the Civil War, were observed and a message to the Mayor was despatched demanding an entrance into the City for he found the gates shut against him.

Thus followed Cromwell's well known letter to the Mayor saying he expected the mayor to give him free entry and the Mayor's evasive reply of September 28th 1645.

CROMWELL'S LETTERS TO THE MAYOR

"Sir

*I come not to this city but with a
full resolution to save it and the
Inhabitants thereof from ruine
I have comaunded the Souldyers, upon
payne of death, that noe wrong bee
done, which I shall strictly observe;
only I expect you give me entrance into
the city without necessitateing mee to
force my way, which yf I doe, then it
will not be in my power to save you or
it.*

A of W
p. 148.

*I expect your answeare with in halfe
an howre; and rest*
  Your Serv't
   Oliver Cromwell
Sept 28th, 1645
Five o' Clock at night
To the Mayor of the City of Winchester."

Books
Charters
and Mss
1951
No. 74.

THE MAYORS REPLY

"Sir,
*I have received your letter by your
Trumpett, and in the behalf of the
Citizens and Inhabitants returne you
hearty thanks for your favourable
expressions therin; But withall, I am
to signifie unto you that the delivry
up of the city is not in my power, it
being under the comand of the right
no'ble the Lord Ogle, who hath the
military Governm't thereof.
In the meane tyme I shall use my best
endeavour with the Lord Ogle to
performe the contents of your letter
concerning the city; and rest*
  Your most humble Serv't
   Wm LONGLAND Mayor.
Winton Sept 28 1645"

4th Book of
Ordinance.

Oliver Cromwell must have then called on the Governor to surrender, his 'First Summons', but contrary to his expectation Ogle refused to parley.

While these letters were being exchanged Cromwell learnt that among those in the castle there was the elderly Bishop Walter Curll, who had been translated to Winchester by King Charles in 1632 and was then aged about seventy. Cromwell in spite of his own strong Puritanical views and Parliament had abolished episcopasy, offered the Bishop safe conduct which was bravely refused. There was to be no second chance.

Godwin.
p. 334.

"Wednesday Oct 1
This day by letters from Winchester
we understand that at Cromwells' first
coming against Winchester, having
notice that Doctor Kirl, Bishop of
that diocese, was in the city, sent
to him, and proferred that in respect
of his cloth (if he pleased) he shall
have liberty to come out of the town,
and he would protect him from violence;
which the Bishop not accepting of, our
men soon after forced their passage
into the city."

On the Monday morning Cromwell, finding his offers of safe conduct refused and of a treaty spurned, fired the bridge and gate (probably the South Gate) and after a short dispute he forced an entry and the (Royalist) enemy was driven off and fled into the Castle. The Roundheads with so it was said, the townsmen's consent, then cooped up in the castle 120 horse and 400 foot, and all the malignant gentry and clergy of this Hampshire and Sussex with many Papists and Jesuits. It is hoped the Parliament will give order these delinquents shall trouble them no more.

The town was thus again occupied by Parliament's forces, and as has just been mentioned by the expression "with the townsmen consent" there were some who welcomed the invader.

Late autumn with the nights getting colder the Roundheads would have sought and found shelter in any building still standing. The hard pressed citizens had seen it all before, in '42, '43, after Cheriton in 44,and now again in '45.

It was during the autumn, two years previously Ogle had entered the City and seized and fortified the castle for the King when he cleared the ditches and banks around the castle of any trees shrubs or buildings. Since then engineers had been employed to strengthen the defences. Now the castle stood ready, naked and proudly stark. During the two years the walls had been repaired week places strengthened with stockading, and its store rooms well filled with gunpowder and victuals.

To many Milners reconstraction as shown in the drawings made by James Cave in 1797, appear to be too fanciful, but allowing for some exaggeration and a little civic pride to show off the castle at its best, the drawings present a very fair representation of the mediaeval castle, perhaps permitting a smile at the perfect crenellations.

Milner. J
2nd. Edition
p. 19.

Milner in the preface to his book says of the illustrations

Milner. J.
Gents Mag
Top V.
p. 120.

> *"The east and west view of the ancient*
> *Castle have been drawn under the authors*
> *directions from the slight sketch of that*
> *fortress in Speeds Chorography, from an*
> *attentive consideration of the ruins,*
> *ditched and situation of the same, from*
> *the discoveries that were made in digging*
> *on the spot in the year 1797 and from*
> *certain hints that occur in ancient*
> *writers concerning it. "*

The mediaeval castle, of a Norman foundation, was two thirds the size of Windsor. In its prime it was the creation of King Henry The Third, Henry of Winchester (1216-1272). It ceased to be a Royal residence following a disasterous fire in 1302, and from that time gradually fell into decay.

In simple terms the castle was some 240 metres long by 40 metres wide and ran in a north south direction along the southern half of the west wall of the City, and positioned astride a dominant spur so that it appeared to be atop an isolated hill.

It was divided into three sections. A motte at the south end surrounded by a curtain wall, square in plan with Norman square towers to the west and round or oval towers that had been rebuilt in the mid thirteenth century by King Henry, to the east. Within this enclosure there was a large round shell keep or great tower, omitted from Speeds drawing but shown in a dilapidated state in Schellinks prospect of 1662.

The centre section or ward was also almost square in plan and walled around with towers at each corner, square to the west plus a great central gatehouse facing across a deep ditch with a bridge to the barbican; on the east side in continuation of those of the south ward there were round towers. In this central ward were built the royal apartments and other domestic buildings. Here was the house granted by King James to Sir Benjamin Tichborne which later, by other Royal grants passed to Richard Weston, Earl of Portland, and then to his son Jerome the second Earl, to be followed by the grant of King Charles to Sir William Waller in 1638. The apartments are described in the siege narrative as the Mansion.

Speeds Map.

Schellinks View.

Cave's Illustration.

To the south West of this ward the square tower is referred to in the final stages of the siege as "The Black Tower".

The third and nothern ward, in which was built the Conquerors motte and tower, is nearly triangular in shape. In the thirteenth century the Norman tower was replaced by a new round tower at the extreme northernmost point of the castle. It guarded the entrance into the town by the West Gate and provided a sally port opening up on to the ditches. In the south east corner of this ward was built the Great Hall of the Castle which stands to this day.

At the time of the Civil War the Great Hall was well maintained and used by the County for Quarter Session Government, and as has been shown, was also used for the State Trial of Sir Walter Raleigh, and later for the Court of Eyre. Although damaged during the siege it was used for the trial for the so called 'treason' of Captain Burley in 1649, for his attempt to rescue his Sovereign, King Charles, from the Isle of Wight.

For Burley's Speech see p. 256 below.

The North ward does not appear to have been included in the Royal grants to Tichborne, Weston, or Waller, being held by the County, but it does appear to have been granted to Sir William Waller by Parliament after the castles capture. Waller subsequently sold this portion which included the Hall back to the county in 1647, while the original grant of the central and south wards were sold to the City in 1658.

It would have been unlikely that Ogle with the resources of manpower, money and time available to him, to have put the whole castle into perfect order. He seems to have concentrated his efforts on repairing the perimeter walls rather than the keep.

Guarding the Castle against a determined foe proved to be an impossible task.

There were eight towers to man plus the gate house. 550 metres of wall to patrol, and seven pieces of cannon to service. Allowing for a reserve, reliefs, sickness, domestic duties and for the non combatants which included the Bishop, Ogle's garrison, of something a little under seven hundred, were fully commited.

This therefore was the strategic and gallant castle if Winchester ready to face and defy Cromwell's army whose investing troops completely ringed the fortress at a distance of some 350 paces, where they were out of musket shot and serious harassment by Ogle's small pieces of artillery.

Cromwell's immediate task was to make a reconnaisance with his master gunner Captain Deane and to chose a site for the siege batteries, Vanderboone's mines and the place of assault.

There is no surviving plan of the City and Castle made during or after the siege, the layout of Cromwell's army is conjectural, but based on the fragments of evidence available in the contemporary accounts and the practice and custom of those times in other civil war sieges.

For
St. Clements
Church.
See p. 234
below.

It is suggested that the Lieutenant General's lines ran on the east side of the castle along Southgate street from St. Clements church, known to have been used as a quard house, through the Southgate and then took a wide sweep up the hill on the south side of the castle towards St. James' Church. The lines then keeping its distance would have crossed over Oram's Arbour and returned down through the orchards (Staple Gardens) to St. Clements. There was to be no way out or in.

Gun platforms had to be built, defensive trenches dug, palisades erected and gabions made and filled to protect the guns and their crews against sorties and counter fire from the castles men and guns.

Ogle did indeed make a determined sally and beat the Roundheads from guns which however were soon recovered. An incident dismissed by Cromwell who said,

Anglia Rediviva. p. 130.

> *"We fell to prepare our Batteries,*
> *which we could not perfect, some of*
> *our guns being out of order until*
> *Friday following."*

A. R. p. 128. Quoting Cromwell's Letter.

The siege works therefore took five days to build.

Cromwell's principal battery consisted of the six heavy guns including the Whole Cannon and two Demi Cannon. Also there was the great mortar which could fire a sixty pound shell. These to be suitable placed, to batter the west wall of the castle, might have been positioned near the old Romsey Road water works a position directly opposite the castle wall beneath the Mansion. The position chosen for Oliver Cromwell's Battery had to be within battering range of the wall and it had to be easily accessible from the road. The heaviest gun weighed over three tons and required a team of at least six pairs of oxen or horse. No easy task handling this and the 63 pounds shot and barrels of gunpowder needed to fire it.

Cromwell was a man in a hurry and would chose as easy and accessible spot for his battery as possible, perhaps even taking into use and remodelling the sconce built by Hopton. The site is indicated on Taylor's map.

Taylor's Map.

It is possible a second battery was established on the east side of the castle above the site of old St. Thomas' church, this would have been well positioned to batter the east wall of the middle ward and opposite the main battery on the other side of the castle.

The relevant quotation for this suggestion, taken from the "Exact Journal", is ambiguous but says,

Quoted by Godwin. p. 335.

"Lieutenant General Cromwell having planted his mortar piece and great cannon against the castle and one party at St Thomas's going to the Minster and another at St Lawrence, as also good strength on both battle sides"

One may wonder by the uncertainess of those words whether one of the smaller guns brought from Portsmouth or Farnham while being hauled into position through the South Gate, was not turned to face the Cathedral and in a fit of religious fervour and petulance was aimed at the great West Window and a shot or two loosed off to destroy the detested images depicted in the mediaeval glass. Thus giving rise to the legend that the glass in the west window was destroyed by Cromwell's guns. This suggestion is made to provide a reason for the tradition. For this to have occured the guns would have to be sited close to the Cathedral at point black range (up to 350 paces) to achieve the accuracy recuired for such a deliberate action.

"One party at St. Thomas's going to the Minster"

The reference in the Exact Journal to St. Lawrence situated in the very centre of the city is difficult to interpret. The expression 'good strength on both battle sides' might infer that Cromwell's troops were placed on both sides of the castle, as has been suggested, and where the battle was to take place, meaning that the investing troops were placed inside the city as well as outside.

In confirmation of this there is yet another tradition, and that well founded, that during Cromwell's siege the Parliamentarian headquarters within the town were at No 24 St. Thomas Street.

Another incident in respect of the despoiling of the Cathedral which may be related to the period of waiting for the siege batteries to open fire was recorderd by John Chase, the Chapter Clerk who so assiduously strove to preserve the Cathedrals muniments,

He wrote,

> *"The 1 & Second of October 1646*
> *22 Car R, not onlie the Chapter*
> *House and mine office but also the*
> *Muniment house, was the second tyme*
> *by the army and Soldiery broken up*
> *and all my lidger register books*
> *taken away the Records Charters,*
> *deeds writings and muniments lost,*
> *the common seale taken away, and*
> *divers of the writings and charters*
> *burnt, divers throwen into the River,*
> *divers large parchments being made*
> *into kytes withall to flie in the aire,*
> *and many other old books lost to the*
> *utter spoyling and destruction of the*
> *same muniment and chapter house many*
> *of the deeds and writings may be*
> *supposed to have been kept and layen*
> *here for many hundred of years as by*
> *the dates herewith taken by me and*
> *mention in this book may appere.*
>
> *per me JOHN CHASE."*

W. C. D.
II p. 57.

Chase's dates of the first and second of October would seem to be correct. The soldiery might have been Colonel Norton's troops flushed with their empty triumph over the unarmed Clubmen and now here in the Cathedral led by an old soldier who had witnessed the earlier ransacking of the Cathedral back in '42, who knew his way to the muniment house hoping to find more silver.

However Chase dating to the year 1646 cannot be correct for by that time the muniments were in charge of Parliament's solicitor of sequestration John Woodman who had been appointed, shortly after the fall of the castle, on the 29th November '45.

Besides Winchester had been "disgarrisoned" in June of '46.

During those first few days of October '45, while the Cathedral was again being ransacked, there were frantic preparations being made for the assault on the castle. At that particular moment Cromwell was absent from Winchester having gone north to meet Sir William Waller approaching from Reading with a supply train. It was not until Friday evening the 3rd that the batteries were ready and on Saturday morning the Lieutenant General arrived back in Winchester to find himself in a strong and positive

"Posture to Parley".

To announce this Oliver Cromwell fired a single salvo as a signal to Ogle that the battering would begin and then sent the Governor his

"Second Summons"

to surrender which was contemptuously rejected.

On the morrow the bombardment began.

Chapter 18

THE CASTLE BATTERED

SATURDAY the 4th October 1645.
Cromwell from a position of undoubted strength himself said,

> "Our Battery was six guns which
> being finished after once firing of
> them round I sent a Second Summons
> for a Treaty which they refused
> whereupon we went on with our work"

A. R.
p. 128.

Orders for the bombardment to start were apparently delayed for quite a while until the civilities were complete. Mercurius Civicus relates,

> "Sir William Ogle, governor of the
> Castle (lately made a Lord by His
> Majesty) refused upon summons to
> accept any parley at all, one reason
> thereof was that on Saturday, the
> convoy coming from Reading, Lieutenant
> General Cromwell and Sir William Waller
> with them, they supposed it was relief
> coming to them."

Quoted by
Godwin.
p. 335.

While messages were passing between Cromwell and Ogle the opportunity was taken by an apprehensive Bishop Curll to send to Cromwell a message to say he

> "was sorry that he had not accepted
> of Lieutenant General Cromwells former
> proffer, and being better informed,
> did now desire the benefit thereof."

*"Unto which, answer was returned
that he (the Bishop) had refused
the former proffer and had gone with
the soldiers into the Castle; he was
not capable of that favour, and in
case he were taken in the Castle he
was esteemed a prisoner of war, and
just now (the batteries being raised)
be liable to such conditions as the
rest of those that were in the Casle
should be brought unto."*

or as reported of the Bishop in the "Exact Journal"

Quoted by
Portal.
p. 37.

*"Afterwards, the Castle being begun
to be battered by 2 peeces of Ordnance,
he sent to the Lieut General, giving
him thanks for the great favour offered
to him, and being more sensible what it
was he desired the enjoyment of it, to
whom the wise Lieut-General replied,
that since he made not use of the
cortesy, but wilfully did run away from
it, he must partake of the same condition
as the others who are in the Castle, and
if he were taken he must expect to be
used as a prisoner of war."*

C. S. P.
1645/47
p. 198.

Psychological warfare fully appreciated by Cromwell in his efforts to obtain a quick submission, but also he realised the necessity of keeping up the verve of his own troops during this period of uneasy hush, that precedes a battle, while the opposing forces brace themselves for the conflict, and are keyed up in a mixture of exhileration and fear. Cromwell therefore issued a warrant authorising the payment of 5s/-, storm money, to every foot soldier present at the capture of the Castle.

Not only was this an incentive to the soldiers, even though such payments carried the stricture of no looting. In the event it is likely to have been paid by the town to avoid being plundered although no mention of such payment amounting to 1,400 Pounds was made until 1662, two years after the Restoration.

See p. 247.
below.

Without any further delay Cromwell gave orders for the batteries to open fire. The Parliamentarians then entered upon their work with zeal and

> *"began to play with their cannon,*
> *and played six continually, one*
> *after another as fast they could*
> *charge and discharge."*

Godwin.
p. 336.

Each gun could fire about three shots an hour allowing time for the gun to be swabbed out and cleared of any possible remains of smouldering gunpowder lest there be a premature explosion. Time was also required to allow the guns to cool down, be reloaded and realigned.

By darkness the cannon fell quiet but already a breach had been made which compelled Ogle to send Major R Clarke with 50 soldiers to guard during the night.

Perhaps quiet from the thunder of the guns, but not entirely so, with the sentries calling out to each other mixed with the long drawn out squeaks of heavily laden carts bringing forward ammunition, shot and powder, mingled with the plunging of horses, and shouts of the wagoners.

All these sounds of preparation for the morrow would carry eerily and echo across the valley.

In the City too, there would have been continuous movement as the guards changed and supplies were brought in. Few would have slept easily that Saturday night.

The Parliamentarians claimed "before day about 40 of them ran away". Exaggeration as was the wont of the reporters but it had some element of truth as admitted by Ogle himself in these two messages written on that Saturday night during another period of endeavour by Cromwell to get Ogle to accept a third summons to treat.

Godwin.
p. 355.

Ogle to Cromwell,
> *"Sir*
> *I have received a sad summons, and desire*
> *that this enclosed may be conveyed from*
> > *Your servant*
> *Winston Castle   OGLE.*
> *4th October 45*

> *Sir,*
> *Upon the opening of your sad message*
> *by your drum, there was a mistake between*
> *your men and mine, for there was a man*
> *making an escape from the castle, at whom*
> *your men and mine did shoot, not knowing*
> *in the dark who he was, and the man is*
> *killed.   OGLE."*

Ogle continued in his refusal to parley although he asked for and was granted a safe conduct for his desparately sick wife Charity, who unhappily died before reaching her home at Stoke Charity.

Sensationalism over a tragedy and a tinge of cynical gloating by the press is clearly not new as expressed by Joshua Sprigg in his Anglia Rediva who tells the story this way,

A. R.
p. 130.

> *"And another summons God sent them, in*
> *the middle of their Battery, his lady,*
> *to whom our Lieutenant Generalhad given*
> *leave to come forth, and had gone some*
> *miles out of the town, died, by whom the*
> *Governor had during her life 1,000 L. a*
> *year, now lost by her death."*

So ended Saturday.

The next day Sunday the 5th of October, the Lord's Day was "spent in preaching and prayer whilst our gunners were battering".

A. R.
p. 130.

Cromwell had no scruples about allowing the bombardment to go on during the Sabbath, to him it would have been the Lord's work they were undertaking, nothing should delay it.

The Castle was then to suffer a day long battering, subjected to the crash of the heavy shot every two or three minutes. Every quarter of an hour or so there was the swish of a shell followed by the crump of an explosion followed by the noise of falling and crashing masonry, added to which was the occasional shriek of a wounded man or horse.

To add to the confusion smoke from the guns and fires in the castle drifted across the battle arena as eager and anxious faces on both sides watched or suffered the onslaught, even in wonderment, at the display presented by Captain Deane's great cannon and mortar fire.

Somewhere the sappers were preparing their mines and when two of these went up whoosh in a great flash of flame and cloud of smoke surely even those Roundheads amidst their Sabbath day prayers would have raised a cheer.

That day two hundred shot were fired and sixty grenadoes or shells from the mortars, truly a tremendous battering and bombardment.

It should not be thought that the garrison were passive during the cannonade, Ogle's own guns quite uninhibitedly firing into the centre of the City if there were enemy there to be shot at. So reported Sprigge.

> "The chiefest street of the Town the
> enemy (The Royalists) played upon,
> whereby divers passengers were wounded
> and some killed, in which street my
> quarters were, I have that cause to
> blesse God for my preservation."

A. R.
p. 130.

By Sunday evening a great breach next to the Black Tower wide enough for thirty men to go in abreast had been made.

Mercurius
Civicus.

> *"The grenadoes had done very much*
> *good execution; one of them broke*
> *into the great hall and killed three*
> *men, and another beat the red flag*
> *of defiance, which the enemy (Ogle's*
> *garrison) had hung out, all to pieces,*
> *so that none could discern what became*
> *of it."*

Or the same report in the more colourful manner of Sprigge.

A. R.
p. 130.

> *"We plaid them with our granadoes*
> *from our Mortar peeces, with the best*
> *effect that I have seen, which brake*
> *down the Mansion house in many places,*
> *cut off a Commissioner of theirs by the*
> *thighs, the most austere and wretched*
> *instrument in that country, and at last*
> *blew up their flag of defiance into the*
> *aire, and tore the Pinacle in peeces*
> *upon which it stood.*
>   *Indeed, the guns played so fast and*
> *the business was so well followed that*
> *we could hear them, and they perceiving*
> *what a straight they were in, and how*
> *the house began to tumble upon their*
> *heads, thought that we should presently*
> *enter, and that they should all be*
> *killed."*

After a week of suspense and two days of continuous battering the morale of Ogle's garrison was on the point of collapse. The cry was,

"A parley, a parley for the Lord's
sake a parley. O for God's sake grant
a parley.
  Articles, articles, O let us have
articles for Gods sake; we will yield
to any reasonable articles; will ye
not hear us for a parley."

Lord Ogle later confessed

Ogle.
Ms 27402.

"That the soldiers and some officers
wanted a treaty and told him that if
he would not treat, they would treat
with out him, (and that) thirty
soldiers did run away over the works
in one night."

The confidence of the garrison must have been shattered by the size of the breach made in the wall and expectation that the castle would be stormed any moment, but as it began to get dark they knew they had to wait yet another tense night before the asault could take place. Perhaps they had seen Cromwell making his reconaissance. Cromwell himself wrote of the breach wide enough for thirty men to enter abreast.

"after about 200 shot we thought
stormable and purposed on Monday
to attempt it."

A. R.
p. 128.

The Royalists now fearing there would be no quarter if stormed, their morale broke completely.

"Sir Humphrey Bennet and all the officers
except the two Major Clerks demanded a
Council, where at they all, except the two
Majors Robert and Henry Clark, deserved a
treaty."

A request for a treaty was then drawn up and presented to the Governor which Lord Ogle put in his pocket as if dismissing the matter; whereupon Sir John Pawlet exclaimed "My Lord you are too hard on us" to which Ogle replied "I am in sadness both for the treaty, and for my lady's death".

This was the moment of tragedy for Lord Ogle, he had heard of the death of his wife Charity that morning, they had been married eighteen years, he had seen her children the Philips boys grow up, he had witnessed the loss of the elder boy Thomas in a skirmish in January and had been obliged in order to save the life of James to make him surrender himself before the siege. He had lost all his family now he was to lose the Castle on which he had lavished so much energy and fortune for the King over the last two years and in his loyal defiance had seen many a man killed. A moment of real despair.

Composing himself he yielded to the clamour of his officers and the realities of the situation and so sat down to compose a letter to Cromwell asking for a parley. This was immediately accepted by the Lieutenant general but the articles were not agreed without lengthy and prolonged negotiations.

"Sir, I have received formerly a letter from you, wherein you desire to avoid the effusion of Christian blood, to which you received my answer that I was as willing as yourself.

But having received no reply (to advance) your desires, I have thought fit to desire a treaty whereby we might pitch up some means, both for the effecting of that, and the preservation of this place. And that I may receive your letter with all convenience, I desire that neither officer or soldier of your party may come off their guards, and I shall take the like course with mine.

Sir I am

Winton Castle,   *Your humble servant*
at eight at night   *OGLE*
October 5 1645.

M. C.

"The Lords day we spent in preaching
and prayer whilst our gunners were
battering, and at 8 a clock at night
we received a letter from the Governor
for a treaty, which I have brought
with me. (up to London)
  Colonel Hammond, and Major Harrison
were sent into the Castle on our party,
Sir Edward Ford, and a Mayor of theirs
were sent to us;
  The whole night was spent about it,
our men standing upon some speciall
terms with them, and very desirous
were we to accept Sir Edward Ford and
(Sir Humphrey) Benet, to be our
prisoners.
  By eight of the clock on Monday
morning, it was agreed they should
depart out of the Castle at five of
the clock according to these articles.

A. R.
p. 130.

p. 131.

ARTICLES OF SURRENDER

"Articles agreed upon the 5 of
October 1645
Between the Right honourable
    William Viscount Ogle,
governor of the garrison of the
Castle of Winton, of the one part
and Col Robert Hammond,
and Major Thomas Harrison, on the
behalf of Lieutenant gen.
    Oliver Cromwell, of the other
party, for the surrender of the
said Castle."

A. R.
p. 131.

A. R.
p. 131.

H. M. C.
Report 13.
Vol 1
p. 182.

"1. That the Lord Ogle shall deliver up
the Castle of Winchester, with all
arms, ordnance ammunition, provision
and all furniture of war whatsoever,
without imbezelment, waste or spoil,
unto that officer or officers as shall
be appointed by the said Lieutenant gen.
to morrow, being Monday the 6 of October,
by three of the clock after Noon.

2. That the said Lord Ogle shall have his own
Colours and one hundred fixt Arms for
the guard, and one hundred men to carry them

3. That the Lord Ogle and all the Officers
in commissions, shall march out of the said
castle with their own horse and arms, and
their own proper goods unto Woodstock,
whither they shall be safely conveyed

4. That there shall be allowed to the Lord
Ogle and his Officers six carriages for the
transporting of their goods aforesaid

5. That all the Officers, Gentlemen,
Clergiemen, and inhabitants within the
guards (desiring it) may live at their
own homes, free from all violence and
injury of the Parliaments forces

6. That the Lord Ogle Shall give Sufficient
hostages for the perfomance of the articles
here constituted on their part to be
perfomed, also for the safe return of the
Convoy."

Chapter 19

THE CASTLE TAKEN

There is a tradition the Articles to the Treaty were negotiated in 24 St. Thomas Street.

When consent had been reached Cromwell agreed to them and "sent Colonel Hammond and Major Harrison into him" who also agreed the Articles. Presumably Cromwell meant that Ogle had agreed also.

The peace treaty signed and hostages exchanged the weary combattants slept. At eight o'clock the next morning a token number of Parliamentarians entered the castle to check the stores and to prevent spoilation, the Royalists not being required to march out until the afternoon of Monday the 6th October.

One of the first to enter was Joshua Sprigge who reported on the strength of the defences and booty gained. This information must have immediately passed to Cromwell who included a summary of the arms and supplies taken, in his official report to his Commander in Chief, Sir Thomas Fairfax and to the Speaker of the House, William Lenthall.

Who better to retell the whole story of the siege, battering, and taking of the castle than the Lieutenant General himself. He dictated his report and had copies made which where at once despatched by his secretary and Hugh Peters to London.

The news of Cromwell's success had however already reached London and was handsomely paid for as this short note tells. Mr Spavin "the messenger that brought the good news had 50 Pounds given him by the Commons. A very good work to reward all men that do service."

The narrative or diary of events having been set out with the use of several excerpts from Cromwell's own report the whole letter is now repeated so that its full tenor may be uninterruptedly appreciated.

CROMWELL'S LETTER TO FAIRFAX AND
THE SPEAKER

"Sir,
*   I came to Winchester on the Lords day*
being the 28th of September, with Colonel
Pickering commanding his own, Colonel
Montagues, and Sir Hardresse Wallers
regiments.
*   After some dispute with the Governour,*
we entred the Town; I summoned the
Castle, was denied, where upon we fell to
prepare our Batteries, which we could not
perfect (some of our Guns being out of
order) untill Friday following.
*   Our Battery was six guns, which being*
finished, after once firing of them
round. I sent a second Summons for a
Treaty, which they refused, whereupon we
went on with our work and made a breach
in the wall neer the Black tower, which
after about 200 shot, we thought
stormable, and puposed on Monday morning
to attempt it.
*   On Sunday night about ten of the clock,*
the Governour beat a Parley, desiring to
treat. I agreed unto it; and sent
Colonel Hammond and Major Harrison in to
him, who agreed unto these inclosed
Articles.
*   Sir, This is the addition of another*
mercy; You see, God is not weary in
doing you good; I confesse, Sir, his
favour to you is as visible, when he
comes by his power upon the hearts of his
enemies, making them quit places of
strength to you. as when he gives courage
to your Souldiers to attempt hard things.

A. R. III.
p. 128.

p. 129.

-177-

His goodnesse is, in this, much to be
acknowledged; for the Castle was well
manned with 680 Horse and Foot, there
being neer 200 Gentlemen, Officers and
their servants; Well victualled with 1500
weight of Cheese, very great store of
Wheat and Beare, neer 20 Barrels of
Powder (and) 7 peeces of Cannon, the Works
were exceedingly good and strong.
*   It is very likely it would have cost*
much blood to have gained it by storm; we
have not lost 12 men. This is repeated to
you, that God may have all the praise,
for it is all his due.
        Sir I rest
            Your most humble servant
                OLIVER CROMWELL"

A. R.
p. 129.

NOTE - In the original there is a postscript in which Cromwell excuses himself for having given Mr Chichely a pass to go to Cambridgeshire to see his sick wife, and stating he had desired Mr Peters to communicate some things about the army which may not be fit to commit to writing.

H. M. C.
Report 13.
p. 282.

Beare = a kind of corn.

LIEUTENANT GENERAL OLIVER CROMWELL

Cromwell came to Winchester on 28th September 1645 and laid siege to the City taking the Castle on the 5th October. It is a calumny to suggest he was in any way responsible for damage to the Cathedral.
(Robert Walker - Courtesy National Portrait Gallery)

HUGH PETER'S COMMENTS GIVEN
THE HOUSE

A. R.
p. 132.

*"The Castle was manned with 700 men,
divers of them Reformaoes; the chief men
I saw there were Viscount Ogle their
Governour, Sir John Pawlet an old
soldiers, Sir William Courtney and Colonel
Bennet, also Doctor Curle the Bishop of
Winchester, who came forth to our
quarters in the morning with whom I spent
an houre or two who with tears and much
importunity desired the Lieut Generals
favour to excuse his not accepting the
offer he made unto him in his first
entring the town. He desired of me a
guard to his lodging, lest the souldiers
should use violence to him and his
Chaplain, who were in their long Gowns
and Cassocks, and he was accordingly
safely conveyed home.*

p. 133.

*I do verily believe that they will
hardly bring to Woodstock 200 men.*

*It did much affect us to see what an
enemy we had to deal with, who themselves
being Judges, could not chose but say
that our God is not as their God.*

*And this is the nineteenth garrison
hath been taken this summer, through God's
goodnesse; and he that will not take his
share in this common joy is either stupid
or envious.*

*The fruits of what is already done are
great; amongst the rest, what I saw upon
the way, all sorts travelling upon their
occasions freely to their own homes with
Carriages and Wains, many Inns filled
with guests, the former face of things
returning upon us in several kinds; yea,
now we ride with safety from Dover to the
middle of Devonshire."*

Joshua Sprigge reported

"These articles being concluded on, I
was forthwith sent into the castle to   A. R.
take a view of it before my departure,
where I found a peece of ground improved
to the best advantage; for when we
entred by battery, we had 6 distinct
works; and a Draw bridge to passe through
so that it was doubtlesse a very strong
peece, and well appointed, as may appear
by this ensuing note of the ammunition
and provisions we found there. Viz

SPRIGG'S LIST	MERCURIUS CIVICUS
7 Peeces of Ordnance	*4 Great Pieces*
	Three less pieces
17 Barrels of Powder	=
2000 Weight of Musquet bullet	
800 Weight of Match	*700 Muskets*
	(500 fire arms)
	200 Pikes halberds
	& other weapon
	200 pairs of bandoliers
	100 horses.
38 Hogsheads of Beefe and Pork	=
15000 Weight of Cheese	=
800 Pounds of Butter	=
140 Quarters of Wheat and Meale	*40 or 148*
3 Hogsheads of French Wine	*3or 4*
10 Quarters of Salt	
20 Bushels of Oatmeale	
70 Dozen of Candles	*With divers crucifixes*
	and Popish pictures
30 Load of Wood	=
40 Quarters of Charcoale	=
30 Bushels of Seacole	*for the smith*
14 Sheep	=
4 Quarters of Fresh beef	*ready killed &*
	much powdere
7000 Weight of Biskets	=
112 Hogheads of strong beer	=

Chapter 20

THE ROYALISTS MARCH OUT
OF THE CASTLE

"The fruits of what is already done are great"

IN saying this, Hugh Peters was reffering to the reopening of the trade routes particularly to the West, whose interruption had been worrying Parliament ever since Ogle's seizure of the convoy of cloth at Andover and his constant forays which "ranged and raged all over the country."

By the capture of Ogle's Stronghold Cromwell had achieved Fairfax's main strategic objective of restoring the trade and supply lines between London and his army at Lyme. Within a week he had consolidated the position by taking Basing House; also by these means the Royalist cause in Hampshire was finally defeated. Three years had passed since George Lord Goring had hoisted the King's Colours at Portsmouth.

Loyalty and bravery were not enough to defeat the determination and discipline of Parliament's strong willed men.

Yet in victory there was some magnamity. Cromwell had shown a constant wish to avoid bloodshed, he had written "I come not to this City but with a full resolution to save it and the inhabitants from ruine" Thrice he had summoned Ogle to surrender and when in the end Ogle did yield Cromwell's response was quick and positive in acceptance of Ogle's request for a treaty. Further who would deny the generosity of the terms agreed to in the Articles of Surrender.

It was so easy at that moment of time, and immediately after the event, to say that Ogle had surrendered to "terms more favourable to the garrison's safety and property than to the Governor's honour". Some of the King's friends making no scruble to call the capitulation a deed of treachery.

It is doubtful if any of the critics were present during the siege, or were in a position to know precisely what articles had been agreed to, and, if Ogle had held out longer against such odds, what terms he might have been forced to accept in the inevitable defeat he faced with no hope of relief whatsoever.

For Cromwell's part, he wanted the castle and all it stood for removed as quickly as possible with the least bloodsed. He acheived this objective with the loss of fourteen lives. A very considerable achievement.

Cromwell could therefore afford to be generous and was so.

If the strategic objective had been obtained, what of the tactical victory? Cromwell had an army over ten times the strength of the castle's garrison, he had far superior artillery and ample supplies of shot and powder. His success was assured eventually. Against this demonstration of strength William Ogle may have hung out his flag of defiance with the cry,

> *"Hang out our banner*
> *on the outwards walls*
> *The cry is still*
> *'They come'*   Macbeth.
> *Our castles strength will*   Act V.
> *laugh a siege to scorn."*   Scene V.

Alas for all the Royalist bravado it was not to be.

In accordance with the Articles of Surrender, Ogle's garrison was to march out by 3 o'clock on the Monday afternoon. The impatience of the jubilant Parliamentarians to posses the castle was expressed by Mercurius Civicus whose account of the surrender is given below. Even before that Monday morning it seems a large number of the garrison would reject the Royalist cause and join Parliament's Colours.

With the capitulation complete and the beseigers taken off
their guards, all would want to see, stare and look at the size of
the breach and destruction caused by the battering. In due time
each and ever one of them, in Inn or Tavern, would boast of the
part they had taken in this great victory, and how the great and
mighty castle had fallen, and been so speedily brought to its knees.

To the Roundhead troopers the fall of the castle was to
them the very visible fruit of the victory.

THE SURRENDER

Mercurius
Civicus.

*"There were in the castle 700 men, officers
and common soldiers.*

*There was a great wall where the breach was
made, which our forces must have entered, and
three works each higher than the other, before
they could have taken the castle; and by the
judgement of knowing and experienced soldiers,
they had made it the strongest (piece of)
architect(ure) for that purpose, that the like
is not in England.*

*We lost not above two men in all the time of
the playing so fiercely that day, nor above
twelve or fourteen in all the siege before it.*

Which is to be looked on as a great mercy.

*Our men were to enter at eight of the clock
the next morning, but they could not take
possesion of it till two in the afternoon, by
reason the Governor and some other of the
officers, being unwilling to leave any wine
behinde them, had made themselves drunke-
and Viscount Ogle drunke as a beggar.*

*There went forth out of the castle, besides
officers, 600 common soldiers, most of whom
either went to their homes, or took up arms
for Parliament, so that it is thought the
Governor will not have above one hundred with
him by the time he comes to his place of
rendezvouze."*

Hugh Peters in the House spoke,

> *"Mr Speaker,*
> *I came from Winchester the last night*
> *late, but I had come sooner had not my*
> *Lord Ogle and his company been so unwilling*
> *to part with their sack and strong beer, of*
> *which they drank so liberally at their*
> *farewell that few of them, as it is their*
> *manner, could get up their horses without*
> *help, for the agreement was for their*
> *marching out at three o'clock, but it proved*
> *late through their debauchery."*

Godwin.
p. 340.

The agreed rendezvous for Ogle and his party was Woodstock, north of Oxford. The likely route being through Alresford, Farnham and Windsor. The Articles said Ogle was to have six carriages and a guard of one hundred, which was commanded by Major Henry Clarke, who it will be remembered was loyal to Ogle when confronted by the other officers pleading for a treaty.

It was also agreed that there should be a Parliamentary escort to take them out of Winchester to Tichborne, perhaps they were to halt there for the night. This escort of 14 was commanded by Capt Robotham of Colonel Sheffield's Regiment.

However, shortly after this dejected band of Royalists had left the City they were plundered near Worthy by a strong party of Cromwell's horse. Major Clarke "being stript of his clothes" and Ogle's "carriages taken from him contrary to General Cromwell's articles and protection, and that he (Ogle) had no apparel left."

A messenger must have galloped back to Cromwell with Ogle's complaint for six offenders were quickly arrested, tried by Court Martial and condemned.

As was customary, they were compelled to draw lots to discover which of them was to die.

Justice was swift, exemplary and severe.

Sprigge wrote,

Anglia
Redeviva.
p. 1333.

"But before I leave Winchester, I cannot but observe a remarkable peece of Justice done in the satisfaction to the Enemy for some injury they had sustained at their marching forth of Winchester, by plunder, contrary to the articles, which was done by some troopers; who being apprehended, were afterwards tried by a Councel of War, and condemned to die, and after lots cast for their lives (being six of them) he whose lot it was to die was brought to the place of execution, where with a demonstration of great penitence (so far as the beholders did judge) he suffered death for his offence, which exemplary justice made a good impression upon the Soldiery: The other five were sent with a Convoy to Oxford (together with a full account of this proceeding, to the Governour there, Sir Tho Glenham to be delivered over as prisoners, and to be put to death, or otherwise punished as he should think fit: Which was so well received by the Enemy (to see so much right was doe them) that Sir Tho Glenham returned the prisoners back again, with an acknowledgement of the Lieutenant Generals Noblenesse in being so tender in breach of Articles."

If Ogle's departure was ruffled, that of Bishop Curll was certainly unhappy. The Bishop who had been escorted out of the Castle in the morning under the protection of Hugh Peters, left for London during the afternoon under escort, at the same time as the despatches were sent to the Speaker.

Parliament's Post for October 7th tells

> *"The Bishop who had before a guard*
> *to secure his person (with certain*
> *condition), is now like to partake*
> *amongst them in the common distress.*
> *There is little happiness to be*
> *expected from late repentance."*

Godwin. p. 334.

And Mercurius Civicus said

> *"Dr Kerle the Bishop of Winchester*
> *and all the Cantory, to be referred*
> *to the mercy of Parliament."*

Nevertheless the Bishop who "by the actual laws was now no more than a private clergyman was permitted to retire unmolested. His hereditary property, as well as his revenues being sequestrated, he had no other resourse for his subsistence, other than the bounty of his sister who had a house at Soberton, where he died in 1647."

Milner. J.
II p. 20.

The Bishop's altar tomb is in the south transept of Soberton Church, now renamed the Curll Chapel, but formerly known as the Minchin Chapel.

To Bishop Curll is attributed this saying

> *"A Presbyterian is Such a one as*
> *loves God with all his Soul and hates*
> *his neighbour with all his heart."*

Altham. H. S.
in W. C. R.

Of two Winchester personalities, Viscount Ogle was Court Martialled at the Governor's Lodgings in Oxford on the 12th November 1645 for surrendering Winchester Castle. The Court, clearly aware of the realities of the situation created by the strength of Cromwell's army and siege weapons, even though some of the Royalists suspected treason, exonerated Ogle from any blame.

Add Mss.
27402.
f. 100.

John Jackman declared,
"We have a strong plot to procure
all the garrisons in the King's
possesion to be betrayed as diverse
are, viz the Devizes and Winchester
without even a bloody nose. I say
nothing of Bristol and the rest."

Godwin.
p. 339.

The other Winchester personality was Sir William Waller who was responsible for the earlier pillaging of the City and who now had only arrived on the scene with Cromwell on Saturday morning in time to see his house in the castle battered into ruins. Mercurius Civicus reported

"The Castle being Sir William Waller's,
the Lieutenant General delivered it into
his possesion by the articles of the
surrender bearing date October 5."

As related, Charles I had granted the house within the castle to Sir William Waller in 1638. Parliament's confirmation of Waller's ownership came the following January and seems to have included not only the original grant but also the Great Hall. The house having been destroyed, Waller never returned to live in Winchester or became its Governor.

Milner. J.

V. C. H.
V. p. 12.

Because of the unsettled conditions and fear of a Royalist rising, Parliament decided for the time being, the castle should be garrisoned and on the 14th October '45 nominated Lt Colonel Lower to be its Governor. This nomination was not acceptable to the Hampshire Parliamentarians who immediately wrote to the Speaker nominating Thomas Bettesworth. He was involved in the midnight raid from Southampton on the Cathedral Close, the previous August.

1645   Sir Thomas Jervoise and others wrote to William
Oct 18   Lenthall from Basingstoke,

> *"Desiring that Captain Bettersworth for
> whom they had written to the Committee
> of Both Kingdoms for a Commission to
> command their horse and taken order for
> making him Sheriff, should be appointed
> Governor of Winchester Castle instead of
> Colonel Lower."*

H. M. C.
Report 13
VI. p. 292.

Two days later Captain Bettesworth's appointments were confirmed by the House and agreed to by the Lords.

Portal.
p. 182.

Chapter 21

WINCHESTER AFTER THE SIEGE

A BREAK from the narrative to consider a tradition that Oliver Cromwell's guns fired on the Cathedral from the earthworks on the high ground, one and a half miles to the west of the City, known as Oliver's Battery. This would have been an impossible task for Captain Deane, Cromwell's Master Gunner with the guns and equipment available to him. 17c Guns had not the accuracy required to precisely hit a target, such as the west window of the Cathedral at the extreme range of 2000 yards. A difficult enough task even for a guided missile to day.

"Olivers Battery" an Iron Age enclosure of about an acre in extent surrounded by a four foot embankment has been shown, by archaeological research, to have been abandoned about the year 150 BC, used by the Romans for a very short period in the 1st century. The excavations made in 1931 by W.J. Andrews showed a single vallum with the enclosure almost square in shape bearing no relation whatsoever to military fieldworks of the Civil War period. In one place the vallum was broken to make an easy entrance into the enclosure. The only evidence for a Civil War period of occupaton was a single spur and a pair of farriers pincers, found during a previous search in 1875 and a mid 17c glass bottle found by Andrews in the excavations of 1931.

Andrews.
H. F. C.
XII. p. 163.

Olivers Battery clearly was not used as a gun platform. It may have acquired its name by being used by Cromwell for parking his artillery as they approached from Romsey, out of reach from a raiding party from the castle, while the siege works were being prepared.

The first mention of the earthworks in connection with Cromwell is on T Milne's map of 1791 when he used the name "Oliver Cromwells camp" and marked it diagramatically as a typical small 17c fortification with bastion at the corners. The title "Cromwells Bty" is given on Greenwoods map of 1826. On the present issue of the Ordnance Survey 1/50,000 series the site is named "Oliver Cromwell's Battery". SU 459288.

There is another but larger low banked enclosure of three acres called "Olivers Battery" only 1200 yards north of Basing House. From the descriptions of the siege of that great House, Cromwell's battery was sited elsewhere to the south and very much closer to the House for the walls to have been breached. A third Iron Age camp with the designation Oliver's Battery is at Abbotstone about midway between Winchester and Basing House using the old tracks across the downs and up the Candover valley which conceivably could have been used as a camping ground for the Cromwell's siege artillery while waiting for the works to be completed in readiness to assault that House.

It is remarkable that these three ancient camps should be named after Oliver Cromwell who was only active in Hampshire for a month.

A pre Civil War description of the City in 1635 has been given by Lieut Hammond, but what if the state of Winchester ten years later and immediately after Cromwells departure?

The South Gate had been forced for the second time and would have been in a wrecked state. Gone were all the little orchards and gardens around the Castle which now stood guant and bare with the signs of war in the breaches made to its walls and towers. Inside the castle the Earl of Portland's house, so recently repaired and beautified and which had been passed on to Sir William Waller, lay in ruins utterly destroyed by Cromwell's battering.

The Great Hall of the Castle, in which Hammond had seen and described the Court of Eyre sitting in all its pomp and ceremonial grandeur, now had a gaping hole in the roof and the interior devasted by one of the granados charged with musket shot which had killed three men in the hall. Was it this shot that had peppered the Round Table with musket shot? The hall was not used again until Michaelmas 1647, the Quarter Sessions having to be transferred to Wolvesey.

Furley.
p. 16.

Inside the town, below the West Gate and to the upper part of the High Street, within the old parish of St Clements most of the houses were burnt or damaged and the church of St Clement itself had lost part of its roof. It had been used by the Roundheads as a guard room which they had left "miserably ransacked and torn to pieces so as to be rendered useless as a church. Later it was used "as a place to lay faggots in, yea, wherein to receive oxen, horses etc at time of fairs."

A "Friend"
See p. 234
below.

John Woodman who was appointed Receiver over the Dean and Chapter's affairs reported many leasehold tenements had been pulled down and burnt during the War. Winchester College records tell of the house of Peter Chamberlain, a tenant who lived next to the castle, being burnt out. It is very remarkable that this is only damage to College property mentioned in their records during those troublesome days.

Kirby.
Annals of
Win' Col'
p. 333.

It is unlikely that any buildings were standing on the west side of Gold Street (Southgate St) between the street and the castle. Midway along this street, down a steep bank, stood the old St Thomas's Church in a ruinous condition. It was restored at the Restoration of 1660, demolished in 1845 and rebuilt on its present site in Southgate Street and is now in the care of the County Council.

St Lawrence's Church in the very centre of the City was wrecked and unsafe for meeting, its seats miserably ransacked and torn. Patched up it was used, for a short while as a school after the Restoration, until rebuilt and given its present roof and aisless form.

It will be remembered that Joshua Sprigg complained how the Royalists "played upon the chiefest Street of the town" adding to the devastation and distress.

In the middle of the High Street, on the north side just below its junction with Parchment Street (Nos 113-114) stood the Church of St Mary Kalender, already in ruins in 1630 except for its tower. During the War it was robbed of its bells by the Royalists which were taken off into the Castle; fortunately recovered but then sold the proceeds being used to restore St Thomas' Church.

The only church fit for a congregation to meet in was St Maurice, restored in 1630 and then used for Services strictly in accordance with the Directory of Worship. This church, except for the tower was demolished in 1842 and rebuilt on the same site. The second church was demolished and the site cleared in 1957, again except for the much patched mediaeval tower.

Demolished under the supervision of the writer.

Little St Swithun's Church over Kingsgate was also severly damaged and the parish had to be united with St Michael's in Kingsgate Street.

St Swithun's was let during the Commonwealth period to "one Robert Allen, his wife delivered of children at one end and a hogsty made of the other." This church now happily restored and kept in a good state of repair and in use today.

One other devasted church was St Peter Colebrook which was then left to decay. In 1660 it was described as being "an inconsiderable little placeno use made of it for above these fourteen years, extremely untiled, the covering almost gone, grass nettles weeds growing in the body of it."

The mediaeval Wolvesey castle, a great fortified palace of the Bishops of Winchester had been in decline since the Reformation and had become a farmstead and administrative headquarters of the Bishops' estates. It does not seem to have been used occupied for military purposes during the war other than a convenient billet. The Militias equipment and stores kept there had been removed by Parliament before hostilities commenced.

Hammond. See p. 254. below.

Greatrex. J. Register of the Common Seal.

Godwin.
p. 341.

Furley.

Turner. B. C. T.
Winchester
p. 128 n. 32

Wren. C
Parentalia.
II. p. 21.

See page
164 above.

Wolvesey was probably in a fair state of repair for the buildings had been put into some sort of order at the time of the State Trials of Lords Cobham and Grey, and of Sir Walter Raleigh in 1603, but the restoration then was never fully completed. In 1645 immediately after the siege and taking of Winchester Parliament ordered Sir William Waller and the Committee for Hants not only to consider the need to garrison the Castle but also "Woolsey House". The following year Wolvesey was used by the County for Quarter Sessions from Easter of that year until Michaelmas 1647. Without any orders or instructions to demolish the House it apparently remained in use until after the Restoration still being taxed for 23 hearths in 1664. Bishop Morley lived at Farnham and did not commission Wren to build a new palace at Winchester untill some twenty years later.

Thus had the venerable City been devastated looted and laid waste over a period of three years. It had suffered military occupation by Royalists and Parliamentarians alike. Thrice it had been pillaged. It had suffered heavy fines and its Civic Plate surrendered, trade interrupted, buildings damaged and left unrepaired. The City had suffered everything that war brings except a massive and destructive fire.

Its Cathedral had been ravaged, its window broken leaving the building open to the elements and deserted by the clergy. In the Close all the houses lay empty and looted yet soon to be reoccupied by Parliamentarian sympathisers led by Nicholas Love who seized the Dean's house.

A description of the spoilation of the "Muniment House" the second time on the 1st and 2nd October, while the army was waiting for the bombardment to commence and Cromwell was away and therefore not able to exert his own strong influence on discipline, has already been given.

Further confirmation that the second destruction of the
Muniment House took place in October 1645 and not in 1646 is
given by Chase himself in his own writings and by this Order of the
Committee of Parliament for the County of Hants of the 29th
November 1645.

> *"John Woodman, Solicitor within the*
> *City of Winton shall have the house*
> *in the Close, late in the possession*
> *of Henry Foyle, delinquent, during*
> *pleasure for laying up and preserving*   W. C. D.
> *sequestrated goods of Papists and*   II. p. 71.
> *delinquents."*

It is evident that Parliament was quick to seize on the Office
of The Dean and Chapter to secure for themselves the revenues
due.

Chase does not seem to have access to the Muniment House
until 1650 when he was then permitted to recover lost records
and wrote the memo given below, when he appears to be acting
professionally for the Parliamentary Committee, the office of
The Dean and Chapter having been abolished.

> *"After the muniment house was*
> *(the first and Second October 1646*
> *22 Car Reg) by the Army and Souldiery*
> *the second time broken upp, I haveing*
> *obtained an order from the Committee of*   W. C. D.
> *Parliament for the County of Southampton*   II. p. 58.
> *and sitting in the Close of the said*
> *Church, began serch and inquirie, and*   &
> *by meanes made I found and got into my*   xxvii.
> *custody as followeth*
>
> *I ordered this about*
> *22 & 24 Aug 1650"*

It is in the list of muniments prepared by Chase that one finds two significant endorsements pinpointing the second spoilation to 1645 for he records the recovery of King Adelwulfs Charta on Nov 25 1645 and the Charter of Eadwig he endorsed "Inventa 1645".

W. C. D. II.
p. 60. No

p. 62. No 957

Further in the margin of the Register of the Common Seal, John Chase wrote 25 leaves of the Register (Viz ff 31-57) were missing on 2 Oct 1645 during the Civil War but after careful searching they were found and restored to their place on 2 June 1648.

Greatrex.
p. xi. n. 1.

Two further documents written in the diligent John Chase's hand, although not altogether sure in which year some events took place.

"Delivered up 1650   Thirteen lidger bookes

Given to Mr Rd Love at Crondale
5 Sbr 1650

One old Inspeximus of divers charters
with the Confirmances thereof touching
the faire to be holden upon St Giles
Hill by the Bishops of Winchester and
their officers, which I found and was
given me by Tupper the butcher all
soyled and found by him in Winchester
High Street; and also a copie thereof
in paper eaten with rats, wherein the
liberties and tolls are mencioned Etc."

W. C. D. II.
p. 58.

&
xxvii. n. 1.

Sad to relate that was not the end of the spoilation of the muniments for John Woodman sold some of the books and manuscripts to a merchant or agent in London named as Thomas Matthews, a grocer as described in the subsequent trial of Woodman for embezzlement of the records which took place on January 22nd 1651/2. Many of the books were recovered but were ordered by Parliament to be sent to Winchester College.

p. 71.

Chapter 22

POLITICAL PRESSURES

BY the summer of 1646 Parliamentary dominance in the south had brought an uneasy peace. On the 29th June Parliament decided

> *"That the Town and Garrison of*
> *Winchester be forthwith disgarrisoned"*

The City relieved, as they hoped of this final burden of the war with troopers billeted in the City struggled to re-assert itself. Given below is a minute of the City Government which illustrates quite a different sort of struggle that was going on between the 'Old Order' and 'Puritanism'. It was about The Winchester Races, the annual race meeting which brought excitement, gaiety and trade to the City. Should they be permitted? With some hesitancy they were and continued to be run on the downs some two miles to the north of the City towards Worthy Down. The course was still marked, as late as 1826 on Greenwood's Map.

THE RACES July 1646

> *"It is agreed by the said assembly*
> *that Ralph Riggs Esq Maior of the*
> *said City shall have security under*
> *the City seale to save him harmless*   H. N. & Q.
> *for being engaged for the race cupp*   IV. p. 103.
> *as shall be advised by the Council*
> *of the said Maior"*

This is the same troublesome Riggs who was in ill odour with the Royalists over taking the City Maces into the Cathedral, purloining the proceeds from the sale of the bronze statues of King James and King Charles, and here he is finding a political excuse for his Puritanical views by not attending the Race Meeting and possibly being fined by the Council for not carrying out an old and established Mayoral duty.

The next year from the Coffer accounts there is this entry of monies paid out:-

> *"May 18 1647*
> *£10 to Sir William Kingsmill Knight*
> *Easter last towards the race cupp."*

By 1657 the "Races" had become entirely acceptable.

City Coffer
Accounts.
H. N. & Q
VII. p. 64

> *"Paid out then to Captain Palmer £30 to*
> *buy a race cupp in accordance with the*
> *Lord Richard Cromwell on behalf of the*
> *Gentlemen of the County."*

Later in 1647 the Royalists in the Corporation felt strong enough to ask the King to nominate the Royalist Ferdinand Bye as Town Clerk. The nomination became a cause celebre. The format of the Kings reply and that he was able to do so at this time is interesting.

Archives of
Winchester.
p. 188.

> *"Charles Rex.*
> *Trusty and well beloved, we greet you well*
> *Whereas we understand that your Towne*
> *Clerkes place is voyde by the decease of*
> *that officer; and whereas we understand that*
> *Ferdinand Bye of that City hath been*
> *formally ymployed in that office, and is a*
> *person of ability to execute it, by being*
> *one that hath well deserved of us; we*
> *therefore upon his humble peticon, are*
> *graciously pleased to recommend him to your*
> *present election to succeed the sayd Town*
> *Clerke deceased, wherein you will express*
> *your readiness to comply with our desires,*
> *and give good contentment, when we shall*
> *heare you have done accordingly.*
> *Given at Hampton Court 13 Sept 1647."*

The election of Bye was opposed by John Lisle, recorder of the City, on the grounds that he had been in the service for the King against Parliament. In his stead Lisle nominated Stephen Welsteede Gent' to the sayd office for that he had served the Parliament as Clerke or Agent to the Committee of Parliament for Sequestration. Then followed the direct result of political pressure.

> *"And divers of ye said Committee*
> *then likewise appeared on the behalf*
> *of the sayd Stephen Weltsteed for as*
> *much as this Citye was then under the*
> *power of ye Parliament and the Committee*
> *the sitting in the Close and the sayd*
> *John Lisle being then one of the*
> *Committee, and a person then in great*
> *power"*

The appointment of Welsteed was reluctantly accepted. The above quotation is taken from the renewed petition of Ferdinand Bye made after the Restoration in 1660. King Charles II using the same format as his father wrote in reply to the petition

> *"That he may be forthwith admitted*
> *Towne Clerke (and that our Citye)*   A of W.
> *will comply with our desires and give*   p. 189.
> *us good contentment when we shall*
> *heare you have done accordingly.*
> *Whitehall 17 sept 1660."*

As another example of the political pressures brought to bear on the Corporation, by the coterie of Parliamentarians in the Close this order signed by three prominent members of the Committee in the name of Parliament is indicative of their fanaticism. All three became regicides.

The order was in the usual form used by Parliament for the disfranchisement of Royalist "Delinquents".

It will be seen that whereas His Majesty desired compliance to give good contentment, the Parliamentarians required the City to yield Obedience to their orders.

G. N & Q.
V. p. 140.
quoting
Journals of
the House of
Commons.

House of Commons
14 April 1648.

"Ordered

*That according to former ordinance
of Parliament Robert Tucker late
Alderman of Winchester be disfranchised.*

*And the Mayor Aldermen Bailiffs and
Commonalty of the City of Winton are
hereby required and enjoined to
disfranchise the said Robert Tucker.*

*And it is further Ordered that Robert
Matthews late Mayor of Winton be restored
to his place of being Alderman Justice
for this present year, and to the same
place in the said city as other Aldermen
have usually enjoyed the next year after
their mayoralties.*

*And the Mayor Aldermen Bailiffs and
Commonalty of the said City are required
to yield obedience to this order herein.*

*And Mr Wallop, Mr Lisle and Mr Love are
to take care that this Order be sent to
the city and that it is performed in all
particulars thereof."*

In November 1647 there was a Great Alarm in Hampshire, caused by the King's escape from Hampton Court. It was of course not known until later how close to Winchester he had come on his journey through Bishops Sutton and Titchfield to the Isle of Wight, and there only to find himself a prisoner in Carisbrooke Castle.

Captain Robert Burley's attempt to rescue his Sovereign from the Island ended in his trial for treason in the Great Hall of Winchester Castle on January 22 1648. He was condemned by Judge Wilde to suffer the gruesome death of traitor, of being hung drawn and quartered.

Ironical for trying to save the King. The sentence must have sent a shudder through the City, and as no one could be found in Hampshire to carry out the foul deed an executioneer had to be brought from London.

This mediaeval barbarity had been witnessed in Winchester since the thirtenth century when in 1283 one quarter of the body of Prince David of Wales was sent by Edward the First to the City for exposure on the City walls, as an example of the fate of so called traitors.

The Winchester Ordeal was described by Stanford in the middle of the 16c, and now in 1648 it was again to be carried out in Winchester.

> *"That the traytor be drawn from his prison*
> *to the place of execution, as being unworthy*
> *to trad any more upon his mother earth,*
> *backward, with his head downward, for that*
> *he had been retrograde to dutiful courses;*
> *hanged by the neck between heaven and earth,*
> *as not deserving the enjoyment of either,*
> *his privities cut off, as having been*
> *unprofitably beggoten, and unfit to leave*
> *any generation; his bowels burnt, for having*
> *inwardly conceived or concealed treason; his*
> *head cut off, for inventing mischief against*
> *his King and Country; his body quartered and*
> *made a prey for birds, to strike more terror*
> *into others, and to caution them from deserv-*
> *ing the like punishment".*

See p. 256.
below

Capt Burley in his last speech declared more bloodshed would follow his death and denied his judgement was legal saying,

V. C. H.
V. p. 348.

> *"the gentlemen from London had damned him*
> *before they came, the ministers in their*
> *pulpits and the jury at the bar; but that*
> *he was clear from being a traitor"*

C. S. P.

The Parliamentary papers commented,

> *"The death of Capt Burley quartered*
> *at Winchester is little spoken of.*
> *The malignants will have it that he*
> *was quartered in a spring of blood."*

An exceedingly unhappy page in the annals of Winchester, but Burley was not the last to be executed for treason here. Nearly forty years later a grim retribution was exacted when Judge Jefferies, at the Bloody Assizes of 1685, condemed the regicide M.P. for Winchester and lay Master of St Cross, John Lisle's widow, Dame Alice to be burnt at the stake for sheltering refugees from the Monmouth Rebellion. The Church and Town horrified by the sentence, Bishop Mews petitioned the King to mitigate the sentence of Burning-at-the-Stake. The sentence was delayed a few days but only commuted to one of beheading, which was executed in the Square here in Winchester. The plaque marking the spot is a monument and constant reminder of the horrors of Civil War.

Almost a year later towards the end of 1648, after the defeat of the Scots and the failure of the King to submit to the demands of Parliament, the House found itself in the hands of the Army.

Herbert. G.
Charles I.
p. 256.

The Rump Parliament then set up a special "High Court of Justice" to try the King for treason.

H. F. C.
XIX
1. p. 64.

As the first stage of bringing King Charles back to London for his trial, he was taken from Carisbrooke to Hurst castle where after a brief pause he started his journey to Windsor travelling via Winchester Alresford and Farnham.

The King arrived at Winchester on the evening of the 10th December 1648 and was lodged for the night in the security of the Castle. On arrival at the Westgate he was received by the Mayor and Aldermen with all ceremony as though this were a Progress in the days of his power and of former visits to the City in happier times. The Mace was handed to him and formally returned and he was then escorted into the City where many of the local gentry in their best attire had gathered to kiss his hand.

Wedgewood. C. V.
Trial of
Charles I
p. 63.

Herbert.
p. 173.

After King Charles had left the City, the Mayor was reprimanded by the Governor for what he had done and had to tender his apologies to Parliament. There seems to have been no attempt by those in charge of the King to interfere with the customary reception given him.

THE MACE PRESENTED TO THE KING

"Letters from Windsor, that his Majesty removing from Hurst castle, when he came to Winchester, the Mayor and his brethren met him and delivered him the Mace and made a speech to him; that the Commander of that party who guarded the King told the Mayor, that the parliament had voted no more addresses to the King on pain of high treason and by this address they made to him that they were within the danger of being traitors.

Whitelocks
Memorials
p. 484.
  359.

That the Mayor and his brethren humbly asked pardon for it, excusing themselves that they knew not anything of that vote and that they would be more cautions for the future."

Godwin. G. N.
Memorials
of old
Hampshire.
p. 272.

From Windsor the King was conveyed to Whitehall and brought to trial on the 20th January sentenced on the 27th, and executed on Tuesday 30th January 1649.

The custom of formally handing the Mace to a visiting Sovereign, as a mark of the City's Loyalty, happily continues to this day. A rare and cherished privelege of this Ancient City of Winchester.

The Commonwealth proclaimed, further political pressures were soon imposed on the Winchester Institutions. In July 1649 following the Act for the abolishing of Deanes, Deanes and Chapters, Canons, Prebends and other officers and titles belonging to any Cathedral or Collegiate Church -a detailed survey of all the houses and property in the Close was made.

This fascinating survey was published by Stephens and Madge in Winchester Cathedral Documents. The survey is in todays terms a report and valuation of each property giving particulars of accomodation fixtures and extent of the outhouses and gardens. Of especial interest is the names of the prominent Parliamentarians then occupying the houses in 1649.

W. C. D.
II. p. 76.

Nicholas LOVE   in Dean Young's house,
   1608-1682   The Deanery.

The son of Nicholas Love, Warden of Winchester College. (1613-1630) A barrister who succeeded William Ogle as the M.P. for Winchester. He was present at the trial of King Charles and therefore counted a Regicide, although he did not sign the Death Warrant. In 1649 he was one of Parliament's Commissioners appointed to enquire into the affairs of Winchester College. At the restoration he escaped to Switzerland dying at Vevey in 1682.

Robert WALLOP   in Dr Edward Burby's house.
   1601-1667

M.P. for Andover. He sat as a judge on King Charles and although he too was one of those who did not sign the Death Warrant he was nevertheless decared to be a Regicide. He was imprisioned in the Tower in 1660 remaining there until he died in 1667. A Commissioner of Enquiry into Winchester College.

John LISLE	in Dr Francis Alexander's
1610-1664	house.

A barrister, Master of St Cross 1644-49, recorder of Winchester, Lord Commissioner. As one of the managers of the trial of King Charles he was named a Regicide but succeeded in escaping to the Continent only to be assassinated in Lausanne in 1664. His widow 'Dame' Alice Lisle was beheaded in Winchester in 1685, as related. John Lisle was one of the Commissioners of Enquiry at the College.

Francis RIVETT	in Dr Sebastian Smith's house

Commissioner of enquiry to Winchester College.

Sir Henry MILDMAY	in Dr Haswell's house.
Died 1664	

In 1617, he became Master of the King's Jewel House but deserted the King in 1641. He was present at the trial of King Charles. A leading member of Parliament's enquiry into the affairs of Colleges and Schools. At the Winchester College enquiry he personally prepared a list of 14 charges against Warden Harris demanding that he should justify his instructions for "Corporal bowing at the name of Jesus" and that he "Prayed for Lord Ogle and the King's kinne". At the Restoration he was called to account for the King's jewels, sentenced to life imprisonment and died at Antwerp while being transported to Tangier.

Eastgate House, Lord Hopton's headquarters before the Battle of Cheriton, came into possession of the Mildmay Family and was known as Mildmay House. When the House was pulled down in the 19th c., the very fine wrot iron gates from the house were moved to 54 Chesil Street where they can still be seen.

Henry BROMFIELD   in Dr Bucknor's house

Commissioner to Winchester College.

Void   Dr Hinton's house

Humphrey ELLIS   in Dr Edward Metkerke's

One of the two Ministers appointed by Parliament to Winchester.

Leonard COOKE   in Mr John Crooke's
                                 a Fellow of Win' College.

The other of the two Ministers in Winchester.

Richard NORTON   in Dr Edward Stanley's
      1614-1691

Colonel Richard Norton of Southwick and Alresford. An active Parliamentarian in 1642. He was responsible for plundering the City in July '43, took a prominent part in Parliament's success at the Battle of Cheriton in March '44. He suppressed the Clubmen of Hampshire in Sept '45 and was present at the Taking of Winchester in Oct '45. Known as the "Great Incendiary of Hampshire" and by his friend Oliver Cromwell as "Idle Dick"

> *"Given to Presbyterian notions was*
> *purged out by pride; came back and*
> *dwindled ultimately into Royalism."*

William WITHERS   in Dr John Harris' house
       1584-1653   Warden of Winchester Coll'

History
of the
Wither
Family.

St. Michaels
parish
Records.

Kitchen.
H. R. S. 1895.
Manor of
Manydown.
Kirby.
p. 345.

A Parliamentary Deputy Lieutenant. He purchased the Manor of Manydown following the abolition of Deans and Chapters. While in Winchester his daughter Anne married Dr John Potenger School Master of St Mary's College. Their son Charles was babtised on the Thirteenth day of January 1648 about two of the clock in the afternoon and was born January 12 being Wednesday between 4 and 5 in the morning.

Thomas BETTERSWORTH as a Parliamentarian he was the only person allowed to remain in his house in the Close. He was Governor of the castle and Sheriff.

John WOODMAN   in the house leased to
                   William Brown and he had
                   possession of Henry Foyles
                   ostensibly in which to
                   store sequestrated goods.

Parliament's Solicitor for sequestration. He muddled the muniments and accounts and sold books from the Cathedral Library. He was ordered into custody in February 1650/1 the indictment saying John Woodman never included in his return, but appropriated himself, producing a deed, said to be forged, to show that he had purchased the reversion from Trustees for the sale of the Dean and Chapter's lands, and pleading that Brother Ellis (the Minister to whom it had been assigned) was a bastard, and unable to make a will. John Woodman was also indicted for refusing to declare the account and defalcations of over £873.

The Parliamentarians had to allow the old Chapter Clerk, John Chase, to return to the Cathedral and put the muniments back into order.

LEACH.
Win' Coll'
Chapter
XXIII

Kirby.
Chapter
XX

Of the Commissioners, or visitors, appointed by the Parliamentary Committee for regulating Winchester college seven lived in the close, a clique who found security in a still pro Royalist City within the walls of the Close, still locked at night at ten.

The other Commissioners were Colonel Fielder, Robert Reynolds, Francis Allen a former scholar, Richard Major whose daughter had married Oliver Cromwell's son Richard, John Hildersley who later became M.P. for Winchester, Sir Thomas Jervoise, George Marshall the intruded Warden of New College, Thomas Hussey a former scholar and then a Deputy Lieutenant who later became known as the saviour of the Cathedral, and Edward Hooper Governor of Southampton.

An extraordinary large number of people whose task was to report what Statutes should be taken away, and what persons be removed. Warden Harris was ordered to attend and produce the College's Statutes and records. This he did in a forthright and straitforward manner so much so that no changes were made to the statutes and Warden Harris remained in office.

For the Warden to be so well received one must presume Harris had signed the "Engagement" of the 12 October 1649.

Leach.
p. 350.

"I do declare and promise that I
will be true and faithful to the
Commonwealth of England as the same
is now established without a King
or House of Lords."

C. S. P.
Dom.

This declaration was required to be given by General Officers and divers officials and among those specially mentioned who were required to sign were "The Masters Fellows and School Masters in Eton Winchester and Westminster.

It has been said of John Harris

> *"In the difficult whirlpool of that age*
> *he guided through many a storm, with God's*
> *help the ship of which he was captain"*

Wymer.
p. 76.

Certainly the College suffered no damage or any sequestrations although from the accounts kept of the College plate £182/4s of silver was missing at the end of the war. Probably sent to Oxford at the demands of the King in the same manner as plate from the Dean and Chapter and from the City had been demanded.

Further political pressure was soon brought to bear on the pro Royalist Corporation when on the 13th September 1649 a "New Modelled Corporation" was instituted and the Royalists were ejected. Edmund Riggs became Mayor and the Parliamentarian party's tenure was to last until 1st August 1662 when they, in their turn, were expelled from office and removed.

Turner. B. C. T.
in W. C. R.
No. 29.

Chapter 23

THE CASTLE TO BE MADE UNTENABLE

A PROPOSAL to demolish the Castle first arose in the Autumn of 1647 two years after being taken by Cromwell. It came at a time when the County was anxious to re-establish Quarter Session Government in the Great Hall and were compelled to hurriedly negotiate the Halls purchase from its then owner Sir William Waller, who had been granted it by Parliament in compensation for the loss of his House, the 'Mansion', in the Castle.

Waller agreed to sell, his right to the Hall, to Sir Thomas Jervoise, as feo fee for the County for £100. Sir Thomas unable to raise that sum himself had to borrow £50 from Sir Robert Wallop.

The Great Hall was back in use for the September Quarter Sessions and in time for the trial of Captain Burley the following year.

As it happened, although the Hall had been saved, the demolition of the Castle itself was delayed for several years.

In May '48 Parliament alarmed by the Scots and fearing a rising in the South with a seizure of the Castle by the Malignants, ordered Henry Ireton's Regiment of Horse to secure the Town and Castle till some other course could be taken to demolish or secure the Castle.

O. P. Hist
XVII. p. 152.

Nothing was done then, nor is there any evidence how long Ireton's regiment remained in Winchester if at all, before being drawn away north to fight the Scottish invasion at Preston in July.

Parliament still fearful of insurrections and that one might be centred on Winchester with a possible French intervention, the need to demolish the Castle became almost an obsession.

This was at the time when Prince Rupert was in command of a fleet which eventually sailed to Kinsale to support Ormonde in Ireland.
It being said

"The royal cause is all at sea"

Yet for all the supposed military priority the demolition was to be subject to Sir William Waller receiving satisfactory compensation. One would have thought the needs of the New State for security would over ride the satisfaction of any one individual, however prominent and powerful a Parliamentarian Waller was.

The Following extracts taken from the State Papers show how slow progress towards the demolition was. They tell their own story.

1649 June 11
"By an Order in Parliament.
The Council of State to consider how
Winchester Castle may be made untenable
so that no damage may arise thereby,   C. S. P.
and how satisfaction may be made to   1649-50.
Sir Wm Waller for such damage as he   p. 180.
shall sustain by reason thereof."

June 19
That the Castle should be viewed before
being demolished.

September 10
Mr Frost was desired to issue to the
County of Hants a copy of the Order   Portal.
for making Winchester Castle untenable.   p. 41.

September 11
An Engineer to be sent to Winchester
to see the Castle demolished according
to the survey returned; for this he
was to be paid five pounds."

The council wrote to the Winchester Magistrates Messrs Betsworth Moore and Withers on September 26

> *"We formerly ordered Winchester Castle to*
> *be made untenable. We now authorise you to*
> *put the same into execution and to summon*
> *the County to do the work, which we conceive*
> *they will be willing to do to provide for*
> *their future quiet. We enclose a copy of the*
> *Engineers opinion of what is necessary to be*
> *done."*

At the Quarter Session held in the Great Hall at Michaelmas 1649 the above letter was read and it was then ordered by the court

> *"That Mr Bettesworth, and Mr Riggs the*
> *Mayor of Winchester should with all*
> *convenient speed, at the charge of the*
> *County, cause same to be done accordingly"*

and the said gentlemen were by the Court further desired to notify their doings and proceedings therein unto the Council of the State. Clearly there must have been very considerable opposition to any further destruction in the City. By December Parliament had to take more positive and drastic action to make the Castle untenable.

Portal.
p. 42.

C. S. P.
1649-50.

> *"December 16. The Council of State ordered*
> *the Governor of Southampton Major Peter*
> *Murford to 'summon the County to go to*
> *Winchester, to demolish the castle and*
> *wall about it, so that it may not be used*
> *by the disaffected; and likewise to send*
> *forty of his garrison soldiers thither to*
> *keep the peace there while the work is*
> *going on' and they informed him 'that the*
> *Militia Commissioners for the County had*
> *been ordered to supply him with forty*
> *honest men at Southampton during the*
> *employment of his soldiers in that service.'"*

Further delay was imposed while it was decided who should pay.

Portal.
p. 42.

January 13 From the minutes of the Proceedings of the Council of State

*"To write to the Commissioners of the
County of Hants to proceed to demolishing
of Winchester Castle according to former
order. Council thinking it not fit to move
Parliament to defray the charge of the work,
which it is proper for the County to do."*

With the fears of a Royalist landing from France, Parliament had to rebuke the County for the delay and ordered the work to be done in fourteen days, little realising the magnitude of the task in the very strength and size of the structure.

1651 February 21 Council of State to the Militia Commissioners County of Hants.

*"We have before written to you
concerning the making of Winchester
Castle untenable, but it is not yet
done.
    We have intimated the danger that
might come of it, which, if it should
happen, would first have its ill
effects upon that County: We therefore
order that it may be done within
fourteen days after the Assizes, when
you will have occasion to meet, and
can take order for its being done, of
which you are to certify to us, that
we may be satisfied that the danger
feared by that place is prevented."*

1651 March 28 Council of State to Militia
Commissioners of the County of Hants

*"In yours of the 21st you state that
you have begun to make Winchester Castle
untenable; we hope by this time it has
been effectually done, as it might have
been long since, if the orders of the
Council had been pursued."*

C. S. P.
1649-50.

Four and a half years after Cromwell had taken the Castle
its demolition commenced. The contractors accounts, taken from
Richard Cromwell of Hursley's papers were published in 1899
by Portal in his 'The Great Hall of Winchester Castle'.

Portal.
p. 43.

There is insufficient information showing the exact position
of the walls and towers of the Castle on the west and south sides
but the demolition contracts (given below) suggest they allowed
for the demolition of the whole of these two walls.

The first contract, Richard Warder's, was for the demolition
of the West wall and Gatehouse, Richard Warder's contract, the
remainder of the west wall, not already destroyed at the "Breach",
(wide enough for thirty men abreast) including the "Black Tower"
was the responsibility of Leonard George. The South West square
tower and the South wall was in John Wheatland's contract.
Demolition of the South East round tower and continuing round
on the east side was included in Philip Sharp's contract.

This would place the breach opposite the site previously
suggested for Cromwell's Battery of his six heavy siege guns.

The centre oval tower on the east side does not appear to
have been demolished at that time and remained standing, until
the space was required by Sir Christopher Wren for King Charles
II new House in the 1680s, the tower was still in occupation by
the Reverend Henry Compton in 1664.

ACCOUNTS FOR THE DEMOLITION OF THE CASTLE

Portal.
p. 43.

"Mr Durnford's accompt of ye demolishing
Winton Castle from March 21 1650 (1651)
to June 17 1651.

Pounds

March 18 1651

    Agreed with Richard Warder and his
Company to demolish the Gate House,
and lay it level with the passage
going in   22

    Agreed with the same Richard Warder
to demolish the outside West Wall of
the said Castle with the two inside   20
walls to the South and West with part
of the kitchen and other partition
walls.

March 18 1651

    Agreed with the Leonard George
to demolish the Black tower level to
the ground going in.   8

    Agreed with the said Leonard George
to demolish the wall from the
Black tower to the breach within the
walls, and all the old Chappell walls
in the inside there for   10

April 6 1651

    Agreed with Philip Sharpe,
of Twyford to take down the
Rounde Tower towards the South east
and other works for   18

April 12 1651

    Agreed with John Wheatlands
to demolish the square tower towards
the south west and the south inside
wall with other partition walls for."   16

Mr Major of Hursley to the Council of State.
April 21 1651.

> *"Many labourers have been employed towards
> the demolition of the Castle Winton and a
> fair progress has been made therein, and a
> hope expressed that the work will be
> finished in six weeks, but, the foundations
> of the Castle are discovered to be so lowe
> and the wall so thicke under ground, made
> with flint stones, that it is very difficult
> to get beneath it and will be a work of
> longe time and a vast charge if not possible
> to subvert it.*
>
> *It is therefore suggested that it may be
> sufficient to discourage an enemy from
> attempting to make it a place of refuge, if
> the walls are thrown down level with the
> ground, the wells filled up and all the
> timbers and stone and other vendible
> materials sold and removed."*

Letters of
Richard Major
of Hursley.

The towers and walls were raised to the ground and the Castle as a fortified place completely destroyed, the site however was still owned by Sir William Waller. Seven years later the City Council decided to purchase the site little thinking that within twenty five more years the Council would sell it to the King for the token sum of Five Shillings on which to build a new House to be the equal of Versailles.

May 2 1658

City Coffer
Accounts.
H. N & Q.
VII. p. 61.

> *"Taken out of the Cofers to pay Sir William
> Waller for the purchase of the Castle with
> the appurtenances and other materials
> thereunto belonging, the sum of Two hundred
> and three score Pounds.*
>
> *Nicholas Purdue Maior, paid Mr Recorder
> for drawing the deeds and conveyance 3.
> Mr Champion City solicitor enrolling
> Sir W.Waller deeds £2. 6. 3."*

The Castle demolished and levelled Sir William Waller confessed in his "Recollections. Fourth fatherlike chastisement."

> *"It was just with God for the punishment*
> *of my giving way to the plunder of the*
> *Citty of Winchester (whereof I was a freeman*
> *and sworne to maintain and procure the*
> *good thereof as far as I could) to permit*
> *the demolition of my castle at Winchester."*

Sawyer
Cheriton
p. 147.

In 1682 The Corporation did indeed sell the Castle site to King Charles II for 5s/-

Bailey
A of W.
p. 155.

> *"The said castle as it stood defaced and*
> *mutilated with the walls stones and other*
> *loose materials belonging to it and like-*
> *wise the castle fence and ditch containing*
> *by estimation eight acres,*

> *To build on as his Majesty*
> *should think fit."*

Wren Soc'
Papers.
VII. p. 11.

In 1683 to further clear the whole site of the old castle of its walls and buildings the County agreed to the demolition of the great Hall, because of its proximity to the new King's House, on condition that they would be provided with a new hall.

From the layout of the original plans His Majesty's Surveyor, Sir Christopher Wren would have certainly considered the clearance of the Hall to be an absolute necessity to the completion of his grand scheme for the House. But when King Charles II died the next year, and further work on the House abandoned, the Castle Hall was saved from demolition by default of an alternative ever being built.

C. S. P.
Dom 1683.
p. 84.

WILLIAM SCHELLINK'S VIEW OF WINCHESTER 1662

The original etching by William Schellink is in the Ostereichish National Bibliothek Vienna and published in Vol. XXXV of the Walpole Society Papers.
(Copy in Southampton University Library)

Chapter 24

PARLIAMENT ORDERS THE
CATHEDRAL TO BE
PULLED DOWN AND OTHER TROUBLES

THE City so long afflicted by the malice of man and the destructiveness of Civil War now feared the return of the plague, then still endemic. Whether it was for the defence of the City or prevention of disease the self interest of some citizens again came to the fore. In 1643 it was

Trussel.
See
p. 95
above.

*"some not well advised who privatt
profytt before publick good ever
prefferr"*

In 1652 the same comment but under different circumstances is made,

Bailey.
A of W.
p. 111.

*"Where as diverce psons, Inhabitants
of ye City of Winchester tendering and
preferring their owne private ease more
than ye publique good and well being of
the sayd City have refused to pay and
contribute to a skavenger for the
cleaning and desent keeping cleane of
the streets there have beene and continued
very noysome, with putrified dirt, dung
and filth, very undesent and unbeseeming
a place of eminensy or of good government."*

Another trouble was the need to reorganise the old parish structure into two new parishes following the destruction and decay of so many of the old mediaeval churches and houses.

October 29 1652
By the COMMISSIONERS FOR PLUNDERED MINISTERS

> *"Upon consideracion had of the Petition*
> *of the Mayor, Bayliffs, and Commonalty*
> *of the Citty of Winchester, in the County*
> *of Southampton, thereby alledging that*
> *there are within the said Citty the several*
> *parish churches of Clements, Thomas*
> *Swithins Kingsgate, Lawrence, Calender,*
> *Maurice & Peteers Colbrooke, divers or*
> *most of which Churches are very ruinous*
> *and fallen much into decay, and that the*
> *same have stood void and destitute of*
> *Ministers for divers years now past;*
>
> *And the sayd parishes are soe small that*
> *they may be fifty be reduced into two*
> *parishes; It is therefore ordered that*
> *the parish Churches of Calender, Maurice,*
> *& Peteer's Colebrook aforesaid be united,*
> *and that the parishioners and Inhabitants*
> *of the said severall parishes doe resort*
> *unto the said Church of Maurice for*
> *publique Worship, and that the severall*
> *other parishes of Clement, Thomas, Lawrence,*
> *and Swithins Kingsgate be also united,*
> *and that the respective parishioners and*
> *inhabitants thereof doe resort unto the*
> *Parish Church of Thomas aforesaid for*
> *publique Wirship.*
>
> *And that the two Ministers placed in*
> *the said Citty by authority of Parliament*
> *doe officiate and preach the Gospell to*
> *the Inhabitants of the said Citty in the*
> *aforesaid Churches of Thomas & Maurice,*

unless good causes shalbe shewen to the
contrary before this Committee on the
second day of December next, whereof
notice is to be given to the Inhabitants
of the sayd respective parishes in the
publique places of meeting in the sayd
City. And it is further ordered that the
Mayor and Commonalty of the sayd Citty
doe make enquiry what goods chattels,
and materials, are belonging to the
sayd several parish churches, and make
retorne thereof to this committee by
the said day.   Jon DOVE
John BARKER
Ja NELTHORPE."

The two Ministers, who were living in the security of the Close, were Humphrey Ellis and Leonard Cooke.

The document was endorsed on the margin in a contemporary hand,

"What, the Black Saints on earthe
unsainted those glorious Saints
in heaven."

On the 9th December the commissioners, after repeating the above preamble, further reported and confirmed an order to divide the City into but two parishes those of Thomas and Maurice.

Gents Mag.
p. 118.

"noe cause hath beene as yett shewen
to the contrary, although it appeareth
that the sayd Order was duly published
in the said Citty;"

*"It is therefore Ordered that the sayd
former order as to the Union be confirmed,
and that the sayd Churches be united
according to the purport and tenure thereof,
and that the aforesayd Ministers doe
officiate and preach the gospell diligently
to the Inhabitants of the sayd Citty within
the sayd Churches of Maurice and Thomas,
and receive and enjoy tithes, rents, duties,
and profitts whatsoever of or belonging to
the sayd respective churches til further
Order shalbe taken in the premisses, and
all person and persons are required to give
all due obedience hereunto accordingly. And
it is furthered Ordered that the Mayor and
Aldermen of the said Citty doe secure the
goods, chattels and materialls of or
belonging to the sayd severall Churches
till further Ordered therein, and to be
disposed according as they shall receive
furthe direction.*

Tho. LISTER
Gilb. MILLINGTON
Jo. GOODWYN
Will. HAY."

Gents Mag.
p. 118.

A new peril arose in 1653. One which united the whole City who rose in defence of their Cathedral threatened with demolition by Parliament. They had seen their homes pillaged, their livelihood disrupted and their churches ransacked and ruined. They had faced shot, fire and disease. They had witnessed the destruction of their Castle. The threat to the Cathedral was real and ominous and not to be suffered by any one whatever their religion or politics, Royalist or Puritan.

The threat arose from a Parliamentary Committee set up in 1651, to consider the fate of the Cathedral Churches. Which should be suffered to stand and what to be taken down. They advised Parliament

B. A. Assoc.
1845
p. 109.

See p. 236
below.

> *"That all Cathedral Churches where there*
> *are other churches or chapels sufficient*
> *for the people to meet in for the worship*
> *of God be surveyed, pulled down and sold*
> *and be employed for a stock for the use*
> *of the poor."*

On the list of Cathedral Churches to be demolished was

> *"Trinity Church neare Winton-*
> *Like to be expensive."*

Demolition that year, 1653, had already started in Lincoln, fortunately stayed. And Peterborough was only saved by the inhabitants agreeing to bear the cost of the services.

By good fortune, on the Parliamentary Committee called to consider Winchester was Alderman Hussie, a good friend of Trinity Church. He was a scholar of The College, sat as one of the Commissioners of enquiry on the College, and was a Deputy Lieutenant of the County.

Thomas Hussey was the chairman of the committee which had to deal with Winchester Cathedral. By adjourning the proceedings he was able to warn his friends in Winchester of Parliament's proposals and so "quickened" the Mayor and Commonalty to make a resolution to save the Cathedral and to prepare a Petition against it being pulled down.

PETITION AGAINST PULLING DOWN THE CHURCH

*"The Humble petition of the
inhabitants of the countie of Southton
and of the City and suburbs of Winchester.*

*Sheweth that whereas frequent reports
have of late come often to our ears
concerninge the destroyinge and pullinge
downe of Trinitye Church theare scituate
an auntient and most beautiful structure,
the most convenient and spacious place of
assemblinge for the hearinge of Gods word
whear many thousands of Soules may be served
and satisfied (if you continue able and
faithful Ministers amongst us) with the same
spiritual provision, and there beinge noe
other place in the Citty can contain a
third part of the number.*
  *We therefore out of our zeal for the
propogation of the Gospel and not out of
any superstitious conceite of holiness
in the walls do humbly desire That goodly
Fabrick maye continue and be preseved as
a place of worship of the onlie true God,
and not made a heape of stones and rubbish,
like that which is commonly called the
Temple of Dagon neare adjoining to it;*
  *Thus we shall looke on you as second
Founders and livinge pillers of it (to
support being as glorious a thinge as to
erect) and in that and in all other places
you shall have the fervent prayers of your
humble petitioners.*

> *Cornelius HOOKER
> Recorder Winton."*

The purport of this petition being there was no other place in which the inhabitants of the Town, Suburbs and County could assemble for Public Worship on such occasions as Assizes. No mention was made of the two Saintless churches Maurice and Thomas or that the City had been divided into just two parishes.

So in this strange way the sacrifice of all the other churches proved to be the saving of the Cathedral.

Two notes on the Petition itself; Cornelius Hooker had been appointed Recorder of the City in 1652. Secondly the Temple of Dagon was probably the ruins of the Carnary, part of which still survives near the south west corner of the Cathedral by the Slype.

As if to stress the importance of Trinity Church with its ring of bells.

"Dec 23 1653.

*Taken out of the cofers and paide
the ringers for ringing ye bells ye
day his Highness the Lord Protector
was proclaimed. XXs."*

No order was made by Parliament, but word must have reached the City by the following Spring of the threat being withdrawn as a subscription list was opened in May for repair of Trinity Church headed by many prominent Parliamentarians.

"May 20 1654.

   Itt being generally knowne that
Trinity Church neere Winton though
it be a very emenent and useful place
for preaching and hearing God's word
yet it doth dayly decay for want of
Reparations.
   We whose names are subscribed to
prevent the mischief that may happen
by delay doe willingly contribute by
way of advance mony for the presentt
towards the reparation of the said
Church such summers as are subscribed
and hereinunder mencioned to our
several names."

Sir Thomas Jervoyce Kt	03	00	00
Robert Wallop Esq	05	00	00
Nich Love Esq	04	00	00
Thos Botteswood Esq	05	00	00
Richard Cobbe Esq	04	00	00
Tho Clerke Esq	02	00	00
John Hook Esq	03	00	00
John Not Esq	03	00	00
Doctor John Harris	05	00	00
Mr Richard Brexton	01	00	00
Mr William Bett	00	10	00
Mr Edmund Riggs	01	00	00

The list is endorsed by John Chase
     Trinity Church
       Cathedrall
         repairs la.
   before ye returne of ye Church which
I had of Maior Betsworth."

By 1658, the wind of change was in the air, Oliver Cromwell the Lord Protector died and when his son Richard was proclaimed, in September only 10s/- was spent on ringing Trinity Church bells to proclaim him, and the small sum of 14s/3 on an Address. Richard Cromwell resigned five months later.

On the 12th May 1660 Charles was proclaimed King in the City, who, Royalist as ever, were happy to spend over twenty five times the amount they had expended on "Tumble Down Dick of Hursley".

"18 May 1660
Taken out of the cofers and paid
for several expenses at the proclayming
our Soveraign Lord The King ye 12th of
this instant as appears by Bill the sum
of £34 2 6."

KING CHARLES PROCLAIMED MAY 1660.

"At Winchester the Maior and Aldermen in
their scarlet gowns met at the Market-Cross
and went down to the Cathedral, where they
heard a very loyal and eloquent sermon
from Mr Complin minister of Avington, near
Winchester.
Marching thence into the High Street, the
Mayor, with the rest of the Corporation
ascended a scafflod covered with red cloth
and then solemnly proclaimed King Charles.
The which ended the musquetteers gave a
gallant volley; then silence being commanded,
the remaining part of the Cathedral singing-
men, whereof Mr Burt a gentlemen of eighty
years of age was one with the Master of the
Choristers and other musical gentlemen sung
a solemn anthem in a room built on purpose
some what above the mayors scafflod, the words
O Lord, make thy servant Charles our gracious
King to rejoice in thy strength, Etc."

On the 8th August 1660 the Office of Dean and Chapter were restored. Dean Young had died at his home at Upper Wallop in 1654, and in his stead was appointed Alexander Hyde, a scholar of Winchester College and a cousin of Edward Hyde Lord Clarendon, was installed.

The Church of the Holy Trinity now happily restored to the dignity of a Cathedral was soon to see again its Plate. The silver was quietly returned, no questions to be asked.

The first Bishop to be appointed after the Restoration was Brian Duppa, formerly Bishop of Salisbury, who was translated to Winchester on the 24th September 1660. It was Bishop Duppa who restored the Bronzes of the Cathedral's Royal patrons King James I and Charles I.

Silver and bronze both saved by friendly hands from the smelters pot.

It is therefore not inappropriate to quote the Duke of Albermarle's letter and to requote Bishop Duppa's on these two subjects.

From the Duke of Albermarle about the Plate.

> *"Being informed that Mr John Dalsh*
> *is troubled by some belonging to the*
> *Cathedral Church of Winchester about*
> *some plate which he was ordered by a*
> *Committee to take away from thence,*
> *I desire that he restoaring all the*
> *plate in his custody belonging to the*
> *said church, you will not let him bee*
> *further troubled about it seeing what*
> *he did was by order, and shall take*
> *it as a favor to*
> > *Yr very loving friend*
> > *ALBERMARLE."*

Alas all robbed in 1791.

THE 15th C. MARKET CROSS

(Winchester City Library's collection of Prints)

Bishop Brian Duppa's letter about the Bronzes.

"Mr Deane and ye rest of yo'r Chapter.
This gent Mr Benjamin Newland of
the Isle of Wight gave me notice yt in
the times of ye late distraction
(wherein the Churches themselves could
not escape plunder).
Two noble Statues in Brass of his now
Majesties Royal Father and Grandfather
were brought to Portsmouth to be sold
by some persons, from whose sacrilegious
hands he bought them with his own money
to preserve them for such a hoped and
happy Restoration.
He kept them at first (as he saith)
underground and afterwards very privately
and brought them now unto me: for which I
paid him £100 out of my own purse; which
I think well bestowed for ye recovery of
those Royal monuments, and shall send
them unto you as a small Testimony of the
honor I owe unto the blessed memory of
their sacred Majesties and the good
affection I bear unto your Church of
Winchester where they were first erected
in the West End of the Quire.
I look upon the gent, as one who for
his reall affection (generaly reported)
unto the Church, justly intitled unto a
favor from the Church, and therefore do
recommend him (upon any occassion which
may be presented to you) unto a kindness
to be shewn unto him, being he might have
made (as I am informed) a much greater
advantage, if he would have sold them
heretofore unto Aliens. So leaving him
unto yo'r favourable consideration, I
commend you to the Grace of the Almighty.
Your very affectionate friend
18 Dec 1660   BR WINTON."

The restorer of the Cathedral plate Albermarle was George Monk, the army commander Knighted and created Duke of Albermarle in 1660 by King Charles, for his resolution in marching the army from the Scottish border, on London and in Parliament demanding the issue of writs for a new Parliament. Only three days after the New Parliament met on the 28th April 1660, it resolved "That the Constitution of England lay in King, Lords and Commons." The motion was passed without dissent.

An important Winchester notability, who helped in the Restoration was Sir John Clobery (at least his monument claims a more prominent part than history assigns him). He settled in Winchester after the Restoration, built Clobery House in Parchment Street, and became Member of Parliament for the City. When he died in 1687 a most elaborate monument to him was erected in the Cathedral Retro Choir, the first monument to be erected since the reign of Queen Elizabeth.

The monument depicts Sir John standing, life size, having a very fine and robust martial figure.

Unfortunately the achievement of military accoutrments and emblems over the pediment has disappeared. His epitaph in latin, and using Canon John Vaughan's translation, tells in diplomatic language how he schemed with General Monk the army's part in bringing about the Restoration.

John Clobery was Knighted at the Restoration on June the 7th and granted the very handsome annual pension of £600. When a few years later an order for the suspension of certain pensions was issued, it was expressly stated that "it was not the King's intention to include that of Sir John Clobery in the order, his being for extraordinary services." His part in the Restoration could not have been insignificant, and his flamboyant monument could leave no one in doubt in Royalist Winchester that Sir John was their hero who brought back the King.

Epitaph to Sir John Clobery.

"Sacred to the memory of
Sir John Clobery, Knight.
A man pre-eminent in every path of life,
He was not only versed in the theory of war,
But translated theory into practice with the happiest of
results
Becoming the prop both of his falling country
And of the House of Stuart.
Coming to London, He and General Monk
Gave effect to the policy which they had first
Discussed in Scotland,
With the result that
Amid the applause of the Nation,
They restored peace to England, and Charles to his throne.
Admidst the din of war and politics
He gave earnest attention to literature,
(A rare example among soldiers)
His unique talents bearing the polish of such learning
That you would have deemed
He had spent his life in a University rather than a camp.
When at length disease enfeebled his powers
He withdrew himself from the care of this life,
That he might the better prepare for Heaven,
In obedience to a principle
Which guided him through life.
He died in the year of our Lord, 1687,
Aged 63.
His widow caused this monument to be erected
As the last proof of her affection."

Sir John Clobery was one of the three officers of his army chosen by Monk to go to London and treat with the Committee of Safety.

With the restoration of the Bishop and the Dean and Chapter came a political agitation by the pro royalists to restore the Old Corporation. Each side whether for King or Parliament issuing their charges and counter charges.

Late in 1660 a "Friend to Winchester" published a tract telling of the affairs of the City while the Parliamentary party held sway.

The tract as printed here has been taken from the proceedings of the British Archaelogical Association of 1845 who held their annual congress in Winchester that year.

The tract is very repetitous and rather tedious, but is worth pursuing because of quite a good account of the state of the churches in the City after the war.

> *"A Vindication of the City of Winchester*
> *against Mis-Representations and Aspersions*
> *cast upon them in a late Printed Paper. By*
> *way of Petition and Articles directed to*
> *the Right Honourable the House of Peers, in*
> *The Business of the Churches of the City.*
> *Seriously commended to be throughly read*
> *and perused by all to whom the said Printed*
> *Paper hath or shall come.*
> *London: printed in the year 1660.*
>
> *It cannot but be esteemed by all in whom*
> *there is the least spark of religion and*
> *honesty, a work very acceptable and Christian,*
> *to heal breaches and reconcile differences*
> *between friends, neighbours and fellow*
> *citizens, that are members of the same*
> *corporation: to say to them (as Abraham to*
> *Lot): 'let there be no strife betwen you for*
> *you are brethren.'*
> *A great difference hath lately broken forth,*
> *and is at present in way of violent*
> *prosecution between the inhabitants and*
> *citizens of the city of Winchester, to the*
> *distracting of the affairs of that city, and*
> *unless stop be put thereto, to the mutual ruin*
> *of one another, though formerly intimate*
> *friendship between divers of those who are now*
> *thus divided; and they still like to continue*
> *neighbours to one another.*

This observed to me an unconcerned person in this difference, a lover of the city,- a friend to both parties, who desires their peace, and laments their differences, and who thoroughly understands the principal matter of controversy between them.

I have thought it necessary thus to proceed in publishing this paper to prevent the mistakes of the one party, who are now prosecutors, and the prejudice of the others that are prosecuted: and as to the things herein respected to show a way of reconciliation between them.

Of the contest the notice I have had, hath been a few days since, by a printed paper, containing a petition in the names of sundry who style themselves therein, Members of the Old Corporation of the City of Winchester, directed to the Right Honourable the House of Lords now in Parliament assembed, and intended against others, who now, and several years past, have not only been members of the same corporation, but also borne the chiefest offices in it: to this petition a paper of articles annexed, as the grounds of prosecution: this paper dipersed into sundry hands, I came to have sight of it; and though I have it not now by me, yet having several times read the same, do so well retain the substance of it as to be able to speak something to many particulars in it.

The petition referring to the annexed articles, I therein find only two, properly and formally drawn up as such; and of these the first containing nothing criminal: but intended as introductory to the second.

The second article containing two things:-

*1st A charge relating to the modellizing
(as it is herein styled) of the government
of that corporation by a pretended act of
the rump parliament; but whereto and to the
several things therein, viz. What they
allege to be the ground of procuring the
act; the persons whom they charge to be the
procurors of it, the effect of it, as of
uniting the members of the old corporation
(as they say in the body of the petition)
and modelling themselves (the defendants) to
be a corporation, as I question not but they
will upon any indifferent hearing appear to
be very great mistakes, so I shall pass them
wholly by, and refer them to that
determination, which, in such hearing, they
may receive, unless as I heartily wish, it
may be prevented by some reconciliation
amongst themselves.*

*2nd But the second thing in that article
is concerning the means they suggested to
have been used for obtaining that pretended
act, which are what hath been done by the
said corporation of the city, relating to
seven churches which they particularly
mention, viz. the churches of St Peter's in
Mercellis, (which I should think should have
been Maccelis): Of Kalender, of St Clement,
St Lawrence, St Thomas, St Swithin, and St
Peter's in Colebrook-street, towards which
the accused are represented to have acted
most horridly, in demolishing, defacing,
altering, and changing, digging up the bones
of the dead, and with several other ways, as
in the said allegations appeareth: and all
to render them persons odious and
sacrilegious to those to whom they are
accused, and whereto, as things best known
by me, I shall indifferently and impartially
speak, for the vindication of the accused,
and undeceiving of the abused, by partial
and untrue representation.*

*1st. Setting down the state of those
churches wherein that now accused as a new
modellizing corporation found them.
2nd. What was the ground of their
charge about them?
3rd. What is it that they have done?
And 4th. a word in conclusion to the
prosecuting party.*

*For the first, in what state the
corporation found the several mentioned
churches of the city.*

*1st For that called St PETER's in MACELLIS,
it hath not been for these hundred years past
reckoned among the churches of that city;
but for that (and I suppose for longer time)
been a very ruinous heap of rubbish; in our
time no more of it to be seen, but pieces of
ruined walls, the like of its steeple, such
as may in some places be seen of the walls
of destroyed abbeys; and hath known to be no
other than a dunghill, a place of all manner
of excrements, and a loathsome, noisome
nuisance, to the parts of the city adjoining
it.*

*2nd For that of KALENDS church, where the
bishop is said formerly to have performed
the ceremonies of his instalment, the more
to be wondered, so little regard should be
shewn unto it; the standing of it being in
the high street and principal place of the
whole city; yet this is not known in the
memory of man to have been a church of any
religious divine service, or fit for that
use: in our times no sign of its belfry, no
roof or covering belonging to it, only a
ghastly sight of two ruinous walls, lying
open for butchers to empty therein the
bellies of their killed beasts, and persons
of all sorts to lay their excrements, that
it became little other than a jakes;*

*the very sight of it so offensive in such
place of the city, that a judge of assizes,
before the window of whose lodgings it
stands, is remembered some time to have
sharply reproved the city, for suffering the
place to stand as it did, Bells there could
be none for them to take away as is alleged;
but the truth thereof is that four bells
said to belong to the church were found in
the castle of that city, when taken by the
parliament's forces and with other goods
there and then so also found, were redeemed
by a sum of money, out of Cromwel's hands
then commander of those forces, by the
committee of the county-and so became
theirs, and were neither that parishes or
the cities longer: yet were by them restored
and given to the city, to be by them
disposed of, as they should think fit.*

*3rd For that of St CLEMENTS, a very
little church, and utterly incapable of
containing any considerable congregation,
yet to be remembered (though not for these
fourteen years past) religious service to be
performed in it; yet this was the church
which in the time of the war, by being made
a court of guard for soldiers, was miserably
ransacked and torn in pieces, rendered
useless as a church, a main part of it
uncovered; and afterwards by one of the old
corporation, and in their time made as I am
informed on good grounds, a place to lay
faggots in, yea to keep hogs in, wherein to
receive oxen, horses &., at times of fairs;
and most part of the parish burnt down in
the war.*

*4th For that of St LAWRENCE church, which with
one more, were in best repair of any in the city;
yet as the former, very small and incapable of
any considerable congregation; and upon an
occasional survey made thereof with other
churches was judged as well as to need
reparation, so for some reasons to be unsafe, and
meeting therein, to be dangerous, and the seats
of it miserably ransacked and torn.*

*5th for that of St THOMAS, one of the most
capacious churches in the city, and wherein as
formerly, so a dozen years since, in time of the
old corporation, were meetings for religious
worship, yet so ruinous then, that the
congregation was necessitated to remove its
meetings thence; and afterwards, so exceedingly
more decaying, as likely wholly especially, the
east end thereof, by the ruine of its principal
arch that supported it, to fall to the ground,
and not without exceeding much charge to be kept
up or repaired.*

*6th For that of St SWITHIN, how ruinous it was,
and for the quality of it and place of its
standing, how unfit for a congregation of the
city to meet in, is well known to all that that
know anything of the state of it: but to dispatch
at once all that concerns this church, which the
corporation are charged to have let to one Robert
Allen, his wife delivered of children at one end
thereof, and a hogsty made of the other: how
little they are concerned therein if it be so
used, let all by this judge: that in the time of
Oliver's usurped protectorship, Mr Nich. Love,
procuring an order for union of some churches and
parishes without the city, got this (as if not a
church belonging to the city) to be united into
that of St Michael's, in Kingsgate-street; and
then challenging right to dispose of it, granted
thereof a lease of years to the said Robert
Allen, which I know to be true, having seen the
lease of it.*

*7th and lastly, for that of St PETER's, in
Colebroke-street, as some of the former, an
inconsiderable little place, no use of it
for above these fourteen years, extreamly
untiled, the covering almost gone;grass,
nettles, weeds, growing in the body of it.*

*Thus is the true state of these churches
mentioned by the petitioners, as found by
that-called new corporation of that city;
and wherein it may be observed, that had it
not been for the cathedral church and
MAURICE church (one other church of the city
not mentioned by the petitioners), that city
had not had one church besides capable or
fit for a congregation to meet in, and
wherein is sore to be lamented the state of
that city, so to suffer their churches to be
so horribly abused, so as to ruine and
decay, that either through poverty could
not, or through wretchedness would not do
anything for reparation of them: and this in
the time of the old corporation, for four
years after the war was ended, soley
holding the government of it.*

*Second. To show upon what grounds the now
accused corporation engaged in what the did
about these churches,
Thus it was in the year 1653, the Rump
parliament sitting, a committee of them was
appointed to consider of cathedral churches;
what of them should be suffered to stand,
and what to be taken down.The votes of this
committee passed concerning divers of these
churches; and at length the cathedral church
of Winchester came under their debate, which
Mr Hussie, of Hampshire, a friend to that
city, and then chairman in that committee,
perceiving, to prevent the passing of a vote
upon it, and to have time to aquaint the city
with it, procured the adjournment of that
committee:*

*the information hereof coming to
the city, at once frighted them with
apprehension of the loss of the cathedral,
and quickened them to consider the state of
their other churches, and brought them to a
resolution to use all means for the
preservation of the cathedral, yet so to
endeavour the reparation of other churches,
that should their endeavours for the
cathedral church fail, they might yet have
places for the city congregations, as also
for the countrey at times of assizes and
other occasions.*

*In this debate, of reparation of other
churches, they determined of the necessity
of two at the least, and these two to be
that of St Thomas and Maurice, for the
conveniency of them, when repaired, as
churches, their capacity to receive
congregations.*

*And as the repairing of all the churches
was to the city, in the present state of it,
impossible, so these two would be
sufficient, as able to receive the city
assemblies, and for the work of their two
ministers, which they then had, and, for
aught they could then see, never likely to
have more; and those so scituate that the
other ruined churches with their parishes
might be to these united, and so the city
equally divided between two such churches.*

*But then they met with another
difficulty: how they should be able to
repair that church of St Thomas. Willing to
contribute towards it they were, but, upon
too just grounds, feared that they should
(as they did) meet with backwardness in
others; rather let all their churches be
ruined, and only talk and complain of it,
than be at the charge of repairing one:
besides they saw the charge would be so
vastly great, that that small and
improverished parish could not possibly bear:*

-237-

they saw a necessity of making use of
materials in other ruined churches to repair
this; that all such would not be sufficient
thereto, without rates on the people; or
with rates on the parish without them; nor
indeed both together, unless in that of
rates there be a junction of other parishes.
But by what authority can they lay such
rates, or use the materials of other
churches? Here they conclude it necessary
of procuring an order for union of parishes,
which would enable them to both, was
necessary, and would be useful to the city
many waies.

Upon this conclusion and the grounds
mentioned, they at once provide two
petitions, one for keeping up their
cathedral, to the committee before whom the
affair of it was pending; the second, for
union of parishes, to the committee styled
for plundered ministers, who exercised such
a power.

This latter petition is granted, but so
that they first appoint an order to be
published in several churches to signify to
the city and all the inhabitants of such
petition for union of parishes presented:
and mentioning a day wherein should be
granted, unless cause could then be shown to
the contrary, which any one that would or
could might then do: and also appointed some
discreet and trusty persons of the city, to
return them a survey of the state of several
churches, whereby they might see whether
they were so ruinous as the petitioners
suggested: all which was done accordingly:
the order read openly by both the ministers
in the several churches wherein they
preached: the survey made both returned
together: and when the day appointed no one
appeared to show cause to the contrary:

the order for union was granted, the consent of the city being premised: and this not in secret, clandestine, but an honest and open way, by concent of corporation and city, and upon such necessary grounds forementioned, is that order for uniting of parishes obtained: and what is now afterwards done upon the several churches will be found to be on these grounds, to these ends, and in pursuance and by authority of this order.

Thirdly Let us now see what this accused corporation have done about these churches severally.

1st Unto the church of St THOMAS, by the aforementioned order for union, were joined the parish of St CLEMENT'S (so burned and ruined in the war, as has been mentioned), with that also of St LAWRENCE.

Some moveable material of these other churches united thereto, (viz.) the three bells and saints' bell of St Clements, with two bells in the steeple of the same St Thomas church, (taken down because the stepple was small and weak, unable to bear more than one bell left in it, and to new build that steeple would too much augment the charge in reparation), were sold towards the re-edifying of it, and the money disposed into the churchwarden's hands, with the consent of the parish, (by which all is now done), to which they are to be accountable; to this are joined the money made of the bells of Kalender church, sold several years before, by order of an assembly of the city whereto they had been given; and two brass statues of King James and King Charles, standing in the cathedral church, much burnt and damaged, and if

*continuing to stand likely to be wholly
spoiled by souldiers, taken down by the then
mayor, in order to their preservation, but
sold by Mr Edmund Biggs, and for ought that
I could ever hear, by his single act; the
money of them recovered is joined to the
rest for the same use: but from St Lawrence
church no more is taken but a few boards of
ruinous seats towards this work.*

*The charge in repairing this church comes
to eight score pounds, not one half thereof
raised by these, sold materials, (so small
and inconsiderable were the several bells
before-mentioned): the rest raised by the
rate on the parish, and voluntary
contributions of divers who are now accused,
and in this very vaste summe, considering
the smallness of these parishes, though now
united into one, and the great poverty of
them.*

*In the reparation of this church, it is
almost wholly new tiled or covered, a pillar
and arch new built, the ruinous seats in it
taken up, to the great loss of the parish
(and grievously to be complained of by the
petitioners), whose church is now wholly new
seated in in a most convenient, decent and
uniform way; the tomb stones over the dead
are also taken up, (but much to be lamented
by the petitioners as it is), presently put
into their place again, and their taking up
was but that they might be fitly placed with
the pavement of the church, which is now new
paved throughout from end to end: and so it
is with much trouble and great charge made a
neat, decent, handsome church: of a parish
church there, I think I may truly say, never
seen the like in that city.*

2. The church of St MAURICE hath, by order of union the parishes of KALENDER and St PETER Colebrooke united to it: the three bells of the latter are, by the consent of the parish, disposed to the churchwardens; one of them joined to four others in this church before, makes a convenient ring: the other two are sold, the churchwardens accountable for them to the parish: somewhat is also here done by way of repair, and this church made a neat, convenient, handsome church.

3. For St PETER Mercellis, reade before the state of it, and let reason judge what the work was to remove such a public nuisance, by freely giving the stone to the inhabitants for their use, (as I hear they did, altho' in the petition the contrary be suggested), and disposing the ground to one of the petitioners to be made a garden, herein well rewarding the favour shewn him, complaining against what himself desired, and is a benefit to him.

4. For KALENDER church reade the state of it before: the ground thereof is disposed for lawful civil uses, for houses and shops to be built thereon: and hereby a filthy nuisance removed from the heart and face of the city; wherein what hurt is done?

5. For the church of St LAWRENCE, reade also of it the state before: whom as hath been said, only a few ruinous seats removed, for seating the church to which it is united: it is now made a school wherein are taught the children of the city, whose coming up and down it may be spurns up some old pavements, But at what small games do such play, who make this matter of complaint in a petition to the House of Lords?

*7. Lastly, the very selfsame with this, is
the case of the church called St PETER's in
Colebrooke Street, united to St Maurice
church, and the state of it reade before
described.*

*Fourthly Let me speak a little to the
gentlemen, my friends and acquaintance,
petitioners in this business:*
*I hope it is a zeal and love to churches
hath made you complain, and not anything of
malice or envy to one another; but let be
considered what matter of controversie you
have with those you accuse, and what cause
of offence against them in all this.*
*In this business of churches, it can only
be about two of them, and their union to
other churches, their being leased to civil
uses their materials disposed to reparation
of them: in what is done about St Peter's in
Mercellis and Calender, what matter of
controversie, they being but ruinous heaps
and filthy nuisances?*
*What of St Swithun, if abused, yet disposed
by other hands, they unconcerned?*
*What of St Lawrence, a school house, and
herein its use not wholly heterogenial or
ecclesiastical?*
*What of St Thomas, at such trouble and
charge repaired?*
*It remains but St Clement's and St Peter's
Colebrooke, about which any matter of
offence and controversie. Is it the union
of these to other churches offends you.
Consider, is union of parishes in your city
strange to you, where having made such a
multitude of churches formerly, as your city
hath decayed, have been united into one
another?*

*I have seen an order of the whole assembly
of your city, now an hundred years old,
determining of four parishes to be only in
your city, viz., of St Thomas, St Lawrence,
Calender, and St Maurice, all other parishes
to them united: your city to be equally
divided between them: no mention made of
your St Clements and St Peter's in
Colebrook, to these united so long since:
you know that of Calender to be fallen to
the ground since, your city much decayed
since, especially bu the late warre so much
of it burned and demolished, and therefore
likely to as fitly reduced into two parishes
now as sufficient for it, as then for four:
but if at this offended, why was your
offence seasonably discovered, when by the
orders published in your churches, you were
required to do so, if you had cause?*

*Why were you silent then, and thereby give
cause of being concluded as consenting? How
unreasonable so many years after to
complain.*

*Are you offended at their being let to
civil uses?*

*Consider, have not divers if not most of
you, the petitioners, consented to it in your
city assemblies, by whose act was it done,
as will, I suppose, be made to appear by
your city books; and then 'quis tulerit
gracchos, etc.?' Who art thou that judges
another and therein condemnest thyself?*

*And is this a strange thing to you? Have
not divers decayed and useless churches so
disposed of in your city, and some of your
petitioners herein concerned? Cannot you see
among you any such old church now a stable
or wharehouse?*

*And who did this? In whose time was it
done?*

When St Clements church was made a
hogstye, in the time of you, the old
corporation, and by one of your members,
that in Colebrook Street in little better
case, where was you complaining, your
pretended zeal for churches?

Why as any of you were parishioners to
them did you not appear for repairing them?

The truth is, you of the old corporation
have let churches become nuisances, and fall
to ruin, and brought those so who succeed,
and are now accused, into great necessities
and use of extraordinary waies to redress
those evils about them, and now you
complain: which is not as if you should be
offended that your churches lie not as
nuisances still. and wholly fallen to the
ground, and that the accused should use any
means (being forced to extraordinary) to
preserve them.

Do you not seem to cloak much of malice
under pretence of zeal for churches?

State the case rightly, and will not this
be the language of the two parties?

They of the new corporation, as you call
them, 'We'll sell useless bells, and
raise money out of our purses to repair St
Thomas Church:'

You of the pretended old, 'No, we'll do
neither, let it wholly fall to the ground,
as it is like to do.'

They 'We'll let St Clements and
Colebrook, to civil uses, that they lie not
as nuisances, but be heled and covered, kept
up to revert to religious use again, as
there may be cause, with satisfaction to the
cost of those to whom they are let, about
them: and this is the only way to keep them
up by:'

But you 'No, let them lie nuisances
still, be utterly ruined.'

This is I am sure is the language of the
actions of both parties.

Friends, I shall assert, had not these you
accuse, done what they did herein, you had
not had one of your parish churches this day
either standing or in capacity for a
congregation to meet in, unless perhaps that
of St Maurice: and I again challenge all of
you, to shew another or better way than they
took, to do what they herein did:
considering the time wherein they did it;
the poverty and necessities of your city and
general ruin fallen upon even all your
churches, principally thro' your neglect.

Do not the accuse and publickly defame men
in print to the world, for what wherein they
have well deserved, but by you, to say the
least, very partially represented.

But they have digged up and thrown about
the street the bones of the dead; a very
great crime if true; but you must prove it;
it is on very good grounds and with much
confidence denied: but suppose you prove it,
where is the fault? In those you accuse?

Look at the leases, see them foreseeing
such an evil, and by expresse condition
therein requireing that no such thing should
be, and providing against it.

I yet advise you to correct one great
mistake in your paper, which done most of
your charge therein is answered, or the
odium of it removed: you twice assert all
this done about the churches to be to obtain
the government of your city in the act you
style for new modellizing it, and to defray
the expences thereof: but how can this be?

That act was obtained in 1649, those
things about the churches done not till four
years after, in 1653 and 1654, and can this
latter then be done for obtaining the
former?

Many other reasons are unanswerably against it: methinks some of you should be parishioners in St Thomas parish, and by what you know of reparations there, and accounts for them have prevented this mistake, and not leave ourselves under suspicions of herein sinning against knowledge.

Gentlemen, I have sometimes mentioned you with distinction of old and new corporations; not that I acknowledge any such thing, but to accomodate myself to your language, not questioning but you may ere long see that distinction by you raised, to be groundless; that is all but one and the same corporation in uninterrupted succession.

What have I herein done to rectify your mistakes, and vindicate the accused, that they suffer not under partial representation, cannot be just cause of offence to any: but may be, if rightly understood and improved, a means to procure peace between you, which I heartily wish for your own comfort and good of your now distracted city."

———

"Quis tulerat Gracchos de seditione querentis"

Who shall endure the Gracchi complaining about sedition.
                    Juvenal.

EPILOGUE

As an epilogue - The Mayors petition to the King of the 15th November 1660 pleading poverty. The City were petitioning His majesty for a Charter to build a canal to Southampton and so encourage trade.

THE MAYORS PETITION TO HIS MAJESTY
15 November 1660

"We the Mayor Baylyffs, and Comonaltie
of the Cittie of Winchester doe certifie
that the sayd Citie, and as the Cronacle
informes us, built by King Rudhudebras,
and was the Royall Seate of the West Saxon
Kings, wherein Egbert and Elfred, two great
Monarchs, were crowned, ye Royal Nuptialls
of King Phillip and Queen Mary there
solemnized, and also divers King and Queens
interred in the Cathedral Church there; and
heretofore famous for riches and trade.
  But by reason of former and ye late Warrs
it is very much ympoverished (Being a
Garrison for the late King, of blessede
memory); and to expresse our affection to
His Majesty lent him a thousand pounds, and
voluntarily sent him to Oxford all our
plate, amounting to three hundred pounds
more; and for our Loyalty were several tymes
most extremely plundered by the Parliament
Party, and the Castle and divers Houses of
great value by them demolished; And att such
tyme as they had gotten the upper hand and
taken the sayd Citie, they forced from us
Fourteen hundred pounds more."

The old order changeth yielding place to new

And god fulfills himself in many ways

Lest one good custom should corrupt the world.

Tennyson.

An extract from

A RELATION OF A SHORT SURVEY

OF THE WESTERN COUNTIES

Made by a Lieutenant of the Military

Company in Norwich in 1635

Edited for the Royal Historical Society by

L.G. Wickham Legg, M.A., F.R.Hist.S.

CAMDEN MISCELLANY VOL. XVI LONDON 1936

Pages 43-51

WINCHESTER

p.43   *"And soe ouer the Downes, till I tumbled
downe a steepy Hill a whole mile to geather,
into that old and ancient City of
Winchester, which is of the same age with
her sister Canterbury, and which was founded
by the same British King, and there took up
my third Sundays rest at the (blank) in
their high, and principall Street there,
which runs from East to Westgate, where I
had as much adoe to obtaine quarter, as I
had in my travell: for this old City was
then crowding full, in respect of that
great, and long unsett, sitting Court was
then held there, where all the Chief of this
faire and goodly County were."*

The Lieutenant of the Norwich Militia was Nowell
Hammond. The continuation of his survey is written into the
general narrative of the events leading up to the Civil War here
in Winchester and may be followed through continuously by
reference back to the pages as indicated.

Hammond continues:-

"I found her scytuated in rich valley..."

See page 7.

44 *The government of this city is by a*
Mayor with his four maces... 7.

The City and her Suburbs doe equally
challenge their shares of her churches... 8."

After this introduction to the churches and the Cathedral
Hammond describes in detail the choir stalls.

44 *"And as above on the Roofe, so over the*
Deanes, Prebends and Quiristers Seats,
is rich Joyeners work; but more remarkable
artificiall, and rare Postures, ravishing
the eyes of the beholders, is a lively,
woody Representation, Portraicts, and
Images, from the Creation, to the Passion,
which though it tooke me some time to take,
yet I thought it nethelesse, not idlely,
ill spent time, for me to decipher the same,
as I found it, and heere to insert itt.
Of the Old Testament on one Side.
1. A representation of the Diety, in 3 Persons.
2. The Angells fall, and description of Hell.
3. The Manner of the Creation, and the Chaos.
4. The Creation of Man.
5. The Creation of Woman.
6. The Temptation, fall and Punishment.
7. The first Sacrifices of Cain and Abell.
45 *8. Cain killing his brother Abell.*
9. Noah warn'd by God to build an Arke.
10. The Arke is built, and the Creatures
preserv'd.
11. Noah is drunke, and his 3 sons describ'd.
12. God calls to Abraham to offer Isaac.
13. Hee goes with his Son, his 3 Servants, fyre,
and Isaac riding on an Asse.

Having described the ornamental panels that were over the choir stalls and later destroyed by waller's troopers, Hammond then describes the organs in the Cathedral.

46   *"The organs in this church are not
          exceeding faire, ..."*   see page   48

and continues in sequence to describe,

46-   *"Her monuments are many fayre and
48   ancient..."*   49-55

Hammond concludes his tour of the Cathedral with a visit to the vestry, and then leaves the Close by the Kings Gate, to visit the College, Wolvesey and St Cross.

49   *"From thence I walk'd out at the Kings
          Gate, on the south of this Cathedrall to
          the Colledge, founded by that worthy good
          Bishop, whom I so lately left sleeping in
          his neat Chappell in the church watch'd
          by three vigilant Schollers.*
50   *Heere I saw a spacious and lofty, neat
          Chappell, a grave Doctor, Warden of the
          Colledge, 12 Fellows, 70 Schollers and
          16 Quiristers, all in their Collegiate
          Surplice Habit at their devotions;
          reading and singing as solemnly as at the
          Cathedrall, and as fayre, and rich an Organ.
           After which ended, I went into their
          strong Freestone Library standing alone by
          it Selfe, in their green yard Cloyster,
          where I met with a curteous, free Gentleman
          one of the Fellowes, who gave me a very
          hearty welcome, both there att that same
          time, and afterwards att his own House.*

50   *From thence I march'd into the Pallace,*
adioying neere to the Colledge, the way,
way, and the City Wall onely, dividing
them, where I was showne many huge, and
spacious Roomes, viz't. The Hall, Great
Chamber, Galleries, Lodging Chambers,
Chappell and Towers, all as voyd of
Furniture as Entertainment.
Some cost extrardinary hath beene but
lately bestowed, about some Roomes
there, to make them for his Majesties
reception, whose comming thither was
lately expected.
  This place is sweetly, and
commodiously seated, by the River
which supplies every office, and Roome
of the House, which stands in need
thereof; And such benefitt doth the
Colledge also reap by this delicate
sweet Sreame.

  By the pleasant Banke whereof, let me
carry you butt one Mile from hence, and
there shall you see that famous Hospitall
founded by that Cardinall, we so lately
left, strongly infolded in Brasse; There
I found a Reverend Divine Master thereof,
who is also Master of a great Revenue
thereby, and these particular he by his
place is inioyn'd beside the dayly
maintenance of 10. old Men 4
dayes in a weeke, Sondayes, Tuesday,
Thursday, and Fryday. There is also 40.
poore Men, and Women, that are Weekly
maintayn'd throughout whole yeere
having a House without the great high
Towr'd Gate, on purpose for them:

And 6. times in a yeere there is a Dole
in bread given to 600. poore People,
every one of them a Loafe, every Dole
taking up a Quarter of wheat, at least;
The rest that comes those Dole dayes
(exceedng that number) passe not away
without an Almes, which is a halfe Penny
in Money;
And what Person or Stranger, of what
degree or quality soever, that shall
happen to come on those dayes, and times
to visit that stately Hospitall, must
also accept, and imbrace this most
charitable Mite of the Donors free Donation.

51   *Here is a fayre Square Court, with very*
handsome, and faire buildings in every Square,
and a Cathedral like Church, more like a
Colledge, then an Hospitall; and the River
giving ample benefitt and pleasure to this
stately Building; this place I found as
Curteous, and respective to Strangers as
the Colledge, where such Inhabitants resides,
as Knowes nothing more then that commendable
quality of Curtesie.
Returning to the City againe, I there found
at the west end of it, upon a high mounted
Hill, a strong and spacious Castle..."

Hammonds description of the castle is given on pages 9&10

"And now I am heere (although it bee a little
digressing and retarding of my Journey, yet)
I could not part from the Stately Hall until I
had both seene and heard the noble Proceedings
of soe high and honourable a Court as did then
sit there whish I could not omit without some
(cursory) Observation and notice off."

The arrival in the City of the Chief Justice of Eyre and his procession to the Great Hall of the castle is described by Hammond on pages 10 & 11

51   *"The Noble Earl of Holland Chief Justice in*
Eyre..."

"CAPTAIN BURLEY

His Speech at the

*Place of execution at Winchester, where
he was hang'd drawn, and quartered, for
endevouring to raise Forces to take away
the KING from the Isle of Wight.*

Feb. 7. 1647. Imprimatur. Gil. Mabbot.

*Printed at London by Robert Ibbitson in
Smithfield, neere the Queens-head Tavern.
1646.*

*Captain Burley being on the ladder ready to dye, he was
moved by a Minister and others to bee humbled, that the Lord
might have mercy upon him, and confesse his sinnes to God,
and particularly the Treason for which he was to dye: hee said,
he was a sinner, but no Traytor.*

*It was told him what a faire tryall he had had, and how
legally he was condemned; he answered that it was true, the
Gentlemen condemned on the Bench, the Ministers in the
Pulpit, and the Gentlemen of the County in their verdicts, but
as yet he was no Traytor.*

*He was told how bloody an act he agitated in seeking to
take away the King through blood: hee answered he was happy
to dye so, and prayed that his blood might be the last.*

*The foulnesse of the act was declared to him, but he
continued obstinate still. Afterwards hee prayed, concluding
with the Lords prayer. Then the hangman pulling his cap over
his eyes, Captaine Burley called upon God, Lord preserve my
soule, Lord Jesus receive my soule, and so was turned of, and
hunged, drawn and quartered."*

APPENDIX 1

JOHN CHASE'S LIST	Chase's Endorsements	HAMMOND'S LIST
List of church Ornaments 29th November 1633 In the chest where ye Seale lyeth		Notes made "in the vestry where I saw many rich Hangings and Cloths" 1635
A ritch Canopy embrored with perle to be carried over the King when his Ma'tie cometh to the Cathedrall church	Stollen by the troopers	A rich, and faire canopie of cloth of gold to carry over the King
A pall of cloth of gold upon dark purple velvett with a cross stripe of brghter gold upon crimson velvet.		One of velvet wrought with gold for the High Altar which was given by Bishop Fox
Another pall paned downwards, 3 of gold and 4 of crimson velvet with flowre de Luces and I.H.S. being the greek characters of Jesus.		others of cloth of Tissue
A narrower pall paned outhwart, 2 of crimson and gold, & 3 blew & gold, with a golden border of another work.		Another of cloth of gold fill'd with Pearle wire.
Another pall paned 6 of gold, 7 of dark blew velvet.		
A narrower of ye same stuff & number of panes.		
A narrow carpett paned 2 of gold, 3 of crimson velvet with Flowre de Luces and I.H.S. and a small border at both ends.	Stollen	
A carpet of 10 panes, fringed red on two edges.		
A small old carpet for ye readers.		

Chase heads his list "In the chest where ye Seale lyeth", this seal was found by the pillaging troopers as Mercurius Aulicus reported when he said "they take away the Common Seale of the church supposing it to be silver"

Four months later when the Chapter was next able to meet, and then at Barton (The Dean and Chapter's farm at St Cross) on the 17th April 1643, they agreed to have a new Seal to replace the one stolen and true to their loyalty to the King they ordered that the new seal should include the engraving of the King's Portrait.

JOHN CHASE'S LIST	Chase's Endorsements	HAMMOND'S LIST
Pulpitt Cloathes		
One of Crimson velve 6 gold with a pane in ye middle of blew 6 gold		
Another of silver tissue & watchet velvet flowre work given by ye Lady Powlett wief of Sr John Powlet of Winton Knt.	Stollen	Note- For Sir John Powlett. See below
Another of redd silk wrought with blazing starrs in gold.		
Another of green damask with flowrepotts of God, and one middle pane of purple velvet and gold.		
Itm three old communion carpets of turky work whereof one is on ye communion table, another in the chapter house & a third in the vestry.	One of these stollen	
Itm 2 white copes.		
Cushions		
One of red velvet with 6 Lyons or One of blew velvet with 6 flowr de Luces or	Stollen	12 faire cushions of red and blew velvet with lions and flower de Luces in them wrought in gold
Three large ritch Cusions of Copestuff, crimson velvet embrodered with gold	One of these stollen	
Three other somewhat shorter of ye same work	One stollen	
Three lesser old cushions with a redd panel over thwart in the middle	One stollen	
A purple velvet cushion embroidered with spred eagles Da gloriam Deo. given by Mr Burby, Archdeacon & Prebendary of this church.		
A new cushion of silver tissue with watchett flower work given by the sd Lady powlett being of the same suit with ye pulpit cloth.		Fair Cushions which were given by Sir John Paulet
2 old decayed cases of cushions with T.S.		
2 other worne cushions, blew, thinly embroderd with gold wire		Note- Sir John POWLETT of Hyde was the second son William the Third Marquis of Winchester by Jane Lambert, He died, 1632
12 square cushions Turky work	5 of these stollen	
4 old ones of corse Irish work		

WALLER PEDIGREE

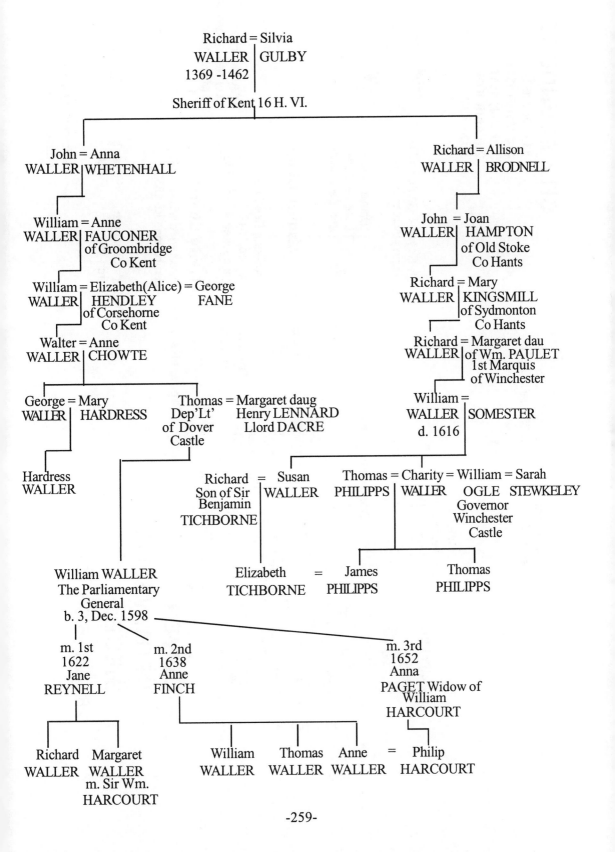

Richard = Silvia
WALLER | GULBY
1369 -1462

Sheriff of Kent 16 H. VI.

John = Anna
WALLER | WHETENHALL

Richard = Allison
WALLER | BRODNELL

William = Anne
WALLER | FAUCONER
of Groombridge
Co Kent

John = Joan
WALLER | HAMPTON
of Old Stoke
Co Hants

William = Elizabeth(Alice) = George
WALLER | HENDLEY | FANE
of Corsehorne
Co Kent

Richard = Mary
WALLER | KINGSMILL
of Sydmonton
Co Hants

Walter = Anne
WALLER | CHOWTE

Richard = Margaret dau
WALLER | of Wm. PAULET
1st Marquis
of Winchester

George = Mary
WALLER | HARDRESS

Thomas = Margaret daug
Dep'Lt' | Henry LENNARD
of Dover | Llord DACRE
Castle

William =
WALLER | SOMESTER
d. 1616

Hardress
WALLER

Richard = Susan
Son of Sir | WALLER
Benjamin
TICHBORNE

Thomas = Charity = William = Sarah
PHILIPPS | WALLER | OGLE | STEWKELEY
Governor
Winchester
Castle

William WALLER
The Parliamentary
General
b. 3, Dec. 1598

Elizabeth =
TICHBORNE

James
PHILIPPS

Thomas
PHILIPPS

m. 1st
1622
Jane
REYNELL

m. 2nd
1638
Anne
FINCH

m. 3rd
1652
Anna
PAGET Widow of
William
HARCOURT

Richard   Margaret
WALLER   WALLER
m. Sir Wm.
HARCOURT

William   Thomas   Anne   =   Philip
WALLER   WALLER   WALLER   HARCOURT

CITY PLUNDERED

13th Dec 1642
3rd March 1643
12th July 1643
7th April 1644
1 Oct 1645

Hopton's HQ

A Royalist Garrison Town
during Winter 1643/4

"Dame" Alice
Lisle beheaded
2nd Sept 1685

Maurice Church

Cathedral Despoiled
14 Dec 1642
Ransacked 1 Oct 1645

Trinity Church

Threatened with
demolition Oct 1652

Sir Arthur Hazelrig's
entry after "Cheriton"
30 March 1644

Fiennes
Billet

Parliamentary Commission
of Enquiry 1649

Waller's departure
30 March '44

Sir William Waller's
entry 12 Dec 1642
& 30 March 1644

Col Brown's
London Regt
Dec 1642

King Charles I
presented with the
City Mews 10 Dec 1648

Grandison delivers
the Castle
Dec 1642

Ogle fortifies
the Castle
Oct 1643
Surrenders
6 Oct 1645

Parliament's
H.Q.

**Thomas'
Church**

Cromwell's Lines

Waller's
Petard
7 April '44

Castle Demolished
March 1657

Cromwell's Lines

Capt Burley's
Treason Trial
Feb 1647

"Breach"

Jan 1644
Hopton's
Sconce

Cromwell's
Battery of
6 Guns
Oct 1645

Cromwell's
Entry
28 Sept 45

OLIVER
CROMWELL'S
SIEGE

28 Sept - 6 Oct 1645

Guard
Room

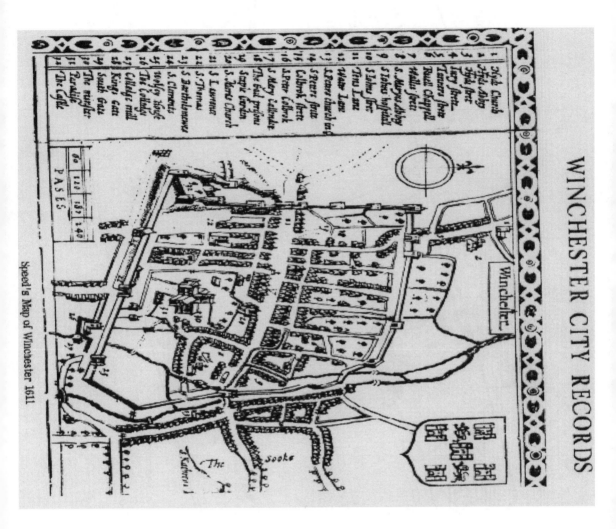

Speed's Map of Winchester 1611

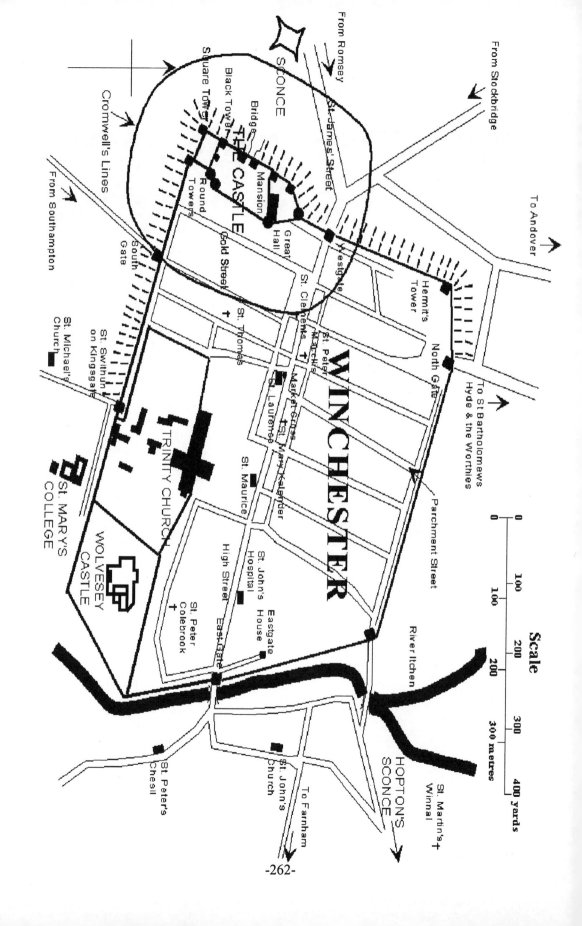

A

B

C

George. L. 213-4.
Gerard. Lord. 94. 97-98.
Gibbons. Christopher. 49.
Glenham. Sir T. 185.
Godwin. Arthur. 74.
Goodwin Jo. 220
Goring. Lord George. 29. 147.
181.
Greenwood. mapmaker. 189.
Grandison. Lord Wm Villiers.
33-5. 41-4. 73. 78-9.
Grey. Colonel. 34. 75-6. 79.
Griffen Edward. 77.
Gwyn. Lieut. 76.

H

Hackett. Fellow of Win' Coll'
39.
Hammond. Lieut Nowell. 7-13.
47. 55. 65. 84. 174-7. 190.
249.
Hampden. John. 79.
Harris, Warden John. 3. 125.
204-8.
Harrison. Major Thomas 174-7.
Haslerigg. Sir Arthur. 83.
124.
Haswell. Dr. 204.
Hay. William. 220.
Hayborne. Major Ralph. 41. 76.
(Hebberne)
Henrietta. Queen. 5.
Henry II. 12.
Henry III of Winchester. 159.
Henry VIII. 16.
Hildersby. John. 207.
Hinton Dr. 205.
Holland Earl of. 10.
Holmes. Thomas Organist 49.
Honeywood. Captain. 75.
Hook. John. 224.
Hooker. C. Recorder. 222.

Hooper. Ed. Parliamentary
Commissioner 207.
Hopton. Ralph. Lord General
of the West and Southern
Counties. 82-132.
Hussey. Chr. Alderman 162.
Hussey. Thomas. 207. 221. 236. 146.
Hyde. Alexander. Dean at the
Restoration. 226.

I

Inchiquin. Lord Murrough
O'Brien. 102.
Ireton. Colonel Henry. 209.

J

Jackman. J. 187.
James I. 1. 2. 12. 16. 95.
159.
Jeffreys. George. Judge. 27.
146. 201.
Jennings. Theodore. 78.
Jerome the Painter. 5. 8. 58.
Jervoise. Sir Thomas.
188. 207. 209. 224.
Jones. Inigo. 6-7. 46. 67.
71.

K

Kercher. Dr. R. 19.
Kingsmill. Dean 55. 197.
Kingsmill. Sir William. 77.
Kirby. T. F. Burser of Win'
College 23. 39.
Knowles. Sir Henry. 77.

L

M

N

O

Okey. Colonel. 154.
Ormonde. Earl of. 210.

P

Palmer. Captain. 197.
Paulet. George. 53.
Paulet. John of Hinton, 55. 77.
        St George. 102. 173. 179.
Paulet. John Marquis of 15.
        Winchester. 88. 92. 109.
Pennington. Isaac. 78.
Peters. Hugh. 155. 176. 179. 181.
Philip of Spain. 51. 58. 247.
Philips. Charity Lady Ogle . 148.
Philips. James. 77. 95. 148.
Philips. Thomas I. 95. 147-8.
Philips. Thomas II. 77. 95. 150. 173
Philpot. George. 77.
Pickering. Colonel. 154.
Potenger. Dr. John 206.
Potts. Captain. 142. 155.
Powlet. Colonel Henry. 88.
Powlet Colonel John. 77.
Powre. Sir Francis. 77.
Purdue. Nicholas. Mayor. 215.
Pym. John. 27

R

Raleigh. Sir Walter 1. 2. 10. 160.
Ranford. taken prisoner to
        Portsmouth 77.
Reynolds. Richard. 207.
Richard of Beorn. 52.
Riggs. Edmund. Mayor. 208. 211.
        224.
Riggs. Ralph. Mayor. 17. 89.
                90. 196.
Rivett. 204.

Robotham. 184.
Roe. Birch's secretary. 135.
Rogers. Lieut. 76.
Ruddry. Lieut. 76.
Rufus. King. 49. 50. 59.
Rupert. Prince. 127. 210.
Ryves. Bruno. 56. 62-3.

S

St Barbe. Capt Francis. 86.
Sands. Henry. 77.
Sands. William. Capt of the
        Militia. 22. 26.
Santbrook. Captain. 143.
Saunders. Gent. 77.
Savage. Cornet. 75.
Say. Master. 83-4.
Schellink. Engraver. 11. 159.
Scott Sir Gilbert 72.
Sharp Philip. 213-4.
Sheffield. Colonel. 184.
Shoveller. Richard. 146.
Simon de Montfort. 24.
Smith. Sir John. 73. 75. 78.
Smith. Sebastian. 204.
Southampton. Earl of. 10. 15.
Spavin the messenger. 176.
Speed. Mapmaker. 11. 158.
Sprigg. Joshua. 169-191.
Stanley. Dr. E. 205.
Stapylton. Sir P. 79.
Sterley. Cornet. 44. 75-8.
Stewkely. Hugh. 96.
Stewkeley Sarah. 96. 120.
Stuart. Lord John. 116.
Sturt. Major. 148.
Swainley. Lieut. 144.
Symonds. Peter. 15.
Symonds. William. 15.

T

U

V

W

Y

A

Aldermen. 7. 11. 15. 20.
        See also under Mayor.
Alresford Fight. 100. 140. 149.
Ambassadors. 1. 12.
Arms and armour 23. 30. 74.
        See also ordnance.
Articles of Surrender.
41. 44. 78. 172-85.
Artillery. See also under
        Ordnance 152-155.
Assizes. 146. 201. 219.
Auxiliaries 119.

B

Bailiff. The Bishops. 3.
Banner, Hang out the 182.
Battalia. 35. 119. 121.
Batter. 40.
Batteries. 162. 166. 168.
        177. 213.
BATTLES
  Alresford. 122.
  Alton Fight 100. 140.
  Bramdean Heath. 121.
  Cheriton. 120.
  Edgehill. 29. 64. 147.
  Marston Moor.
  Naseby. 134. 149. 152. 154.
  Newbury. 86. 145.
  Preston. 209.
  Roundway Down. 86. 88.
Beer. 107. 133. 140-1. 181.
Bells. 3. 16. 69. 78. 239.
  The Great Bells to be tolled
        16.
Billets. 37. 39. 40.
Bishops Saxon. 59.
Biskett. 118.
Black Saints. 219.
Bloody Assize. 27. 146. 201.
Breach in the walls. 38. 143.
        171. 183.
Booty. 33.

Bronzes. 6. 13. 52. 60-72.
226-7. 239.
Burley's Speech. 253.
Brutal appeties. 136.

C

Canal. 247.
Cannon. See ordnance. Captain of the Cuty. 7.
22.
Cavaliers. 32-44.
Carts. 118.
Castle. See under Winchester.
Chapter. Clerk. 3.
        Mettings. 85. 149-0.
Charter City's. 17. 26.
Cheese. 118.
Cheriton Field. 120.
Christ Hospital. 15.
Chronogram. 5. 32.
Churches See under Winchester
Churches as schools 9. 241.
Churches as stables. 111. 112.
Clerk. 53.
Cloth. 89.
Cloth taken at Andover 142.
Clubmen. 150. 151. 205.
Coffer City. 24. 97.
Colours. 34. 35. 56. 74. 175.
        181-2.
Commissioners to Winchester
        College. 207.
        of the County 212-5.
Commissions of array. 27.
Commonwealth. 69. 203.
Communion Table. 19. 31. 36.
Compounding. 43. 45.
Condemned Criminals. 16.
Condition of Surrender 43-4.
Conduct and Coat money. 25.
Conformity 21.
Constitution of England. 228.
Convoy. 141. 175.
Council of State. 212.
Council of War. 107. 153. 185.
Court Martial. 184. 187.
Court of Eyre. 10. 26. 160.
255.
        of Pie Powder.150.
Cromwells Battery. 213.
        Letters. 155. 177.
Crucifixes. 31. 45.
Crusader. 52.

D

Dean and Chapter. 9. 17. 22.
    30-1. 70. 89.
      Abolished. 203.
      Restored. 226. 230. 236.
Delinquents 157. 194. 198.
Deputy Lieuts 26. 28. 36.
Differences. 7. 17-8. 21. 230.
Directory of Worship. 192.
Disfranchisement. 198-9.
Dorset. 99.
Dragoons. 115.
Drinking day. 147.
Drummers and Drums. 25.
Drums beating. 56.
Dutch Engineer. 103. 108. 153.

E

Easter week Races 15.
Engagement The. 207.
Engineers. 103. 108. 210.
Episcopacy. to be abolished
    26. 31. 33.
Eyre Court. 10. 26. 160. 255.

F

Financial aid for H. M. 30
Fine of £600. 83.
Fine of £1400. 79. 168.
Five Members. 27.
Flag of Defiance. 182.
Foraging parties. 126. 145.
Forests. 10. 26.
Fortifications. 108.
Free billet. 26. 103-9.
Free quarter. 83.
French Ambassador. 1.
French Intervention. 210.
Fruits of Victory. 140. 181-3.

G

Gabions. 161.
Gory of the Action. 62. 64.
Governor of the Castle
      Sir William Ogle 94.
      Tho's Bettersworth. 188. 206.
Granado. 155. 170-1. 190.
Grand Remonstrance. 26. 27.
Gun See ordnance.
Gunfoundries 92.
Gunners. 155.
Gunpowder. 94. 126. 152. 158.
    162. 168. 182.
Gunplatform. 161.189.
Gunpowder Treason. 16.

H

Hang draw and quarter. 200.
High Commission court.
His Majesty's Old Army. 144.
Holy Rood Day. 91.
Hoods and Tippets 61.
Hoptons Scoonce. 107-8. 162.
Horse for carriages. 25.
Horse market. 86.
Hostages. 175.
House of Commons. 179.
House of Lords (Peers)
    74. 230. 231. 241.

J

Independency. 33.
Impressed men. 25.
Iron works. 92.
Itchen River. 37. 247.

Jealousy. 133.
Justice. Cromwell's 185.

K

Kent. 82. 92. 115.
Keys of the City, 123-4.

Q

R

S

Sabbath Day. 155. 170.
SAINTS DAYS
      Bartholomew 11.
      George. 15. 16. 52.
      Holy Rood. 91.
      Smithun. 11.
Sally. Ogle's 162.
Sconce. Hoptons 107-8. 162.
School in
      St Johns Chapel. 9.
      St Laurence Church. 241.
Scottish Wars 24. 209.
Sermons. 16. 19.
Sea Power. 92.
Sequestrated Goods. 206.
Sheriff. 1. 2. 11. 17. 36-7.

Shot. 155. 168.
Ship. Money. 13. 17. 26.
Siege Weapons. 147.
Silver cups for H. M. 1.
Skavenger. 217.
Slight defences. 82. 109.
Snow. 108.
Spanish Ambassador. 1.
Speaker Lenthall. 176. 184-6.
Star Chamber. 17. 18.
State tials. 1.
Statues of King James 67-72.
      and King Charles. 89.
Stores in the Castle. 105-8.
      118. 126. 178-0
Storm Money. 167.
Storming of Winchester. 38.
Sugar loafe 20.
Summons. 156-7. 166. 169. 181.
Surplices. 19. 61.
Surrey. 82. 92.
Survey of the close houses. 203.
Sussex. 82. 92. 99. 116.
Sweet Cathedralists. 45.

T

Taxation. 26.
Taylor map. 108. 121. 162.

Thanksgivings. 78.
Town Clerk. 197. 198.
Trade routes. 179.
Trained Bands. 22. 26. 28.
Troyne of Artillery. 155.
Treachery. 181. 187.
Treaty. 173.
Trial of King Charles. 201-3.
Troopers. 32. 37. 61. 68.
Trumpeteer. 147. 156.

U

Uniformity. 19.

V

Vestments. 62.
Vices Foul. 106.
Visitation. Laud's 20.

W

Wallers furniture. 14.
Walls of the City. 17. 24.
Warlike Stores. 29.
Weeping Mothers. 116.
Welsh Wars. 53.
Western Army. 98.
Wheat and Beare. 178.
Winchester Disgarrisoned. 165.
Winchester Goose. 145
Winchester Ordeal 200.
Winchester Taken. 123.
Winter Quarters. 108.
Wiltshire. 82

Magdalen College. 57. 73.
New College. 60. 207.

Peterborough. 221.
Petersfield. 110. 145. 151.
Poole. 92. 155.
Portsmouth. 22. 29. 63. 68.
　　70. 74. 82. 86-7. 103.
　　147. 151-2. 163. 182. 227.
Portsmouth Road. 145.
Preston. 209.

Reading. 98. 116. 165. 166.
Romsey. 86. 99. 103. 108.
　　110. 124-5. 132. 147-8.
Roundway Down. 86. 88. 137.

St Cross. 3. 146. 201. 254.
Salisbury. 147.
Soberton. 186.
Somerset. 34.
Southampton. 22. 77. 90-2.
　　109. 143. 147. 152. 155.
　　211.
Stoke Charity. 12-3. 125. 148.
Sutton Down. 11.
Swathling. 77.

Tangiers. 204.
Taunton. 149.
Tichboorne. 12. 184.
Tichborne Down. 12.
Tower of London. 2.
Twyford. 214.

Upham Church. 110.
Uppark. 91. 99.
Upper Wallop. 150. 226.

Versailles. 215.
Vevey. Switzerland. 203.
Vyne The. 77.

Wallers Ash. 123.
Wallingford. 98.
Wulmer Forest. 11.
Wardour Castle. 92. 114. 144.
West Bere Forest. 12.
West Meon. 116.. 119.
Westminster. 78.

Wherewell. 34. 94.
Whitchurch. 144.
Whitehall. 202.
Windsor. 33. 76. 147. 159.
201-2.

WINCHESTER See below.

Woodstock. 175. 179. 184.
Worthy. 123. 184.

York. 24.

THE CASTLE

The Castle. 8-12. 37-42. 63.
　　127-70.
To be made untenable. 210-3.
To be demolished. 213-5.

Barbican. 11. 12.
Black Tower. 171. 177. 213-4.
Breach in wall. 38. 213-4.
Bridge. 9. 11. 12.
Chapel. 214.
Ditches. 11.
Drawbridge. 180.
Gate. 41.
Gatehouse. 159. 213.
Great Common Hall. 2. 9. 10.
　　27. 160. 187. 190.
　　200. 213.
　To be Demolished. 209. 216.
House. See also Mansion.
　　9. 14. 37. 187. 190.
Keep. 11. 159.
Kings Chambers,. 9. 12.
Kitchens. 9. 214.
Mansion. 159. 162. 171.
Norman. 159.
Round table. 10. 190.
Towers Oval. 159.
　　Round 9. 12. 213-4.
　　Square. 9. 12. 213-4.
　　159.
SITE SOLD by Sir Wm Waller
　　to the City and
　　by City to King
　　Charles II. 215-6.

Surrender Oct 1645. 183.

THE CATHEDRAL

BIBLIOGRAPHY
for the
CIVIL WAR IN WINCHESTER

Abbreviation	Title	Page
Adair.	John Adair. Roundhead General. Macdonald 1969.	34. 65.
A. R.	Anglia Rediva. Compiled by Joshua Sprigge. England's Recovery.	162. 166. 169-70.
ANON.	The anonymous History of Winchester. Porter.	65. 93. 111. 112-3. 136. 200.
A. of W.	Archives of Winchester by Charles Bailey.	24. 104. 156. 197-8. 216.
Baker.	Sir R. Baker's Chronicle.	122.
Berkeley.	Memoirs of Sir John Berkeley. From Baron Maseres Tracts. p 375.	200.
Birch.	Military memoirs of Colonel John Birch. by his secretary Roe.	135.
Blakiston.	J.M.G. Blakiston. Inigo Jones Screen. Win' Cath' Record. Nos 45-47.	6. 13. 71.
Brayley.	E.W. Brayley & J. Britton. 1804. The Beauties of England and Wales. Top' Vol' VI.	47. 66.
Books & Mss.	Books Charters and Manuscripts Exhib' 1951 Win' City.	17. 32. 80. 123. 156.
Bussby.	F. Bussby. Winchester Cathedral. 1979. The Great Screen. W.C.Record. 47-8.	6.
C.S.P. 1625.	Calender of State Papers. Domestic.	90.
C.S.P. Add	Do. 1625-49.	22. 29. 90.
C.S.P. 1637.	Do. Grant of Castle to Sir William Waller. May 1637.	13.
C.S.P. 1644.	Do. Great loss of Cloth at Andover.	141-2.
C.S.P. 1645-6.	Do. The reducing and taking of Winchester.	152-3.
C.S.P. 1649.	Do. Castle to be made untenable.	210.
C.S.P. 1683.	Do. Great hall to be demolished.	216.
Cave.	C.J.P.Cave. The roof Bosses. Friends of Win' Cath.	32.
Clarendon.	Edward Hyde 1st Earl of Clarendon. History of the rebellion. "Broke all the Measures"	129.
County Arch's	C.2484 The King's message to the inhabitants of Win'	80.
Clarendon & Gale.	Henry Earl of Clarendon and Samuel Gale. History & Antiquities of the Cathedral Church. 1715.	6. 13. 47.
D'ewes.	Journal of Sir Samuel D'ewes.Ed by W. Notestein.1923.	18.
D.N.B.	Dictionary of National Biography.	
Edgar.	F.T.R. Edgar. Sir Ralph Hopton. The Kings man in the West.	102. 110.
Eye Witness.	Elias Archer. News Indeed by E.A. 1644. "Winchester Taken".	123.
Fiennes.	Nathaniel Fiennes & Arthur Godwin. Letter to the Lord General of 16th Dec 1642. H.M.C. 5th Report.	36. 37. 42. 44. 62. 74.

Firth.	C.H.Firth. Cromwell's Army. 1902 Storm money.	167.	
	See also C.S.P. 1645 p. 198.		
	The breach 30 men wide.	171.	
"Friend" A.	A Friend of Winchester in the Proceedings of the		
	British Archaeological Association 1845.	8. 69. 191.	
	Reprinted	230.	
Furley.	J.S.Furley. Quarter Session Government in Hampshire	27. 190.	
Gents Mag.	The Gentlemens Magazine Library.English Top' Vol.V.	158. 218.	
Godwin.	G.N.Godwin.The Civil War in Hampshire.	44. 83-4. 89. 94. 98.	
		102-3. 119. 176.	
		184-7. 202.	
Greatrex.	Joan Greatex. Register of the Common Seal. 1978.	192. 195.	
Hammond.	Nowell Hammond. A relation of a short survey of		
	the Western Counties made by a Lieut of the		
	Military Company in Norwich. 1635.	7-11. 22. 48-54. 192.	
	Ed L.G.Wickham Legg. Camden Miscellany XVI.	254.	
H. F. C.	Hampshire Field Cub Proceedings. W.J.Andrews.		
	Olivers Battery.	189.	
H.N.Q. IV.	Hants Notes and Queries. Ch.Eburne shot.	146.	
V.	Do. Warlike Stores.	29.	
	Disfranchisement of Robert Tucker.	199.	
VI.	Do. Attendance of the Mayor in the Cathedral.	17.	
	Bishop Curle's escape in a dung cart.	135.	
VII.	Do. Coffer accounts 1636 for visit Charles I.	5.	
	A Sergeant out of the Low Countries.	22.	
	Fifty pounds lent to Ogle by the City.	97.	
	Sale of Castle by Waller.	215.	
VIII.	Do. the Taking of Winchester castle Dec. 1642.	73.	
	Quotes H.M.C. 13th Report on p. 45.		
Hazelrigg.	Arthur Hazelrigg reports to the House after	124.	
	"Cheriton". Add. Ms 18779. fo. 87.		
H.M.C.	10.	Historical Manuscript Report. Lord Brayes Mss.	
		Norton's report on the Clubmen. p163.	151.
	13.	Portland Mss. Surrender of Winchester Dec 1642.	14. 73. 175.
			178. 188.
Herbert.	Sir Thomas Herbert's Narrative. Charles I in		
	Captivity. Ed. by G.S. Stevenson.	202.	
Jervis.	Simon Jervis. Woodwork in Winchester Cathedral.	5-6.	
Jones.	R.A. Jones. Members of Parliament for Andover.	27.	
	1295-1885		
Journal of the H.C.	Journal of the House of Commons. Re. The reduc-		
	ing of Winchester July 1645.	152.	
	Col Lower to be Governor. 1645.	188.	
K. W. I.	The Kingdoms Weekly Intelligencer. April 1644.	124.	
The Kings Message	The Kings Message to the inhabitants of		
	Winchester. Answer of the Inhabitants. Dec 1642.		
	County Archives. C. 2484.	80-1.	
Kirby.	T. F. Kirby. Annals of Winchester College.	2. 22-3. 39. 66. 150.	
		191. 206-7.	
Kitchen.	G.W.Kitchen. The Manor of Manydown.		
	Hamps' Record Soc.	206.	

Leach.	Arthur. F. Leach. A History of Win' College 1899.	9. 19. 56. 207.
Leigh & Knight.	W.Austin Leigh & M.G.Knight.Chawton Manor. 1911.	76.
Lloyd.	Da.Lloyd.Memoirs of Excellent Personages.1668.	121.
Lloyd Woodland.	W.Lloyd Woodland. The Story of Winchester.	79.
Locke.	A Locke. In Praise of Winchester. 1912.	4.
Ludlow.	Memoirs of Edmund Ludlow Governor of Wardour Castle.	114-5.
Luke.	Sir Samuel Luke's Letter Book. H.M.C. JP4. Ed. by H.G. Tibbutt.	134. 145. 153.
Major.	Richard Major of Hursely's letters. Quoted by Portal. Add Mss 27402.	215.
Matthews.	Betty Matthews. The Music (and organs) of Win' Cath'.	49.
M.A.	Mercurius Aulicus March 1643. Bodleian 4 M 68 Art.	137. 140.
M. Brit. (paper)	Mercurius Britanicus. Brit Lib Benny Collection of Newspapers Vol 1 1603-1693 ref 18a.	145.
M. C.	Mercurius Civicus. Printed in A. Wilkinson's Michaelmersh and its Antiquities.	96. 166-187.
M. R.	Mercurius Rusticus. Soton Univ DA 411 37671.	33. 56-61. 68.
Milner. A.B.	Alfred B. Milner. History of Micheldever. 1924.	54.
Milner. J.	John Milner. History Civil and Ecclesiastical and Survey of the Antiquities of Winchester.	9. 108. 158. 186-7.
Nichols.	John Nichols. Progresses of James I.	1-2.
Nortons.	Thomas M.A.Hervey. History of Colmer & Priors Dean quotes Nortons Letter Book.Add Mss. 21922.	24. 25.
Ogle.	Sir William Ogle Visc Cathalough. An Account of the Siege of Winchester and its surrender by Lord Ogle to Cromwell. Clarendon State Papers. Bodleian 2063.	292.
Ogles Court Martial.	Court Martial of Lord Ogle for the surrender Winchester 12 Nov. 1645. Add Mss. 27402 f. 100.	187.
Ogle's	A True relation of my Lord (William Cavendish	36.
Engagements.	Earl of Newcastle and Lord) Ogle's Engagements 1642-1645. Add Mss 27402 f. 82.	117-134. 172.
Parl' Hist.	The Parliamentary History of England. Essex's Necessity.	130.
	Ireton to seize the Castle.	209.
Perfect Diurnal.	A perfect Diurnal. Burney collection of Newspapers. W254.26 E304.13.	124.
Portal.	Melville Portal. The Great Hall of Winchester Castle.	1. 2. 77. 156. 167. 188. 210. 214.
R.A. Inst.	Royal Archaelogical Insitute Proceedings. Re K Charles Visit 1636.	108.
R.C.H.M.	Royal Commission of Historic Monuments. Newark-on-Trent. The Civil War Siege Works.	
Rushworth.	John Rushwort's Historical Collections. BL. 63-4833.	78. 153.
Sawyer.	Richard Sawyer. The Battle of Cheriton. Ms County Arch.	120.
Saye & Sele.	Lord Saye and Sele in Win' Cath' Record No 24.	64.

Schellinks View.	Schellinks View of Winchester 1662. Walpole Society XXXV (2) Plate 29. Soton Univ. Lib.	11. 159.
Speeds Map.	John Speed Hampshire with inset plan of Winchester c1610 Republished by H. Margary. 1976.	159.
Sterley.	Cornet Sterley. The Eye Witness. Vicars Chronicle. Part quoted by Godwin part by Portal.	43. 35. 75. 76.
Symonds Diary.	Richard Symonds. Bm. Harl 986.	144.
Taylors Map.	Isaac Taylor Map of Hampshire 1759 H Margary 1976	108. 121. 162.
Toynbee.	Margaret Toynbee. King Charles I and Winchester College. Hampshire Field Club. Vol XVIII Pt 1.	5.
True Relation.	A True and Exact relation of a great otherthrow given to the Cavaliers in Winchester by Colonel Hurry, Colonel Brown & some others of the Parliament's Force on Tuesday last Dec 17 1642. County Arch wing T 2438b.	35. 40.
Trussel.	John Trussell. Benefactors to Winchester. Transcript by Tom Atkinson. Loaned to the City by James Osborne of Yale U.S.A.	2. 15. 32-46. 83-95. 119. 130-9.
Turner.	B.C. Turner. Winchester. 1980. Return of the Church Cathedral & Close 1660. W.C.Record. No. 29 1660.	192-3. 208.
Vaughan.	John Vaughan. Winchester Cathedral Monuments.	12-3. 54. 88. 101.
Vicars.	Vicars Parliamentary Chronicle. BM. TT E. 40.22.	34. 38. 45. 62. 124. 126.
V. C. H.	Victoria County History of Hampshire.	72. 187.
Walker.	Sir Edward Walker. Historical Discourses. His Majesty's Happy Progress and Success 1644. "Necessitated H.M. to alter the Scheme of his affairs."	128.
Waller.	Sir William Waller. Recollections. Printed as an appx to the Poetry of Anna Matilda. Birmingham Univ Lib. SPR 375 C6 A17 108154.	24.
Warburton.	Warburton. Memoirs of Prince Rupert and the Cavaliers.	127-8.
Wedgewood.	C.V. Wedgewood. The King's War 1641-7. The Trial of Charles I.	202.
Whitelocke.	Bulstrode Whitelock's Memorials of the English Affairs. Soton Univ DA 390 S OS 7688 7691.	202.
W. C. D. II.	Winchester Cathedral Documents II. Ed. W. R. W. Stephens & F. T. Madge. H. R. S. 1897.	17. 30. 67. 70. 85. 88. 150. 164. 194-5. 203. 222.
W. C. Statutes.	The Statutes Governing the Cathedral Church of Winchester given by King Charles I.	20.
Wren.	Christopher Wren Junior. Parentalia. Re Wolvesey.	193.
Wren Soc.	Wren Society Papers Vol VII. The Kings House.	216.
Wymer.	Norman Wymer. The Story of Winchester. Re Warden Harris.	208.
Young's.	Florence Goodman. The Diary of John Young S.T.P. Dean of Winchester 1616 to the Commonwealth.	3. 5. 8-9. 13. 17-22. 31. 47. 68. 100. 150.
Young. P.	Peter Young. Edgehill.	64. 75.